IMAGES
of America

SUNDANCE

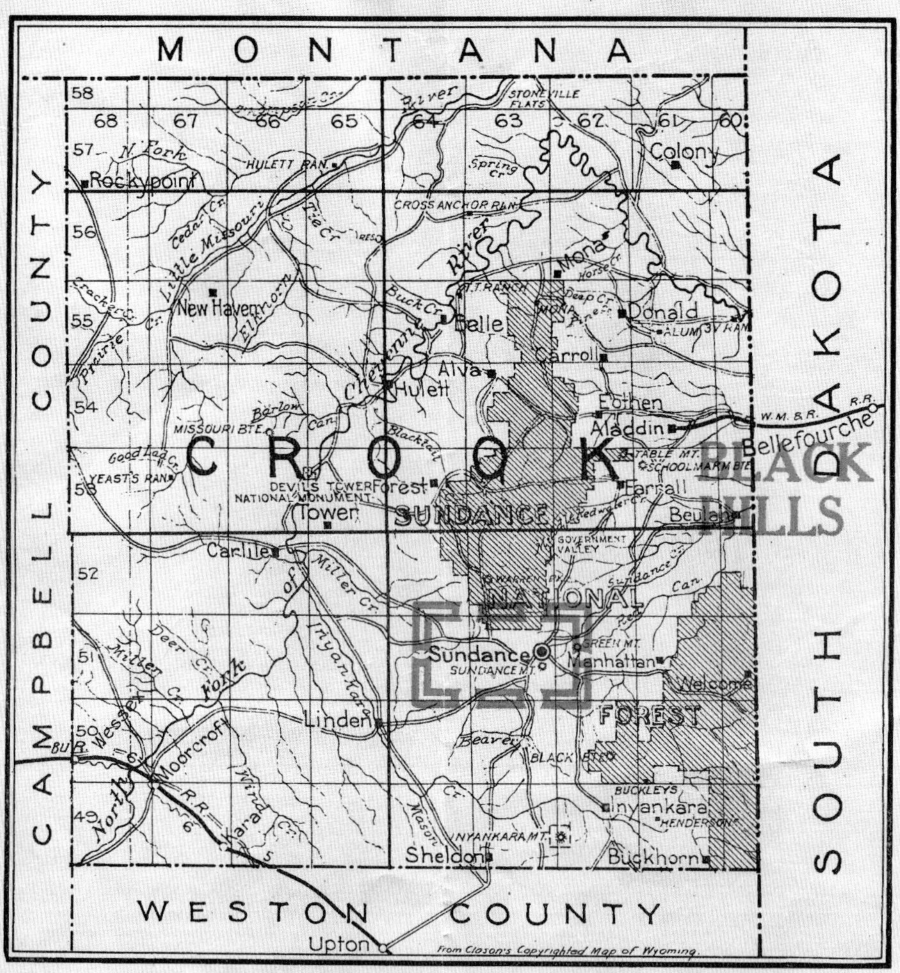

CLASON'S MAP OF CROOK COUNTY, WYOMING

10

This map shows Crook County and the town of Sundance, located in the northeast corner of Wyoming. At the time Sundance was incorporated, it was the only town in the county, making it the obvious choice for county seat. When this map was printed, there were a number of small communities throughout the county. It shows the rivers and streams, including the north fork of the Cheyenne River, called the Belle Fourche River. The map also illustrates the mountains, draws, and canyons. (Courtesy of Crook County Museum.)

On the Cover: This view looks South over Sundance mid-1900. (Courtesy of Crook County Museum.)

IMAGES
of America

SUNDANCE

Rocky Courchaine
and Pam Thompson

ARCADIA
PUBLISHING

ISBN 978-0-7385-8109-5

Published by Arcadia Publishing
Charleston, South Carolina

Printed in the United States of America

Library of Congress Control Number: 2010923456

For all general information contact Arcadia Publishing at:
Telephone 843-853-2070
Fax 843-853-0044
E-mail sales@arcadiapublishing.com
For customer service and orders:
Toll-Free 1-888-313-2665

Visit us on the Internet at www.arcadiapublishing.com

This book is dedicated to the pioneers who took a chance for a better life and came West.

Contents

Acknowledgments

This undertaking could not have been accomplished without the members of the Crook County Museum and Art Gallery Foundation, the Crook County Museum District, the Crook County Historical Society, the Crook County Heritage Association, the Crook County Library, and the many other historical-minded people of Crook County who have kept their stories alive and have given us the opportunity to share these treasured memories with others. Unless otherwise noted, all the images and information used has come from material available at the Crook County Museum. There are so many people who have encouraged us and contributed their support, including our friends and families. We welcomed and appreciated those who offered their research, pictures, and tales of the past. These generous people include Russell Tracy, Mary Garman, Dixie Boyle, Mary Jean Wilson, Sam Henry, Les Hooper, and the Thompson family. And we wish we could thank Ilone Williamson, Mabel Brown, and Edith Thompson for all the information they left behind. Thank you to everyone, especially those whose names escape us right now. We do appreciate everyone's help. Special thanks must be given to Martha Keith for her typing and editing skills and mostly for allowing us to clutter her workspace. And of course we thank our editors at Arcadia for their never-ending patience in dealing with the problems that can arise in the far corners of northeast Wyoming.

INTRODUCTION

Long before the first settlers moved into the area, the Sioux and Cheyenne tribes inhabited the land that would become Crook County. It was not be until after the Custer expedition discovered gold in 1874 that settlers and miners began to flock to the Black Hills. In the early 1800s, many of the people believed that the Dakota mining towns were really in Wyoming. Sometime in the late 1870s, a group organized to request that the Black Hills become part of the Wyoming Territory. The congress of that time did not see things as those Westerners did. They considered northeastern Wyoming nothing more than a piece of this country, where gold nuggets and beefsteaks should not mix together. Not too many years later, congress would be pushing people to come West, where life was mellow and the land was fertile.

The original Crook County was about 102 miles square. Sundance is located about 20 miles from the east border and 45 miles from the north line of the state and at the base of the Bearlodge Mountains, which extend in a broken chain a distance of 25 miles north to northwest. The valley in which the town lies is about 1 mile in width and has been called one of the most picturesque spots that could have ever been selected for a town. Sundance is situated in the pass between the Black Hills and the Bearlodge Mountains, Inyan Kara Mountain, and Green Mountain, and at the base of Sundance Mountain on the north side. This was the most accessible way for the travelers to pass to the Black Hills from the cattle country to the west.

It is through this wide pass that the miners traveled to the gold fields in the Black Hills and the gold fields in Montana to the north. These gold miners were spilling over into the surrounding hills from the gold fields of South Dakota and Montana. Most of the gold found in here was in streams—deposits called "placers." It took tough men to pan for gold because the life of a miner was dangerous and lonely. The danger could come to the miners and farmers alike in many ways. Danger could be found in most every part of their environment. The loneliness came with the vast open spaces; the miles and miles of rolling grass; the deep, moist, quiet canyons; and the endless stars in the dark sky. It is heard in the howl of the coyote and the song of the birds. Sundance Creek, a small mountain stream, flows through the town to meet up with Sand Creek, and together they flow into the Redwater River and then race along to catch up with the Belle Fourche and continue their journey to the mighty Missouri.

Both the town of Sundance and the mountain take their names from the fact that it was here that the native tribes of the area annually gathered to hold their sun dance celebrations. We know from history that Native Americans from a radius of hundreds of miles in each direction annually congregated here to hold these celebrations. These people also found something they were looking for among the four mountains.

A little to the east of town, the valley widens until the Black Hills are reached in about 6 miles distance. A little west of town, the valley also opens out, and some fine agricultural lands are found as well as the outlet to the vast open country beyond. In 1879, the present town site was but a ranch. During the succeeding years, the only business was a road ranch that underwent various changes in ownership. Early in 1883, Sewell Bullard obtained an interest with Albert Hoge, the original homesteader, and a small store was added to the ranch. In 1883, a blacksmith came to set up his shop. A livery barn, a hotel, and even a newspaper followed. Soon other business were arriving and setting up shop. By 1887, Sundance had two banks, three general groceries, supply stores with large stocks of goods on hand, and the school was busting at the seams with hopeful scholars. As the only town in the county, trade was good and that was seen as a sign that the town's future growth would be even greater. The founders felt that since Sundance was located in the pass between the mountains, it was the natural and only roadway leading westward from the Black Hills towns. The future looked very good. It was also highly speculated that a railroad from Deadwood or Rapid City, South Dakota, leading west to the coalfields and to the national parks, must necessarily occupy the Sundance pass. The cattlemen were bringing their herds from places where the grass was less lush to the wide-open plains just west of the town. The railroad would be as good for the cattlemen as the cattle would be for the railroad. Scientific reports were saying that the Bearlodge mining districts all pointed to wonderful opportunities of developing possibilities. The hopeful fathers of this little town did not see that the train might not come, that the minerals might run low, or that the elements were going to test them. In their atmosphere of great expectancy, the town was incorporated October 3, 1887. With the incorporation of the town and with the new and different notice that brought the fledgling town more people, they arrived to see if this was the place for them. Those that wanted to be a part of a growing town arrived, and so did those that just liked to know people were near. The few hardy souls who managed to stay and establish roots were the determined ones. They were also the lucky ones. And they may just have known that.

One

The Mountains

The heart of Crook County in northeastern Wyoming is the Bearlodge mountain range, which is part of the Black Hills. These Black Hills cover an area of about 6,000 square miles, or about the size of Connecticut. For the native tribes, these Paha Sapa, or "Hills that are Black," were and are the literal center of the earth, the place where human beings were first created, the first gathering of the stone, Eden, from where the hoop of the world bends to the four directions. Two thirds of the Black Hills are in South Dakota, and the remaining third is in Wyoming. The Redwater River separates the Bear Lodge from the main range of mountains by a distance of 5 to 10 miles. Warren Peak is the highest peak in this range of mountains at 7,000 feet. The peak is named for G. K. Warren. This peak has been called the crowning points of the Bear Lodge range. Below Warren Peak crouch the shapes of Sundance and Green Mountains. South of Warren Peak lies Inyan Kara. Inyan Kara is also a symbol of the most flamboyant episodes in the career of George Armstrong Custer, that of the Black Hills Expedition of 1874. Between Warren Peak and Inyan Kara lies Sundance Mountain. Charles Schelldorf was 10 years old when he and a couple of friends went to explore the mountain. This was the first time Charles had made it to the top. He lost his footing and fell 150 feet to his death. This one accident has changed the way the people of the community look at the magnificent mountain in their backyard. East of Sundance Mountain is Green Mountain. This is a peaceful little mountain, known for being a nearly perfect circle. It is a shame that Custer did not pay more attention as he traveled under its shadow on his way to his expedition's camp near Inyan Kara.

This picture is looking across Sundance to the east at Green Mountain. Green Mountain is 2.5 miles from the outskirts of town. It stands 5,272 feet above the surrounding countryside. It is one of the few hogbacks that encircles a dome. This dome is an intrusion of magma into the earth's crust. There were four homesteading families who proved up on their claims to the lands of Green Mountain between 1891 and 1914. To prove up on a homestead claim, the homesteader had to live on the land and make continual improvements on it for four years. Then the land would be theirs. Most of these claims were staked in section 17. Section 16 is a state section. State sections were mostly school sections and not to be settled on. The Green Mountain Cemetery was established on the north side of the mountain.

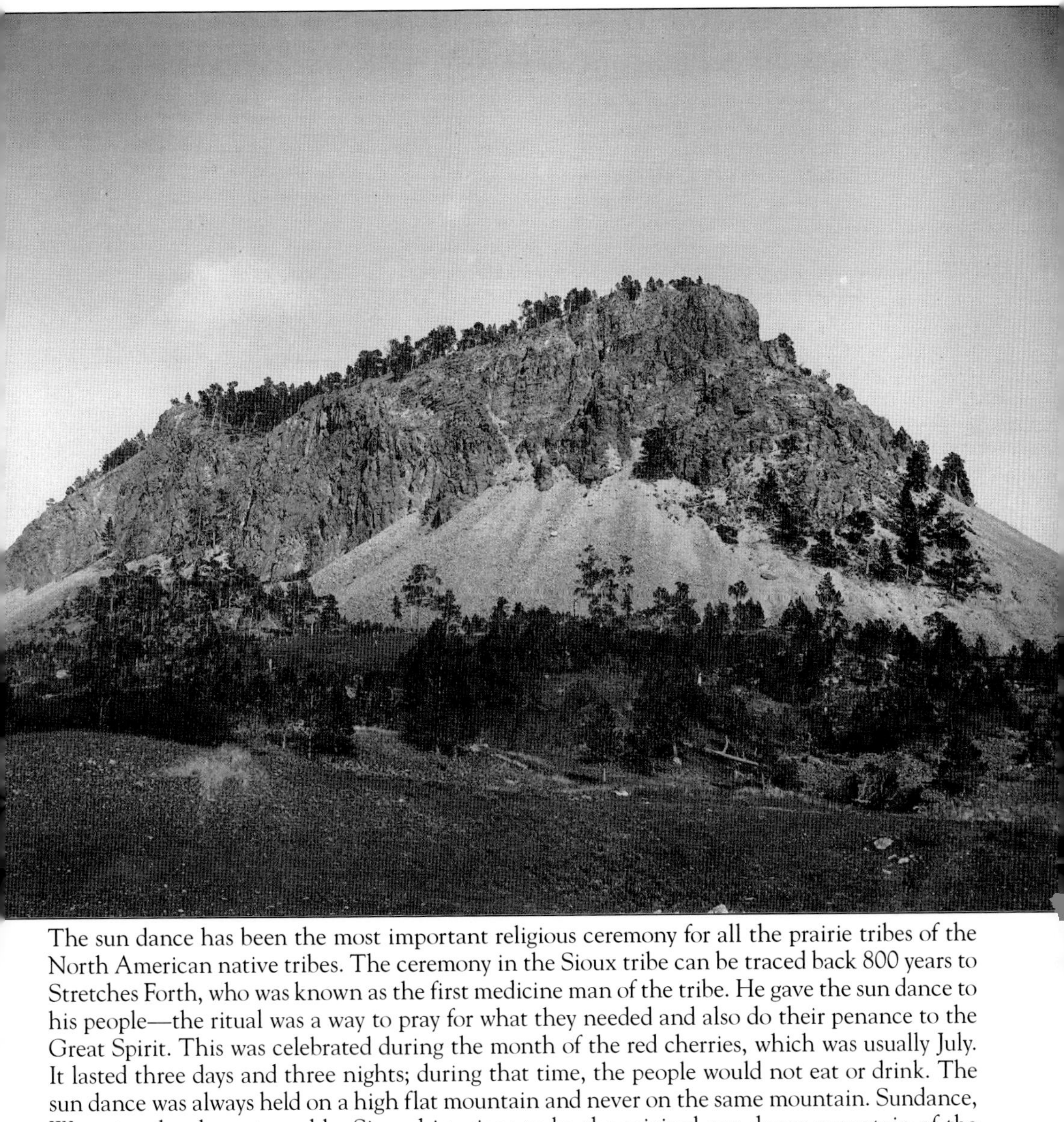

The sun dance has been the most important religious ceremony for all the prairie tribes of the North American native tribes. The ceremony in the Sioux tribe can be traced back 800 years to Stretches Forth, who was known as the first medicine man of the tribe. He gave the sun dance to his people—the ritual was a way to pray for what they needed and also do their penance to the Great Spirit. This was celebrated during the month of the red cherries, which was usually July. It lasted three days and three nights; during that time, the people would not eat or drink. The sun dance was always held on a high flat mountain and never on the same mountain. Sundance, Wyoming, has been traced by Sioux historians to be the original sun dance mountain of the Sioux Nation. This picture shows the north face of the Sundance Mountain.

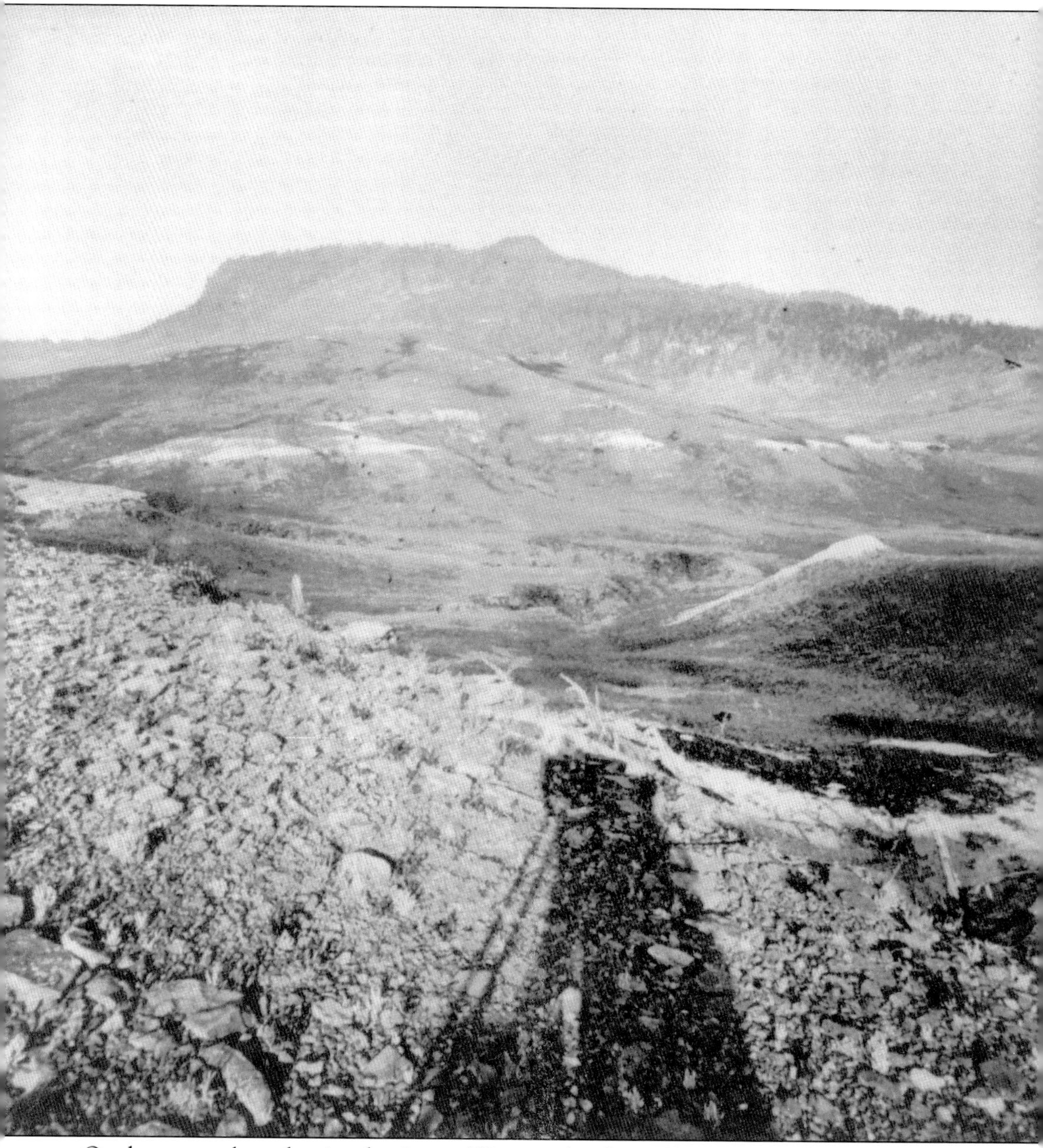

On the western boundary in what is now Wyoming lays Inyan Kara, a misspelling of Inyan Kagha (pronounced *EE-yahn KAH-ga*), the "Holy Mountain." It symbolizes the womb of the woman and is where several tribes pray in thanksgiving for everything the "Creator" has given them, especially the birth of children. The Holy Mountain serves as a symbol of renewal for women as the sweat lodge does for men. It is where the past, present, and future come together in one sacred place. Legend tells of the racetrack, a formation of red clay and stone that surrounds the Black Hills, that was the site of a primordial race between the two-legged birds and the four-legged animals. The birds won, establishing the natural order by which people may kill game for food. This picture was taken by W. H. Illingworth, photographer with the Black Hills Expedition of 1874.

Two

Those Who Passed Through

As early as 1811, Wilson Price Hunt and fur trappers of the Astor Fur Company cut through the northeast corner of Wyoming and Crook County. The credit for being the first into this area is given to Jediah Smith. It is through the journals of trappers that much early knowledge was learned. Before the official government expeditions into the Black Hills began, an Irish nobleman, Sir George Gore, spent the summer of 1854 hunting around Inyan Kara. Jim Bridger is said to have accompanied Sir Gore, even if he did not have much use for the man. In May 1857, 1st Lt. G. K. Warren received orders to ascend the Black Hills and ascertain everything relating to the agricultural and mineral resources and to any obstacles to the construction of rail or common roads. The Warren party traveled along Beaver Creek and made its way toward Inyan Kara. This expedition gave the first real knowledge of the topography and drainage of the region until the Black Hills expedition in 1874. Lt. Col. George Armstrong Custer led this expedition into the Black Hills. Gen. George Crook, the famous Native American fighter, served against the Sioux Indians during the Great Sioux Wars of 1876–1877. He passed this way and gave the county his name. Others that have passed through have been the gold seekers following the trail to the mother lode, and then leaving, as their dreams often faded. The Texas cattlemen passed with the vast herds headed to the plains of Montana. Outlaws have sometimes passed through in a hurry to get away. Presidents have passed this way. Some have stayed a while. In later years, big city gangsters would come to spend quiet time fishing before returning to Chicago.

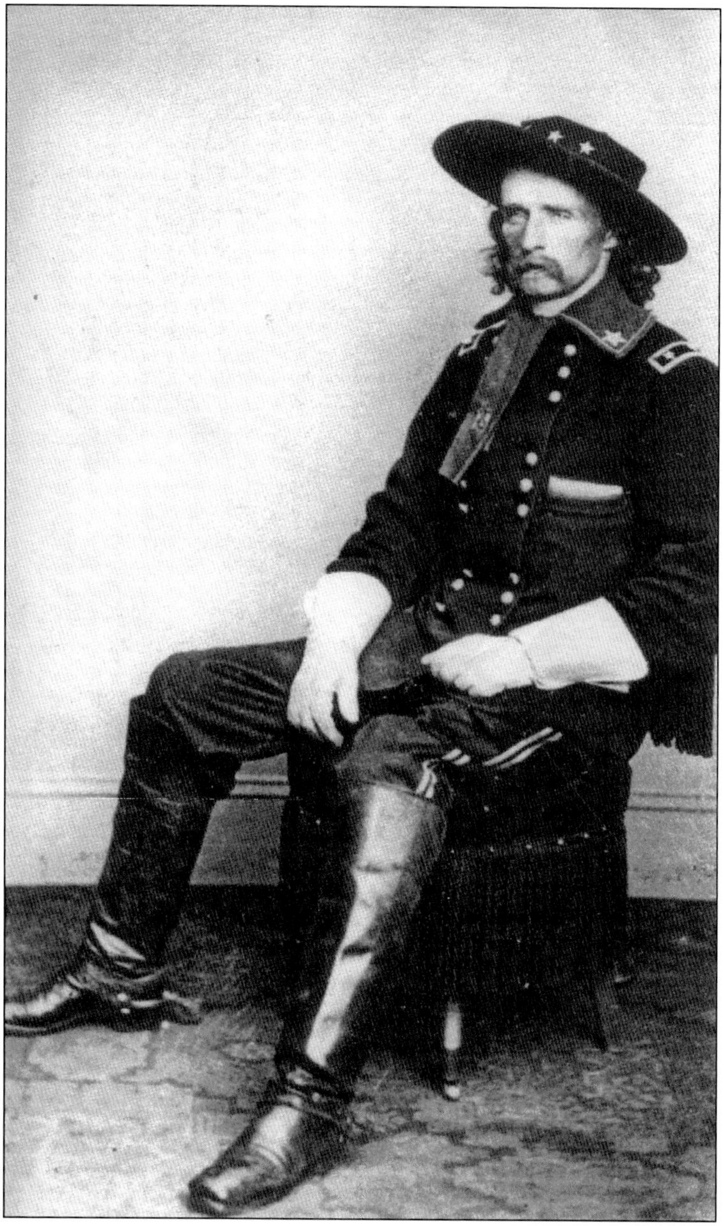

A major military expedition would not enter the Inyan Kara area until 1874, when Lt. Col. George Armstrong Custer (shown) led a group of men into the Black Hills. The expedition was sent to examine the hills and their surrounding area. Custer left Fort Lincoln and entered what would become Wyoming, between the Black Hills and the Bear Lodge Mountains. By July 22, they were camped within 4 miles of Inyan Kara. The next day, it was decided that a small party would proceed to the prominent landmark. Some historians say it was Col. William Ludlow and others say it was Gen. James Forsyth that took his horse over the top. Whichever man was on the top, one of them took a hammer, chisel, and the time to carve "74 CUSTER" into the stone. Above their camp, Custer and his men buried two troopers: Pvt. John Cunningham, who died from a case of dysentery, and Pvt. George Turner, who was shot in a dispute over a hobbled horse. The Crook County Historical Society continues to care for these graves.

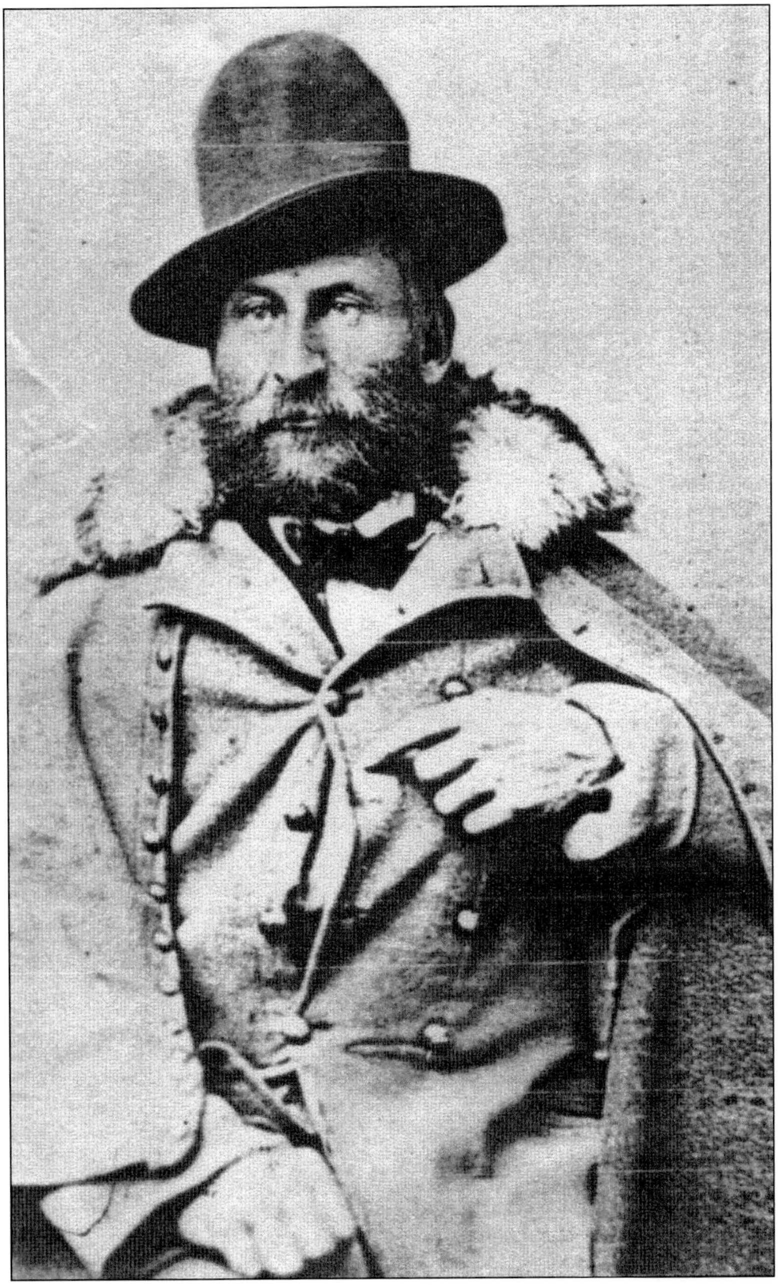

In 1875, after the U.S. government had made several attempts to remove trespassing miners from the Black Hills, the army sent Gen. George Crook (shown) to find the gold seekers and bring them out. Through discussions, the general convinced them it would be in their best interest if they left the area until the government had obtained mining rights for them. General Crook was the commander of the Department of the Platt from 1875 to 1882. In 1879, he spoke for the Ponca tribe and Native American rights during the trial of Standing Bear. He spent his last years speaking out against the unjust treatment of his former Native American adversaries. When he died in 1898, the famous Oglala Lakota chief, Red Cloud, remembered that the general had never lied to them and had given them hope. Crook County, Wyoming, is named in his honor.

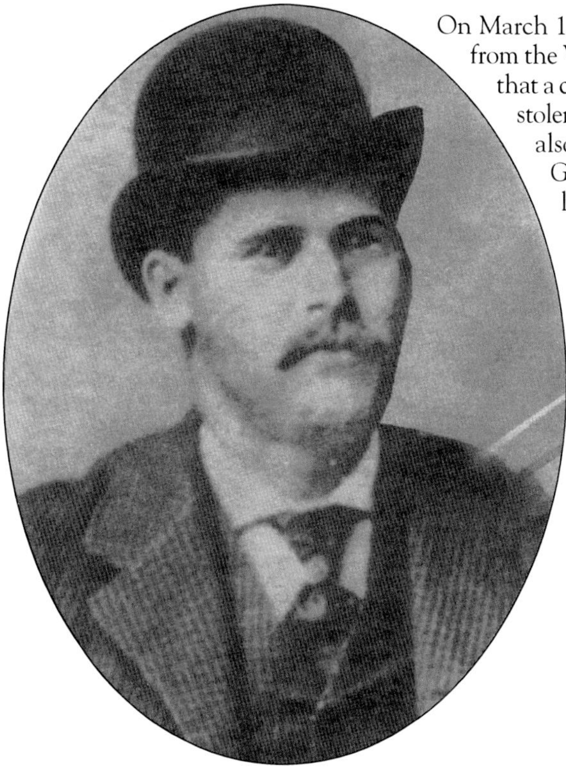

On March 15, 1887, James Widner rode to Sundance from the VVV horse camp on Crow Creek to report that a clean-shaven young man with gray eyes had stolen a horse. A pistol belonging to Widner was also missing. On April 8, 1887, the *Sundance Gazette* reported that Sheriff James Ryan had left for Miles City, Montana, to bring back the kid (in custody) that stole Jim Widner's horse. That "kid" was Harry Longabough, now known as the Sundance Kid.

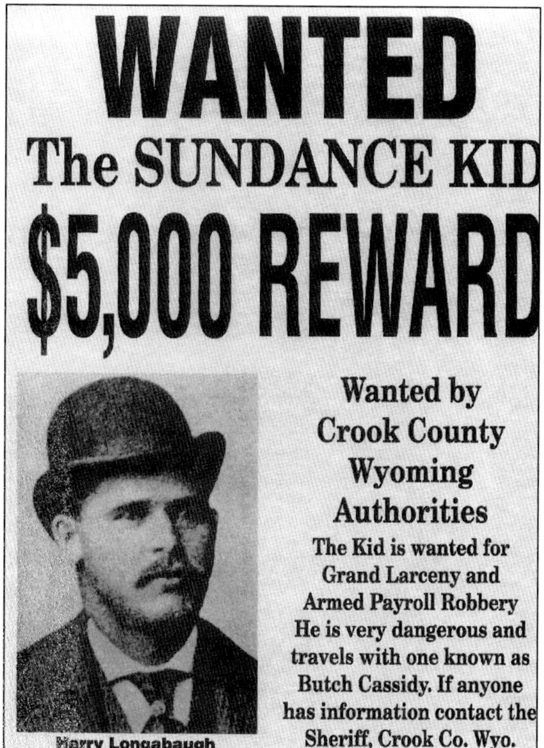

Miles City's newspaper describes how on April 12, 1887, Sheriff Ryan left for Sundance with Longabough. For some reason, Sheriff Ryan decided to return home by way of St. Paul, Minnesota—a big mistake. His prisoner escaped near Duluth. It was Harry who made the next error: he returned to Miles City and was recaptured by Deputy Davis and stock inspector Smith. After arresting Longabough, Davis had to remove three 6-shooters from him. Sheriff Ryan went back to Miles City to retrieve his prisoner. On June 22, 1887, the sheriff and Harry Longabough arrived in Sundance.

Crook County was still in the process of building its first courthouse, but the jail had been complete since April 18. On August 2, 1887, judge William L. Maginnis opened the fall term of district court, and Longabough appeared in court on August 4. There were three indictments against Harry to be considered, but parts of the full indictments are missing. Longabough could not afford an attorney, and so Joseph Stotts was appointed to represent him. The courtroom is pictured here.

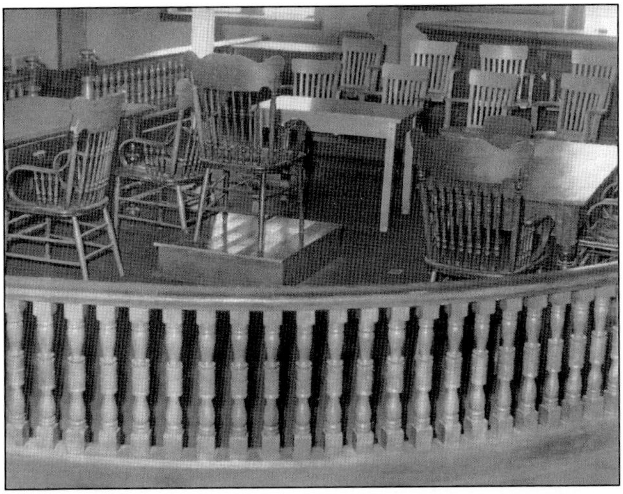

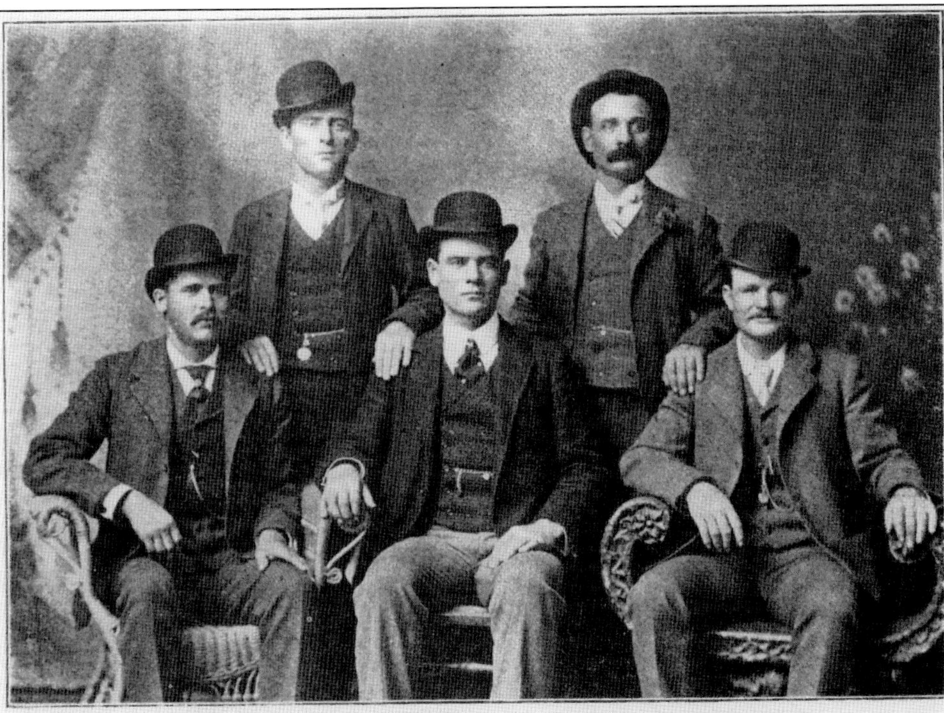

On August 5, 1887, Longabough pled guilty to one count of grand larceny and was sentenced to 18 months of hard labor. On January 22, 1889, the new Crook County prosecuting attorney, H. A. Alden, wrote a letter asking for a pardon for Longabough. On February 4, Gov. Thomas Moonlight issued a letter of pardon since "he is still under 21 years of age and his behavior has been good since confinement." Though Longabough kept quiet for a while after his release, he was not keeping good company. The "Wild Bunch" is pictured from left to right. They are (seated) Harry Longabaugh, the "Sundance Kid"; Ben Kilpatrick; and Robert LeRoy Parker, "Butch Cassidy"; (standing) William Carver and Harvey Logan.

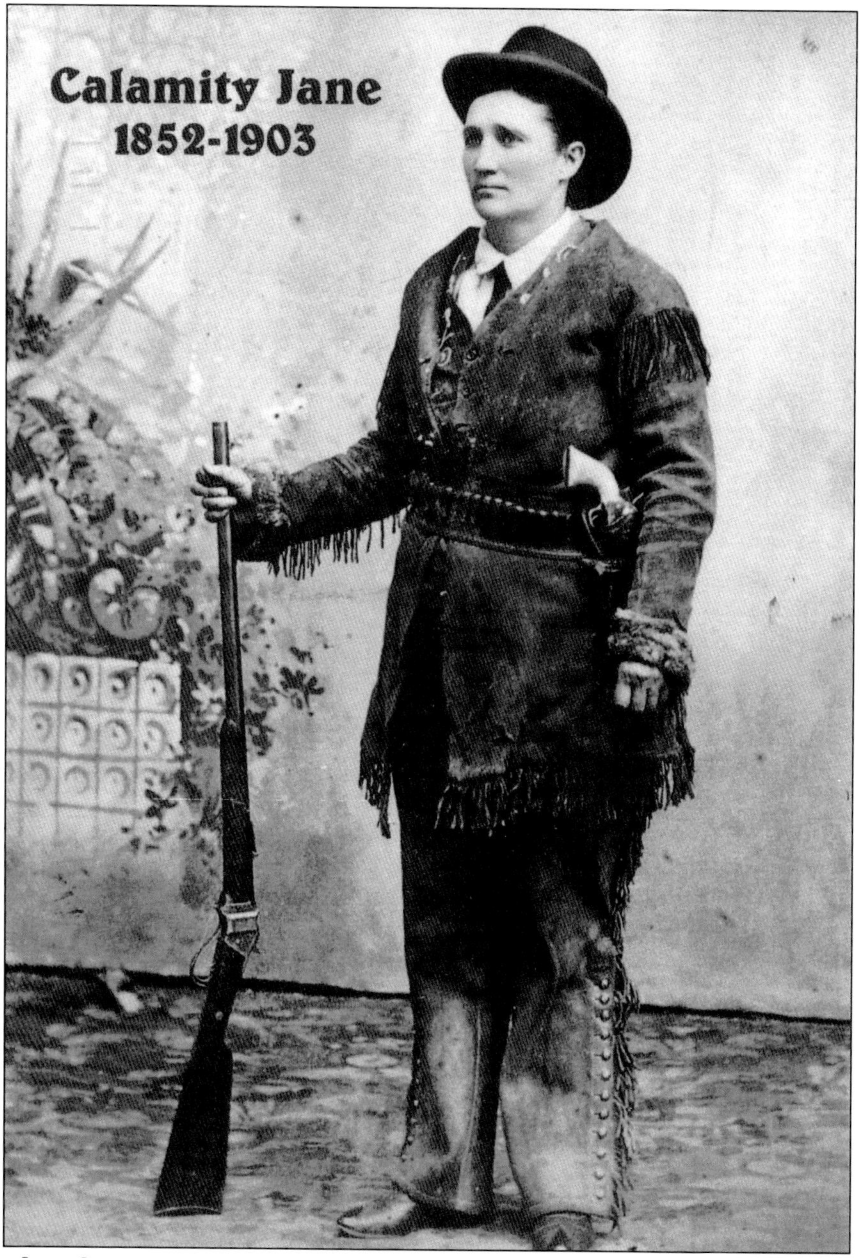

Martha Jane Canary was not a pioneer woman who traveled to Wyoming to till the ground or in any way civilize the West. She was Calamity Jane, a frontier woman who could crack a bull whip, drive a team, spit, curse, and drink with the best. She did not hide the fact that she liked to drink hard liquor more that she liked beer and that she could and would drink until she reached what she called "the howling stage." Calamity stopped in Sundance in June 1903 and found herself a room in the vacant American House Hotel. Businessmen provided her with furniture and groceries, and all seven saloons kept her supplied in her favorite drink. Despite her hard-drinking ways, her kind heart had her sitting with an old freighter as he lay dying. Several weeks later, without a word to anyone, Martha Jane departed Sundance to drift through the other Black Hills communities.

Three

Those Who Stayed

The hardy people who stayed are the ones who laid the foundation for Sundance and the county. The many people who moved out West brought with them their likes, dislikes, fears, and dreams. Much of what they brought was good—knowledge of plants, machinery, and electricity to come would help to take their new community into the modern world. They moved out to a place much different from where they had been. Many times, what had worked for them in the past would not work in the plains and hills of Wyoming. All of this was new and strange. They held close what they had known before, and it gave them comfort. People tend to want things to be the same or as similar as possible to where they came from. It helps them to remember those they left behind. They would do little things to remind them; naming streets after people, places, and events they remembered. Most were proud of where they had been, what they had done, and what they hoped to do now. Those who were not that pleased with what had been or where they had come from hoped to begin again and build a better life for their families and themselves. Those who took the time and effort to learn about what was around them and had the desire to work hard to make a better life succeeded, and those who did not want to or could not, moved on once again.

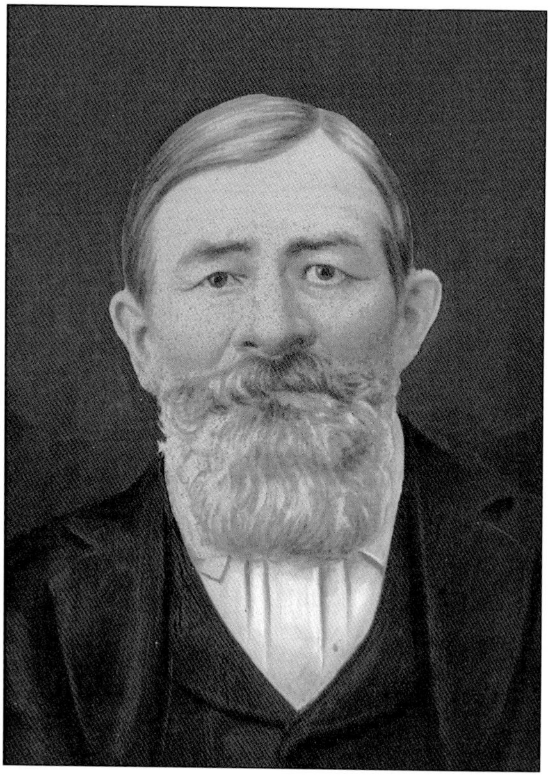

Albert Hoge, one of the original residents of the Black Hills, is indisputably the father of Sundance. He settled in the area in early 1878, building a log cabin near the foot of the Bear Lodge Mountains, where a cold stream from along the cliff provided him a natural buttery. In 1879, he established a mercantile business and trading post, carrying groceries, provisions, canned goods, and ranch supplies, and later he opened and ran a hotel. Hoge maintained an interest in most of the town's businesses for many years. It was at his insistence that the town was named Sundance to honor the mountain and rituals.

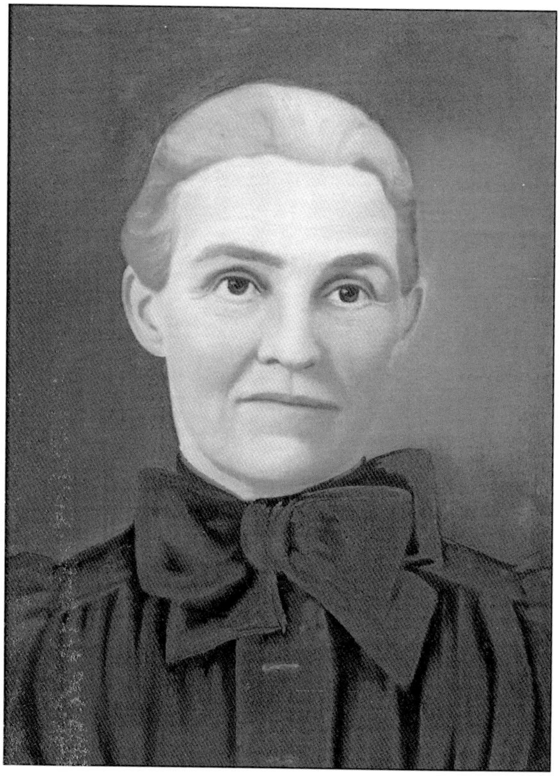

On March 20, 1886, the *Sundance Gazette* reported that Judge A. D. Bishop married Albert Hoge and Sophie E. Durkee at the Sundance Hotel. The new Mrs. Hoge was known by the townspeople as having "good qualities of heart and mind that mark a true woman." A week before, the *Gazette* posted a notice that Sophie proved up and filed with the land office in Cheyenne. Before Sophie married, she made sure to obtain a title to the property that she worked so hard to make her own.

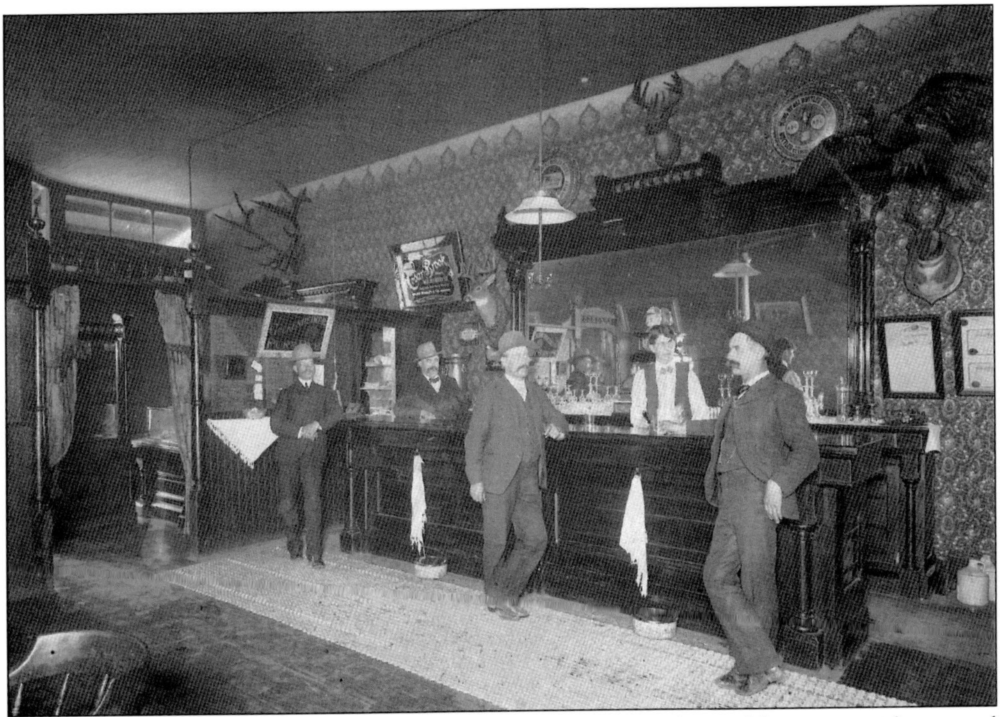

Ezekiel "Zeke" Crewdson has one of the nicest legacies in Sundance. He was considerate and obliging to others. He was always punctual and was known as a careful, capable man. He ran a tonsorial parlor—a barbershop. When the game of baseball came to town in 1886, Ezekiel was one of the first to sign up to play. He was Crook County sheriff from 1905 to 1907. In 1913, his obituary stated that he was probably the least offensive man in Crook County. He is pictured inside Sackett's Dump, joined by friends for some liquid refreshment. From left to right are Ole Swanbury, Charlie Sackett, Ezekiel Crewdson, Charley Taylor behind the bar, and John Propst.

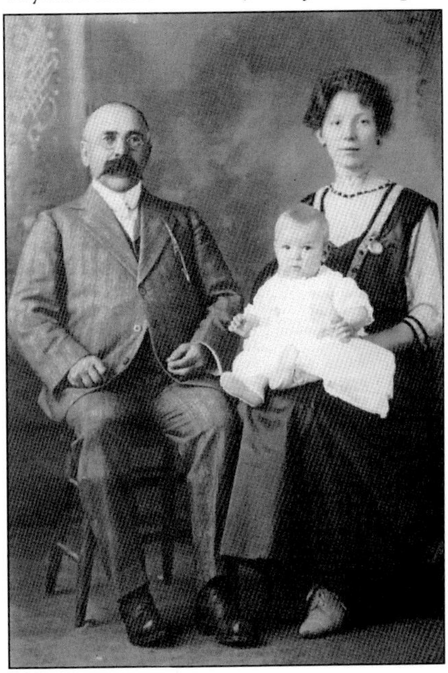

On September 4, 1913, the *Wyoming Blade* reported on the first page that Fred Schloredt and his new bride had returned home to Sundance. Fred had left for Ringelhem, Germany, on June 1, planning to be married upon his arrival. It was not until he had arrived that he was told that the German government required proof that he was not already married. To obtain this proof would have taken at least three months. Fred, not wanting to wait, instead brought his soon-to-be wife to Hoboken, New Jersey, where they were married on August 28, 1913, and returned to Sundance. This picture was taken two years later of Fred, Elfredia, and baby Lee.

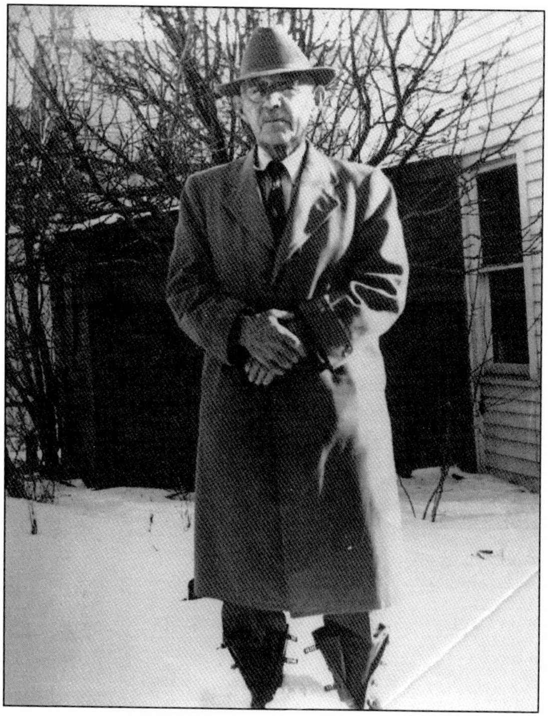

When Dr. Julius Frederick Clarenbach started practicing medicine in Sundance in 1902, he lived at the Zane Hotel. It had a livery stable across the street, which was very convenient for a doctor who might need to hire a rig for an emergency house call. In 1911, the doctor married Jennie Holben, a teacher at the Stanton school south of Sundance. Dr. Clarenbach died at age 80 after 50 years of doctoring the people of Crook County. Old-timers remember him as a gruff but dedicated physician.

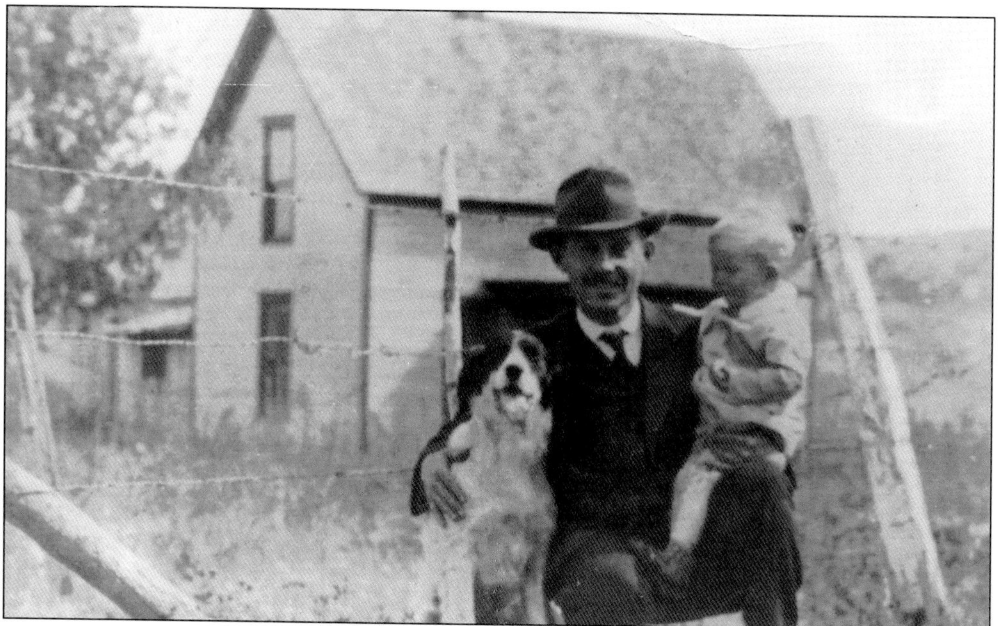

Dr. Clarenbach's first office was a room in the back of Fawkes Sundance Drug Store on Main Street. Its owner and clerks acted as involuntary receptionists—they were kind enough to tell waiting patients when the doctor might be expected back from a house call. Dr. Clarenbach was one of the first doctors in the area to diagnose appendicitis. He saved many in the area who would have been misdiagnosed with a blocked bowel. In 1911, he received a degree in dentistry, adding to his practice. The doctor is pictured in front of the old Dudry house in 1920, holding Ruth Grykowsky.

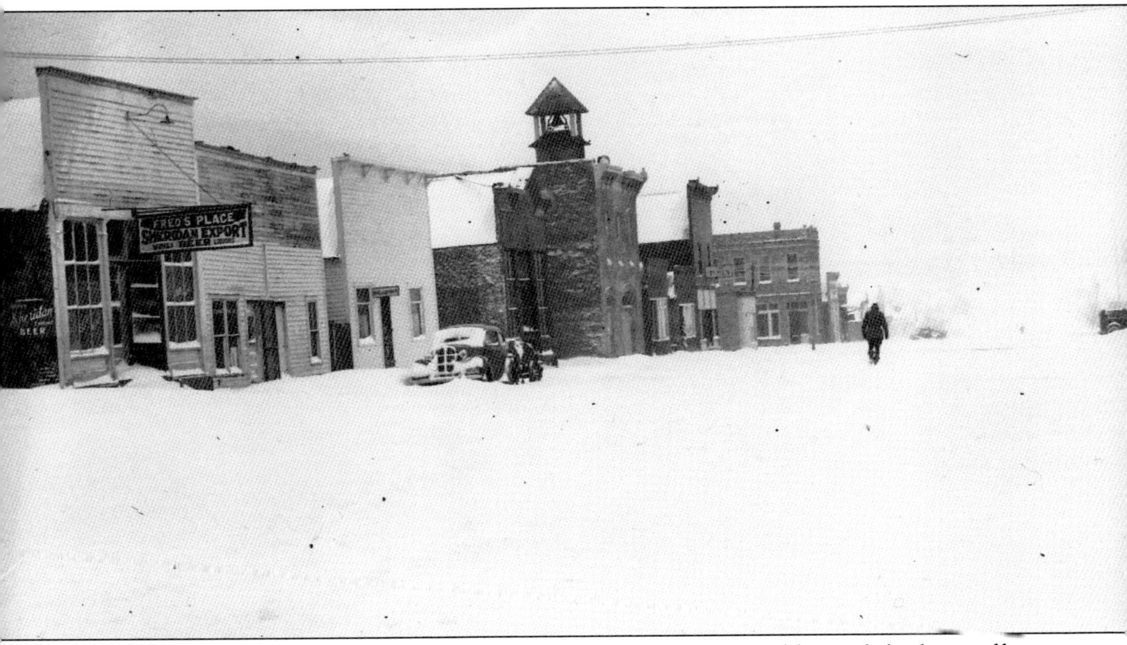

In 1911, with a loan of $500 from Fred Schloredt, Dr. Clarenbach and his wife built an office on Main Street. It stood opposite Frank's dry goods store, which later became Clyde Robert's hardware store. In the early days, Dr. Clarenbach made house calls with a horse and buggy, or a sleigh in winter. In 1935, he bought an automobile and was seen tooling around in a 1931 Model A, still used in parades throughout the county. His office is the third building down, the white one, with his car parked in front. The fifth building, with its bell tower, is city hall.

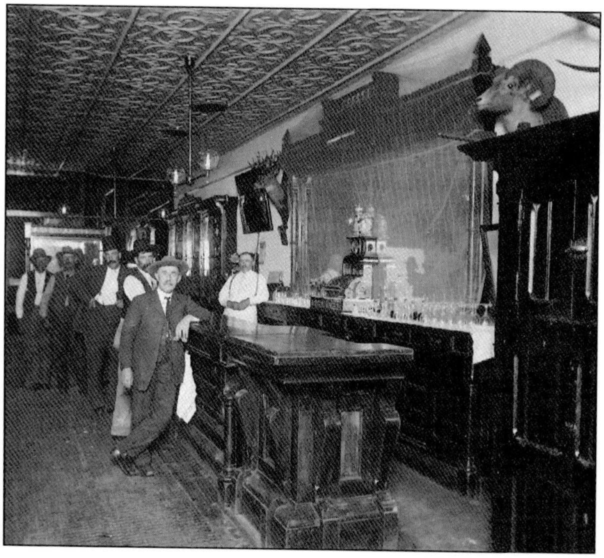

Charlie Sackett was orphaned at 12 years old and began making his way westward, working many jobs as he crossed the country. When he arrived in Sundance in 1890, he decided to stay put. He established Sackett's Palace Saloon on the corner of Second and Main Streets. His friends called it "Sackett's Dump." He sold fine cigars, wine, and liquor and was said to have the finest saloon in town—the Palace had wood floors and oak chairs. Pictured from left to right are the following: unidentified, Judge George Ashdown, Charley Kirby, E. D. Brandeberry, and Abe Frank. Charlie Sackett is behind the bar. Netting covers the mirror.

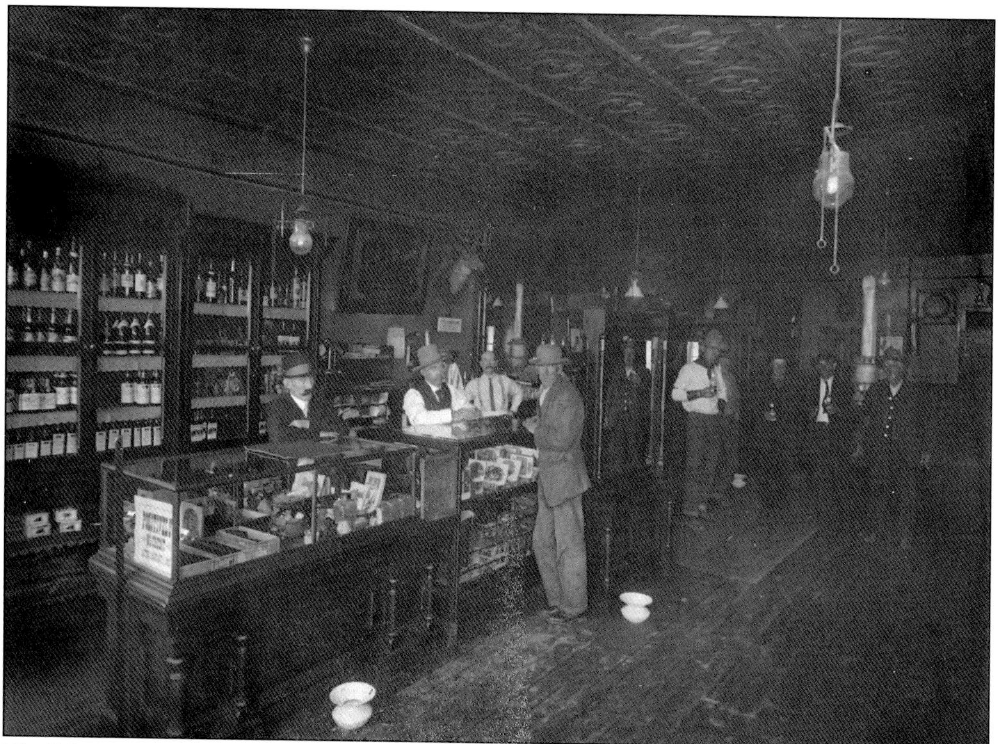

The July 6, 1900, *Crook County Monitor* advertised some of Sackett's Palace Saloon's offerings. You could get Overholt and Guchenheimer seven-year-old rye whiskey for 50¢ a pint; 1889 Belmont bourbon was sold for 75¢ a pint; and Old Jordan 1892 whiskey was 50¢ a pint. Soda, mineral waters, and beers were also available. This picture shows the pressed tin ceiling and spittoons set up along the floor. Most of the men in this picture are unidentified. Charlie Sackett is the second man from the left at his usual spot behind the bar.

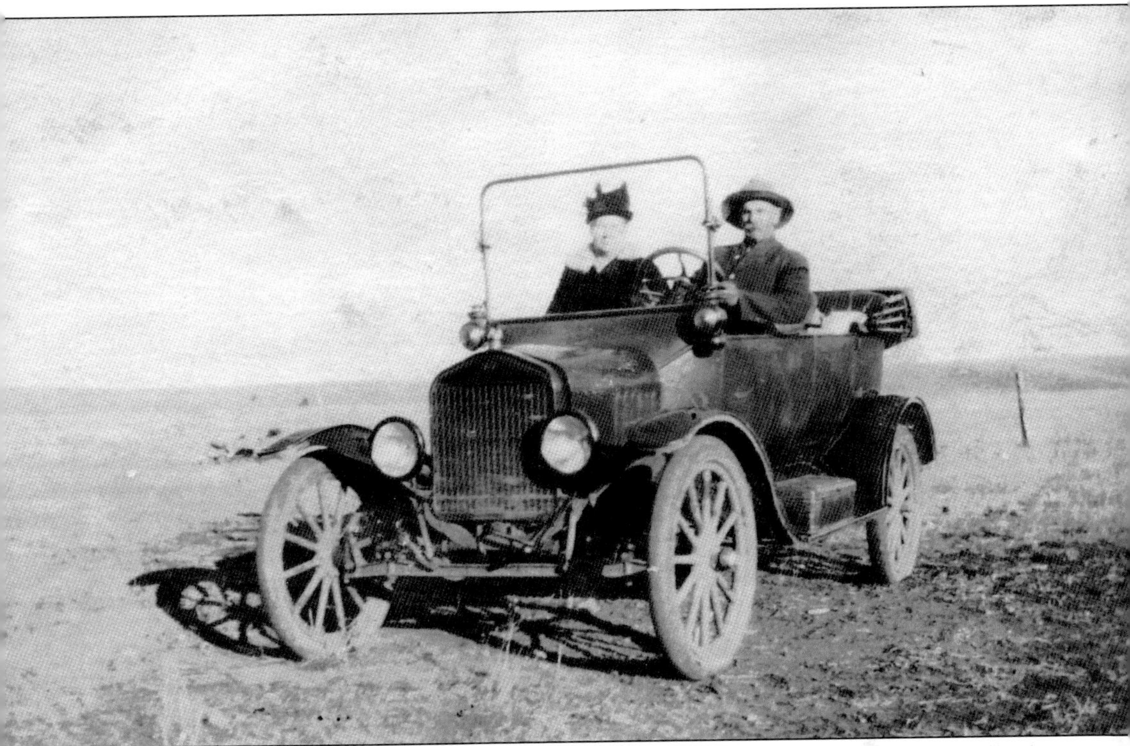

Willard S. Good and his wife, Melissa, (pictured) were born in Rabbit Hash, Kentucky. Willard freighted from South Dakota and Nebraska into Wyoming. In 1878, he returned to Kentucky and married Melissa Gainor, a widow with a son, James. Melissa and Willard homesteaded west of Sundance. Willard loved horses. He raised good Percheron and Clydesdale horses. He would not tolerate mistreatment of animals and would often put a stop to others mistreating their animals. His granddaughter told the story of Willard's friends saying that if they were ever reincarnated, they would like to be one of Willard Good's animals.

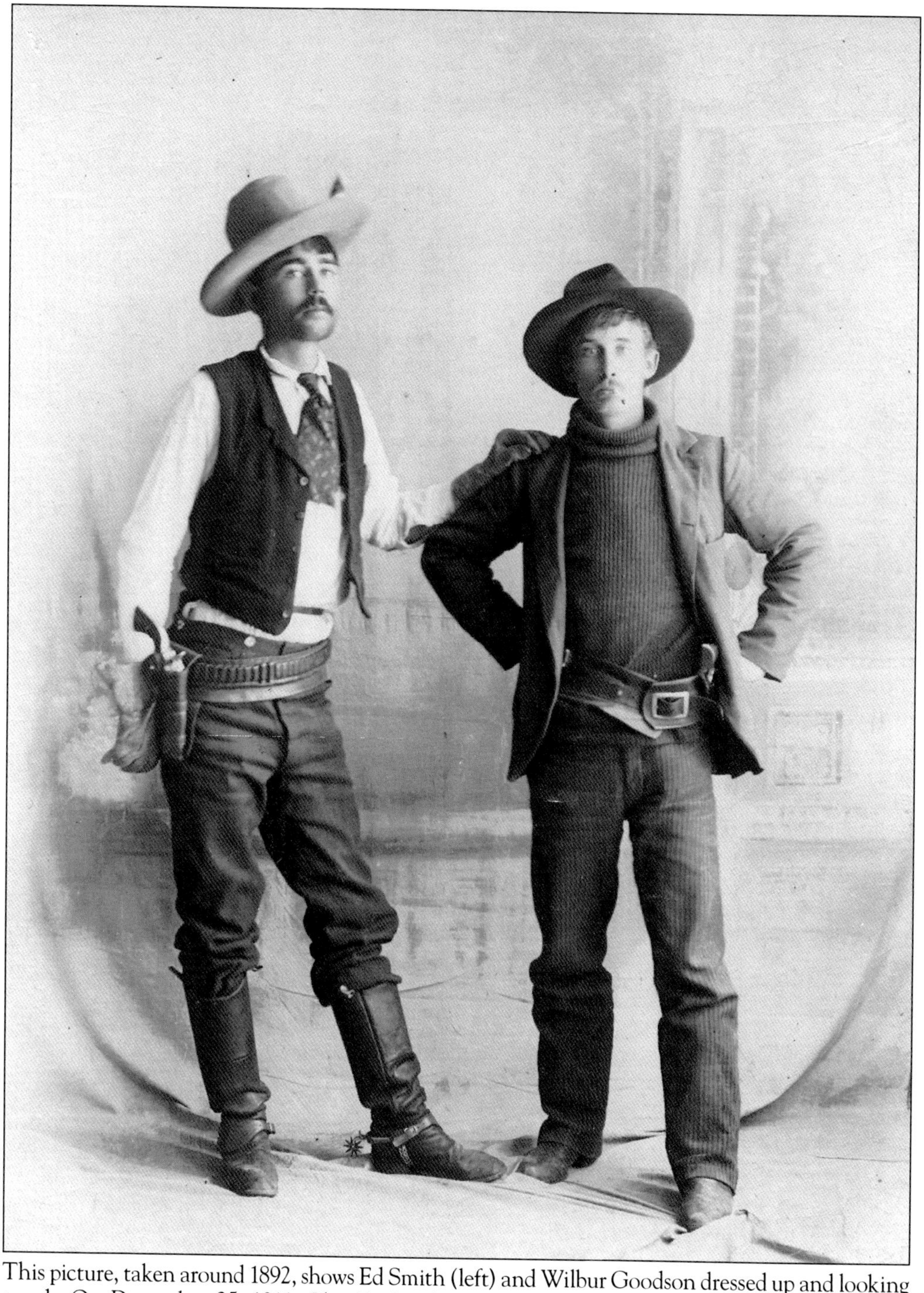

This picture, taken around 1892, shows Ed Smith (left) and Wilbur Goodson dressed up and looking tough. On December 25, 1911, Cleo Richardson married Wilber Goodson at the Richardson ranch. Wilber's parents were Gilbert and Ella Goodson. Wilber was born in Spearfish because the cavalry had moved the family into town for protection from roving Native Americans. Wilber played the violin for barn and school dances and was a forest ranger at the Geyser Creek ranger station from 1910 until 1918. Wilber died July 23, 1938.

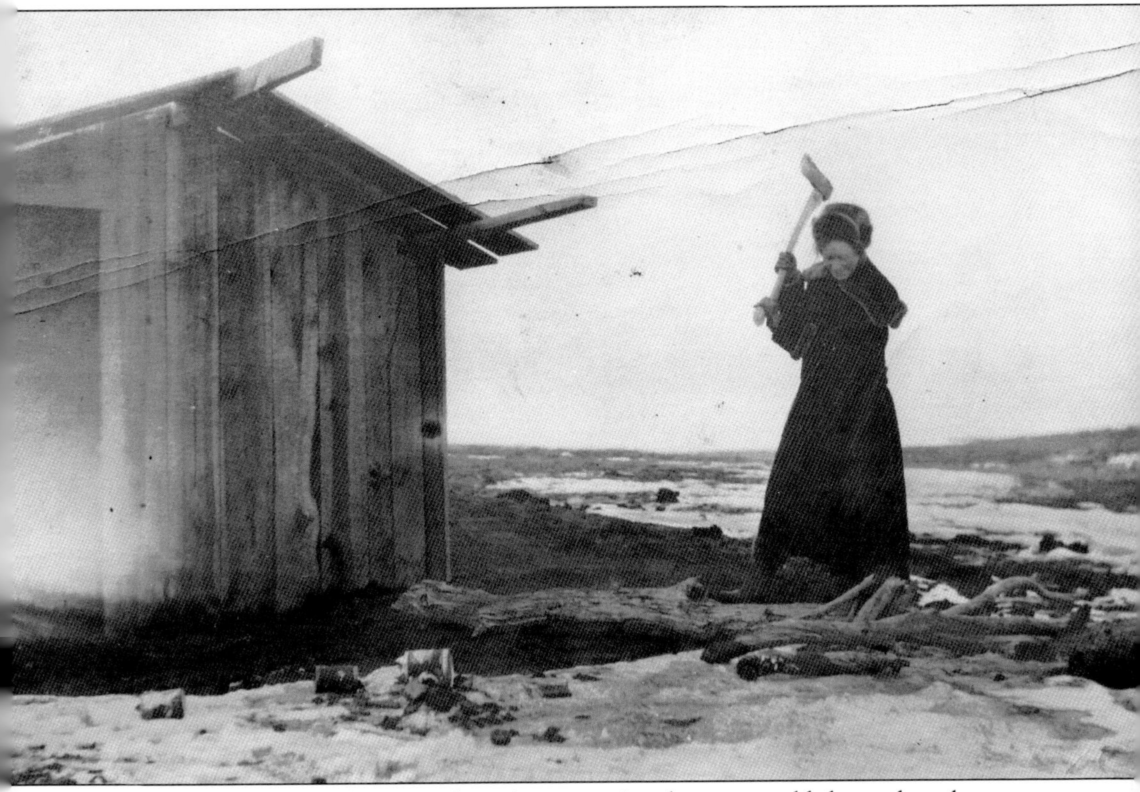

Many women came west to homestead on their own. Land agents could show where lots were available for homesteading, but many people simply set off on horseback or on foot looking for their own land that would give them a better life. To claim a plot, they would need to record it at the nearest land office and make a small payment to hold it in their name until they had "proved up" on the homestead. Once they had shelter, a source of water, and a fuel supply for heat and cooking, they would have to show that they had continued living on the plot and had made an effort to improve what had been there. This could mean building dams, fences, crops, and barns. After this, it was home. Single women often had as much success as men. Many would become teachers and also work their land. These ladies were considered good catches because they had paying jobs and owned property.

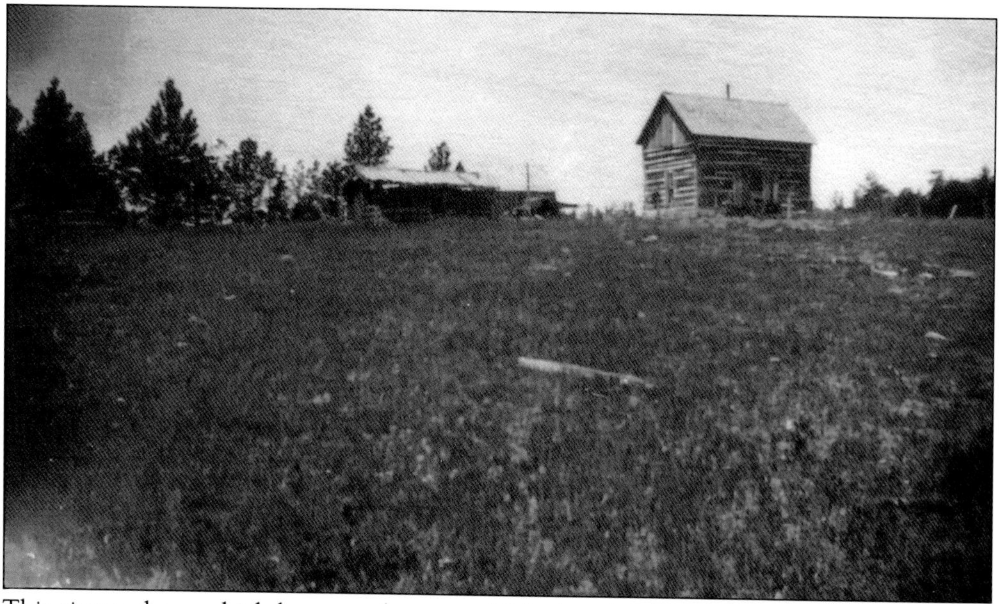

This picture shows a high lonesome homestead. The logs for the two-story house and the barn came from the forest trees in the background. The logs used in building this homestead were hand-hewed or hand-peeled and carefully set into place.

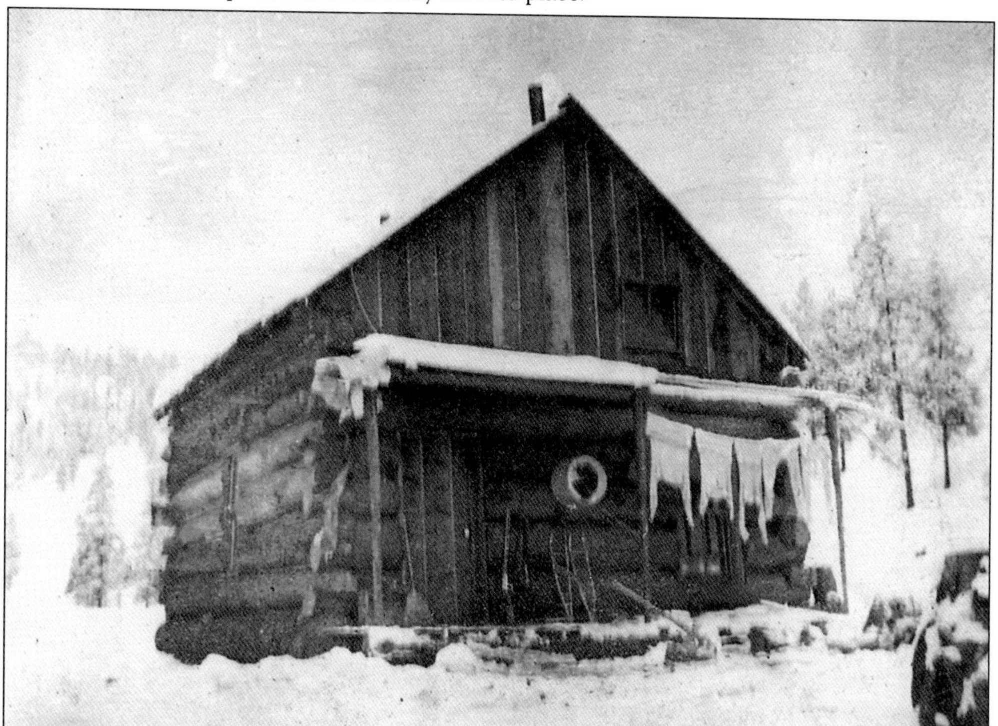

The picture of this cabin was taken in 1911 on a cold winter day. The lady of the house still hung her laundry out. Freeze-dried had a different meaning in 1911. The snowshoes are by the door as is the broom and washtub. The rifle is within arm's reach as you come out the door. This family is ready for the winter.

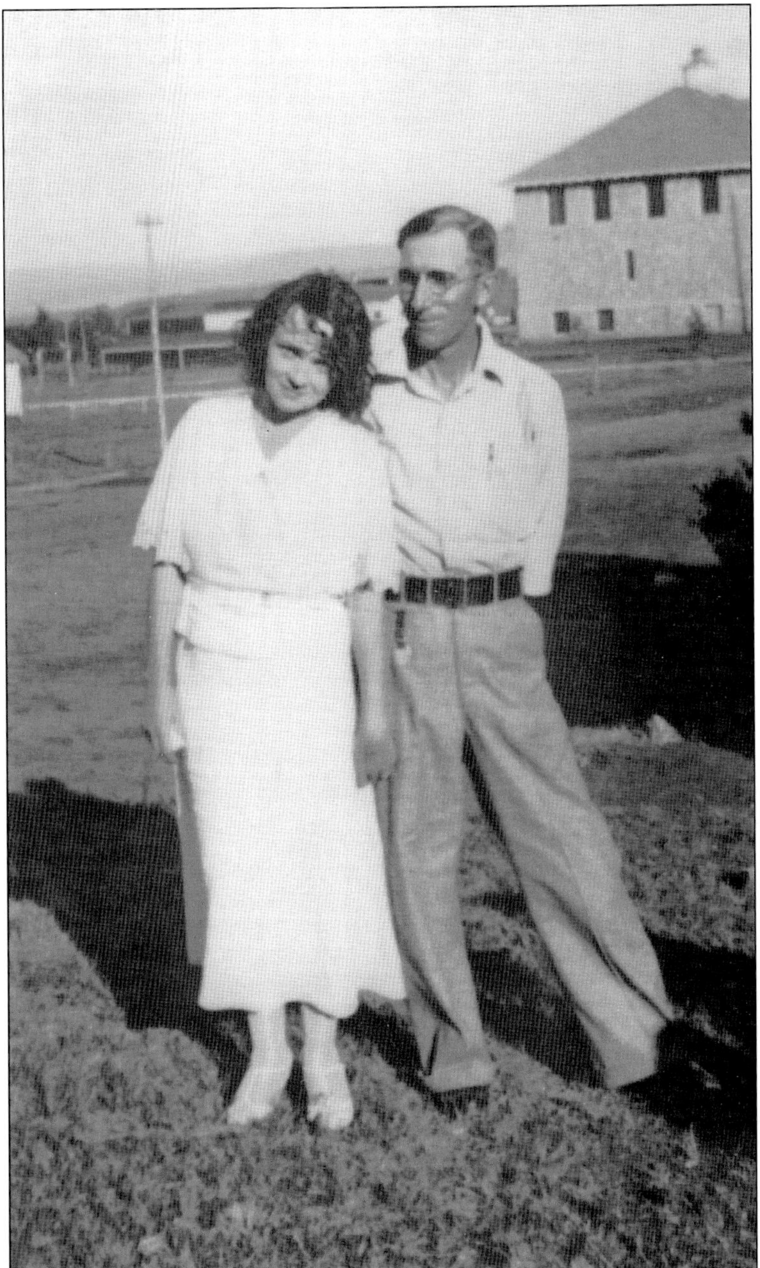

This is a picture of Earl L. and Lillian M. Kipp taken on the lawn of the courthouse square. Earl and Lillian arrived in Sundance in 1926 with six children and no job. With the Great Depression just around the corner, prospects for a job looked slim. They moved into the second floor of the Sundance Shoe and Harness Shop, which belonged to Lily's parents, Anton and Margaret Nelson. It was located on the north side of Main Street between Second and Third Streets. Earl worked as a carpenter and painter in Sundance and then on a road construction crew on the road between Beulah and Sundance. In 1934, they purchased a house on the north end of Main Street. By this time, there were two more children in the family; four more would be born in the house, making 12 total.

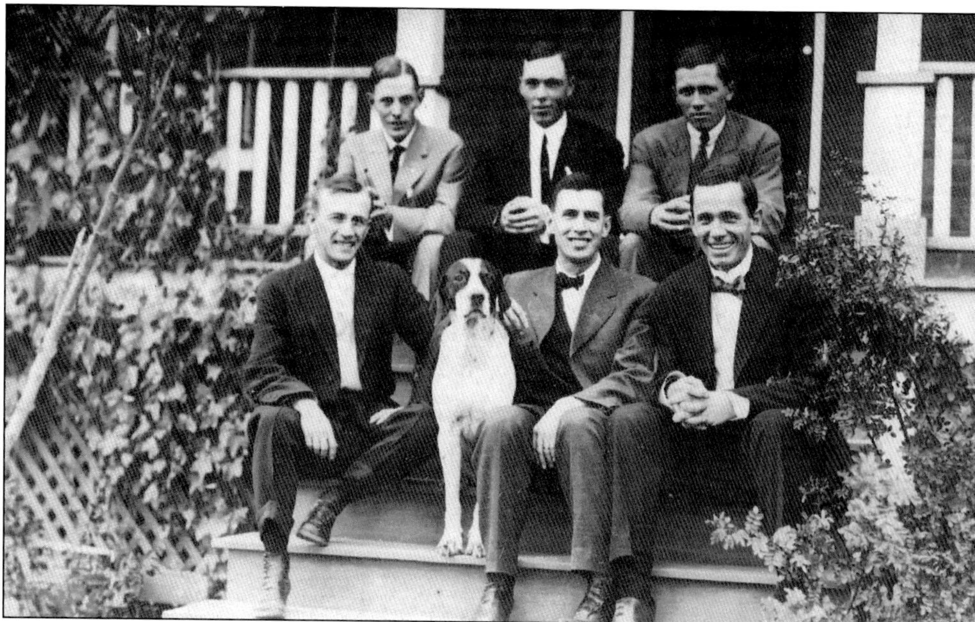

From left to right are (first row) Clif Ruggles, Rover the dog, Harry Ilsley, and Ted Brockett; (second row) Edwin Rounds, Harry Attebarry, and Herb Brockett. This is most of the Sundance Bearcat team sitting on the front steps of a Sundance home. When Edwin was 16 and working in a Sundance drugstore, Calamity Jane stopped him on the street and asked him to tie her bonnet strings. Edwin Rounds tied a neat bow knot amid the laughter from the men along the sidewalk.

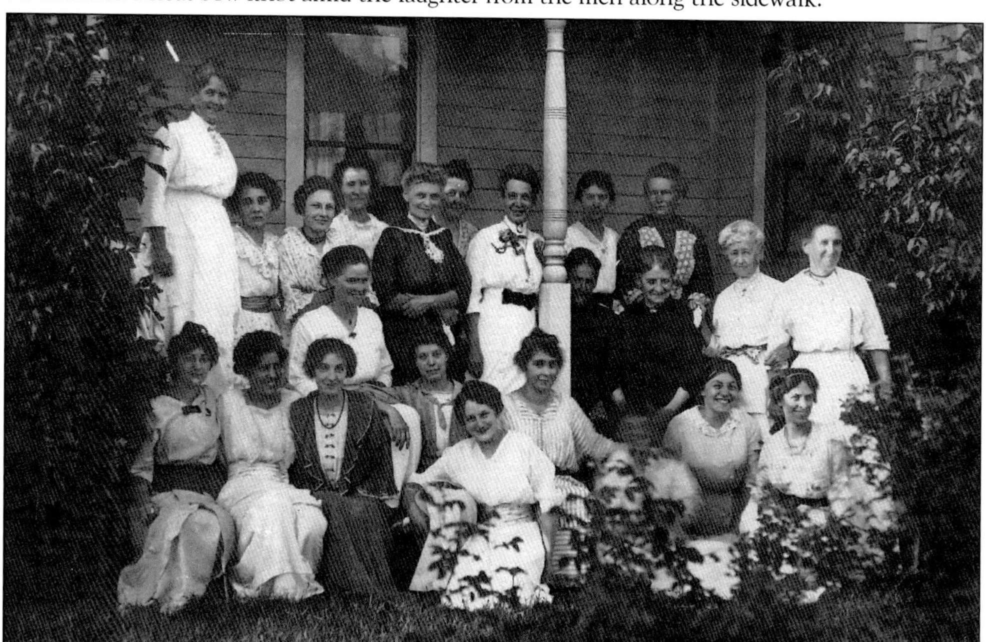

This is a picture of friends of Mrs. W. E. Brockett and her daughter-in-law Anne Mae Brockett on the Brockett front porch. Here are 22 of the finest ladies the community assembled to enjoy each other's company and maybe to discuss the importance of using their right to vote in an upcoming election. After all, this is the "Equality State."

This is the William "W. J." Jonathan and Effie Victor Williamson family in 1913. William and Effie, married in 1887, were parents of nine. The children pictured here, in no order, are Vennie Zeffie, Ima Della, Inez Edma, Lillie Ethel, Josie Elvery, Emmett, Walter, Charles, and Maurice. W. J. opened a grocery store and filling station at the corner of West and Cleveland Streets in 1927. The *Sundance Times* reported that he always greeted his customers pleasantly. He served as city councilman, school board treasurer, and mayor for two terms. The family was remembered as hardworking, fun-loving residents of Sundance.

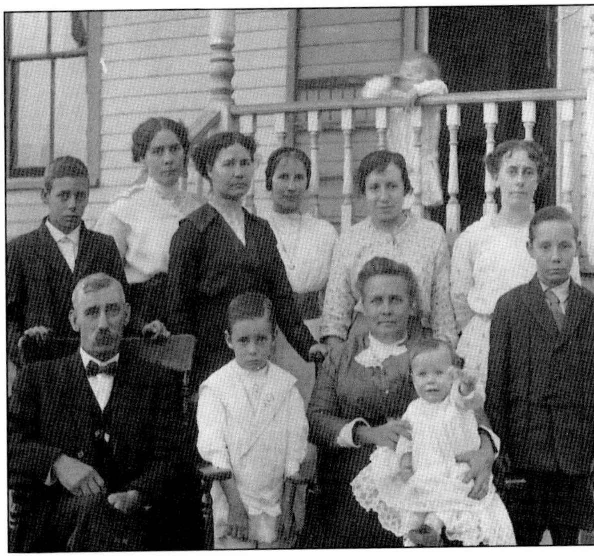

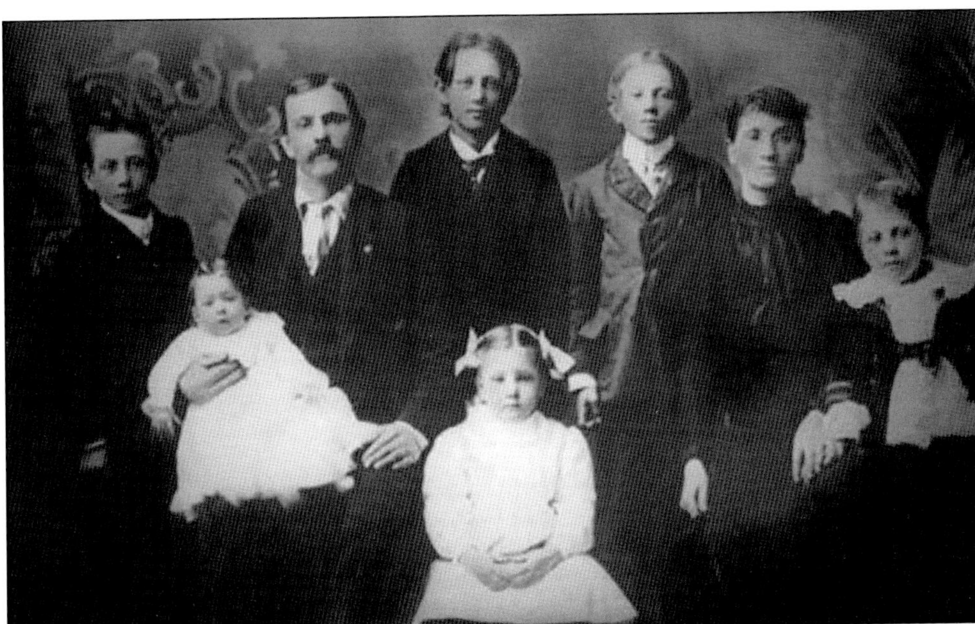

Clement Absolom and Mary Etta Busby Good married in 1887 and had seven children. Two died at an early age. Those remaining were William, Fred, Walter, Lawrence, and Etta. Mary Etta passed away in 1903, leaving Clement to raise their family. In 1910, he won the bid to dig ditches to provide reliable drinking water, and in 1913, he was hired as town marshal and water commissioner. William served as deputy marshal for a while but decided there was more money to be had in the mines. Fred had several business ventures, including a meat market and a saloon. Lawrence had garages. Walter became a surveyor for the Bureau of Land Management. Etta married twice and moved to California. Clement's obituary noted the passing of a respected pioneer.

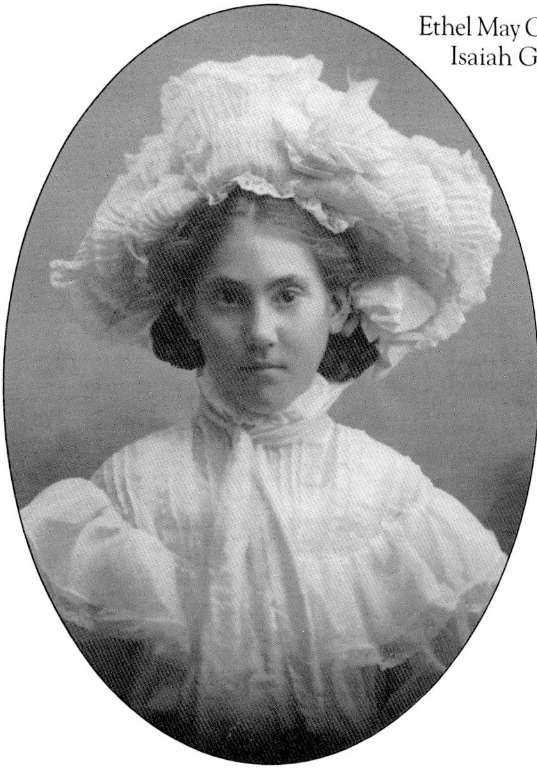

Ethel May Gould was the youngest of Nettie and Augustus Isaiah Gould's seven children. She never married.

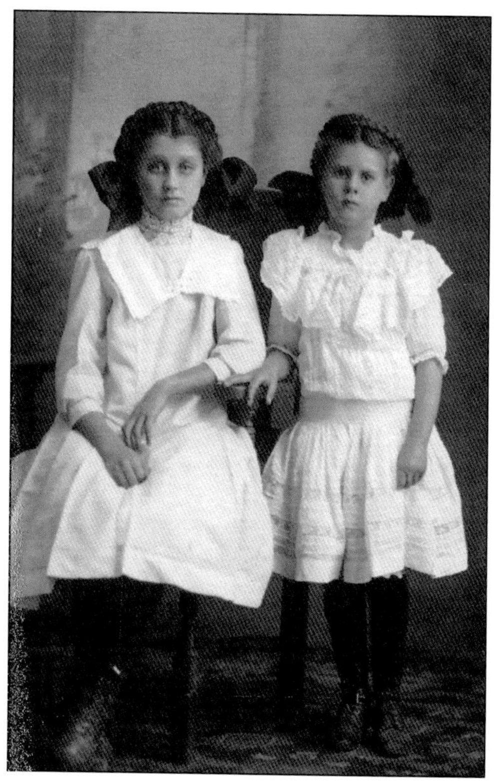

Nettie Pearl Gould married Frank Humphrey when she was 14 and he was 23 in 1889. Their girls, Bernice and Myrtle Humphrey, are pictured here.

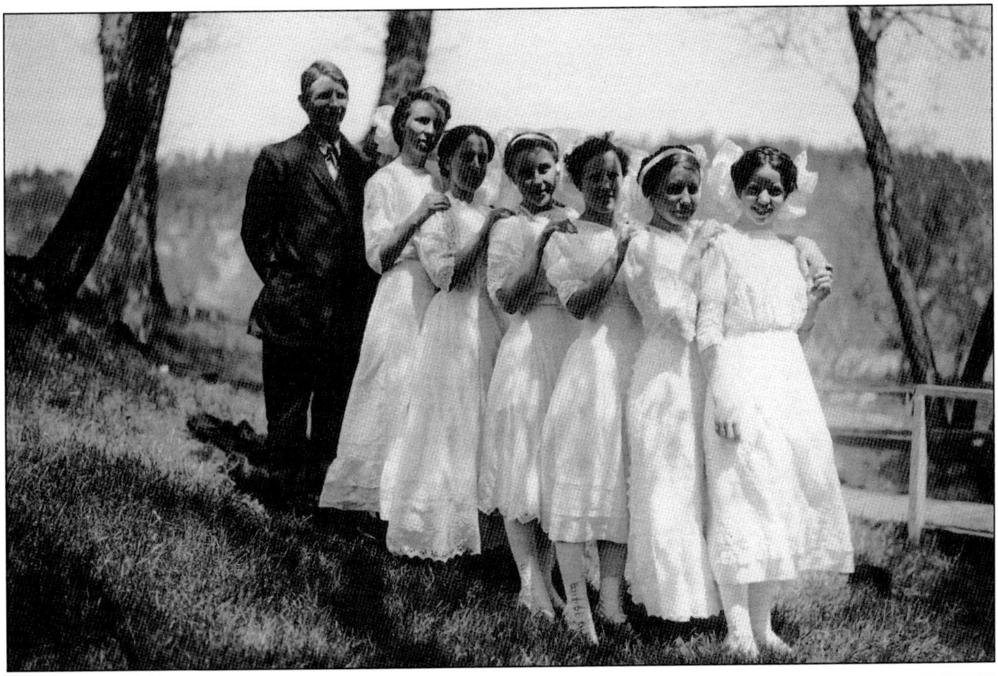

This unidentified family and friends are out to enjoy a Sunday afternoon. The proud father looks over these ladies all dressed in white. The lace and hair bows look so crisp. The girls in the shorter dresses show off their white high-button shoes.

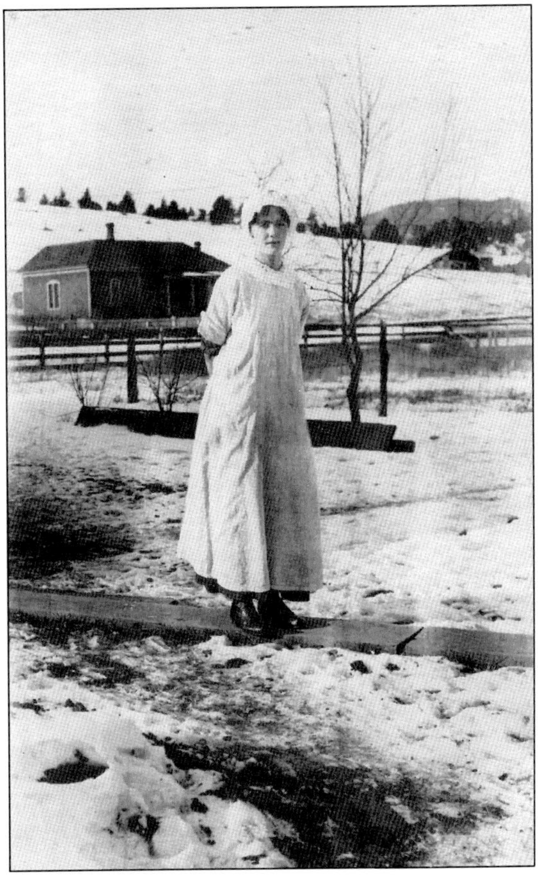

And then came Monday morning. There were floors to scrub and clothes to wash, bleach, starch, and iron. There would be wood to chop. The kitchen stove used a lot of wood to bake the bread and keep the iron hot. This unidentified lady of the house has on the open-backed dress she uses as her apron.

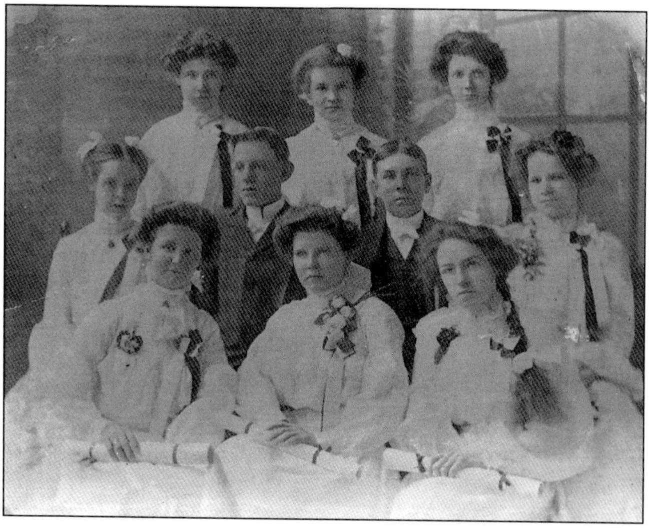

It was not every day that you could put on your best high-necked dress—or in the case of the gentlemen, your best starched collar—and have your picture taken. This group may have been part of a wedding party. Seated from left to right are (first row) Lila Bruner-Zimmerschied, Maude Pearson-Wakeman, and Hazel Foster; (second row) Frances Rounds, Edwin Rounds, J. C. Baldwin, and Mary Tom; (third row) Mary Alice Goods-Schloredt, Clair Baker, and Mrs. Rathbun.

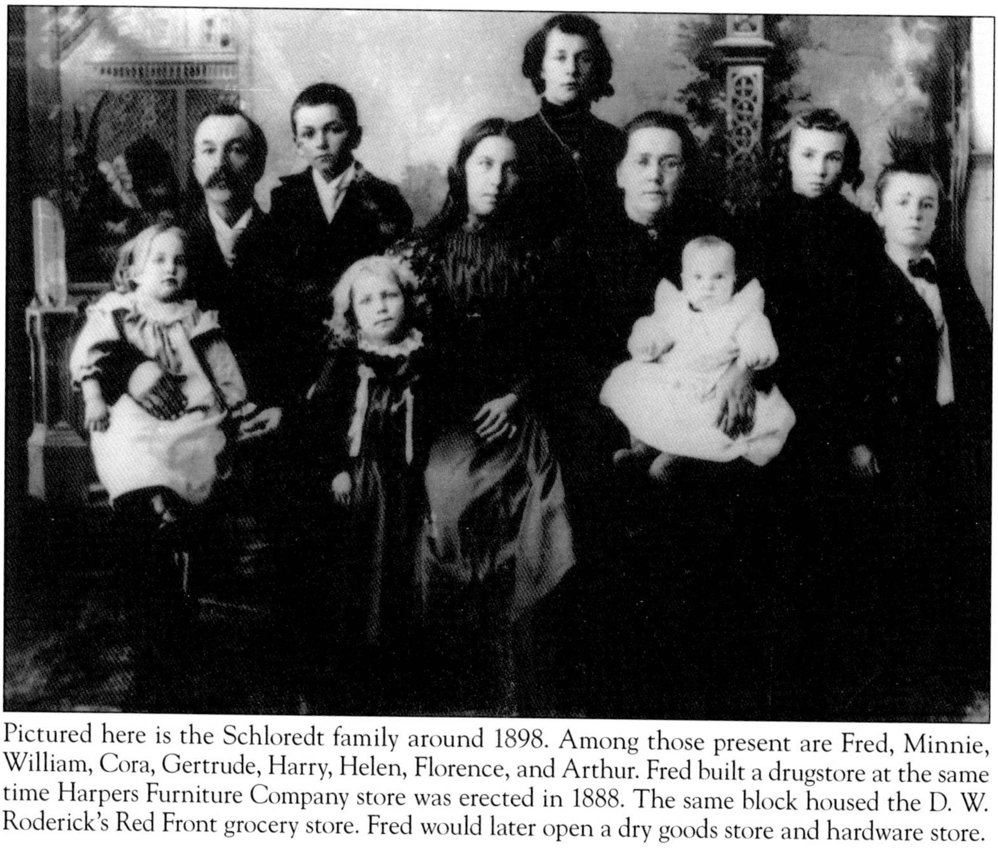

Pictured here is the Schloredt family around 1898. Among those present are Fred, Minnie, William, Cora, Gertrude, Harry, Helen, Florence, and Arthur. Fred built a drugstore at the same time Harpers Furniture Company store was erected in 1888. The same block housed the D. W. Roderick's Red Front grocery store. Fred would later open a dry goods store and hardware store.

Four

The Land They Used

People have been coming to the northeast corner of Wyoming for many years to give the land a chance to make their lives better. The land was free for the taking when the cattlemen arrived in Wyoming. There were no fences or towns or homesteaders. The miners staked claims out on the land for their mine. The original Homestead Act enabled many early settlers to try their hand at framing the plains and valleys. There was a mindset to settle the West and to bring unused lands into production. The ground was hard and packed, not used to being turned upside down. There was rolling prairie waiting for the plow. The assumption was that this was extremely fertile soil and everything should grow easily. And with these men came their families, and with families came gardens, flowers, and vegetables. There were rivers, creeks, and springs to supply all the water a person could use. There were vast virgin forests to be harvested. With the timber from these forests, homes, barns, and businesses were built and trains would move. It was long, hard work to take this land and make it give back everything they wanted from it. The miners, ranchers, farmers, loggers, and sheep men all did their very best to give back to the land as much as they took. This is a land that invokes respect, and it is with that respect that the people cared for it. They watched for what the land needed to keep it safe and healthy. With all of this, some of them made a go of it and squeezed every drop they could from a land that does not like to share itself.

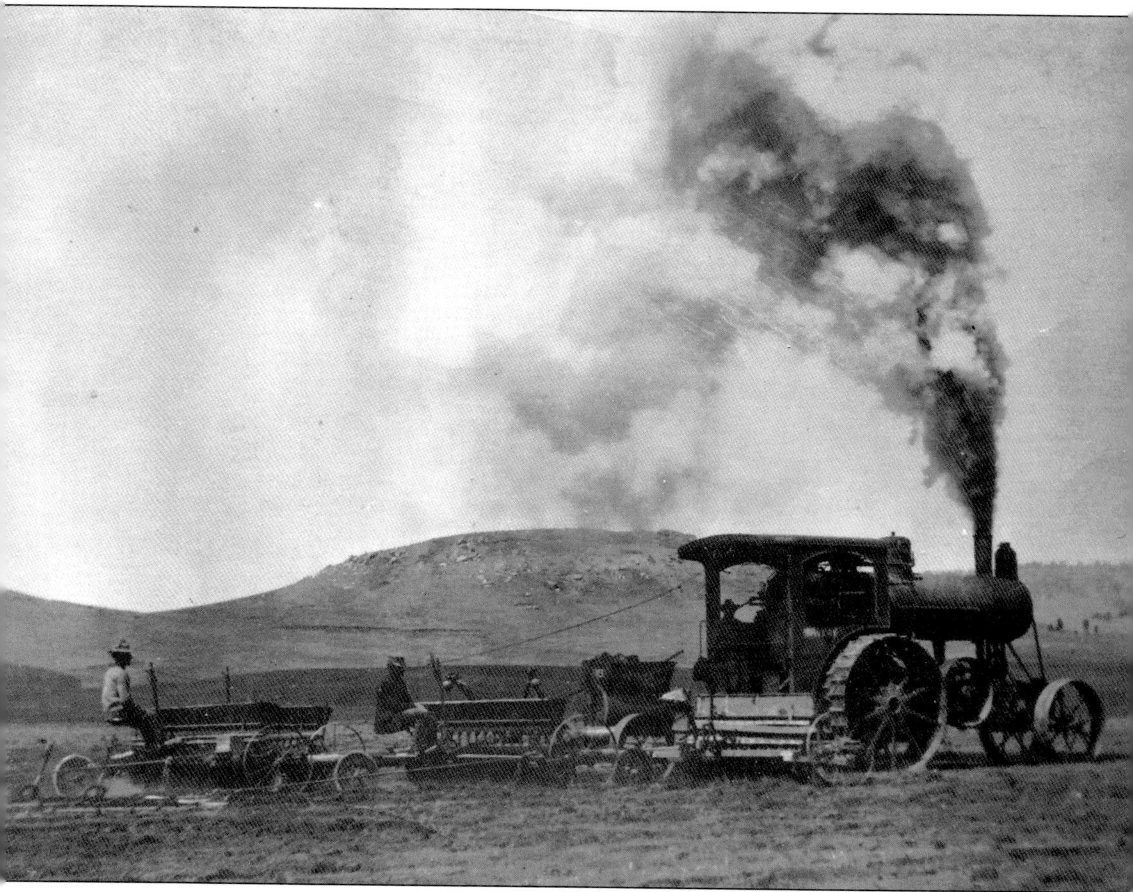

In 1911, the state board of horticulture stated that Crook County had the richest farmland in Wyoming, judged by the nature of vegetation found upon it. Even without irrigation, the average yield per acre was about 24 bushels of wheat, 60 bushels of barley, 31 bushels of corn, and 129 bushels of potatoes. By using irrigation, a yield per acre could double. According to the pamphlet, there were thousands of acres of government land in the county that could be adopted for agriculture. Pictured here is a 1910 Reeves eight-plow steam tractor pulling two grain drills.

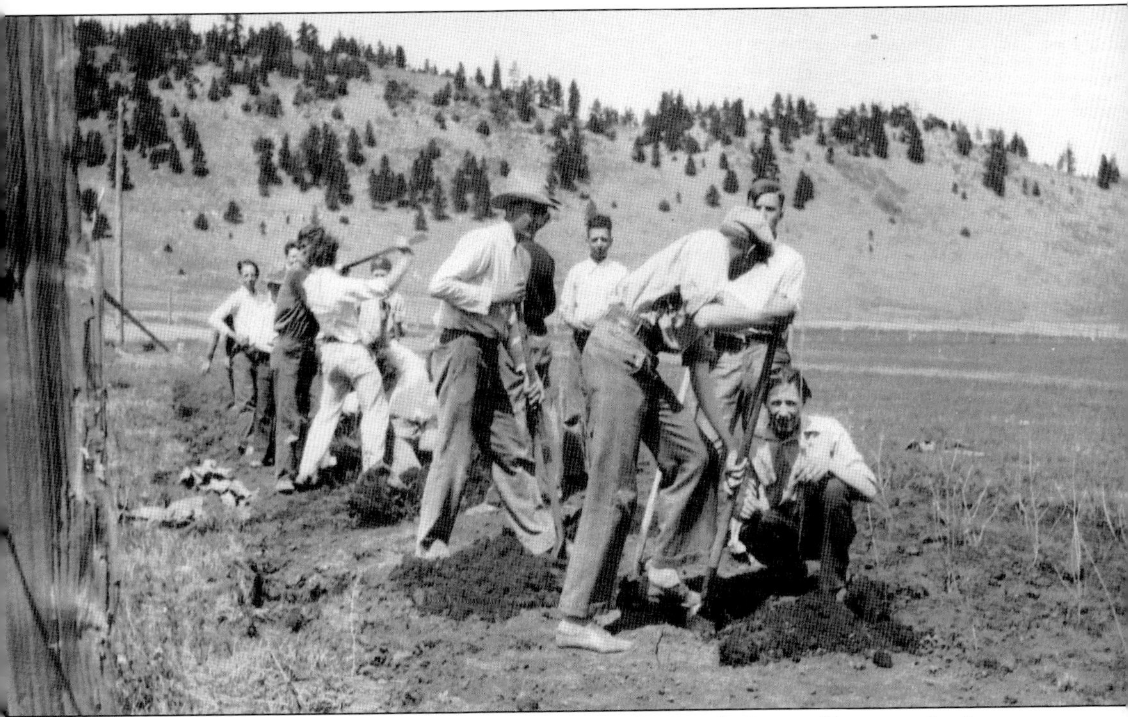

This 1932 picture shows a group of men planting trees at the Crook County Fairgrounds. Among those pictured are Victor Cole, Gerald Blakeman, Elbridge Cole, and Curley Marion McLaughlin. Sundance and many other places were just coming out of the Great Depression and Dust Bowl years. These men could have been working under the Great Plains Program of the New Deal, which was designed to help stabilize the soil and to lessen the wind's effects. This included contour planting, terraces, and windbreaks.

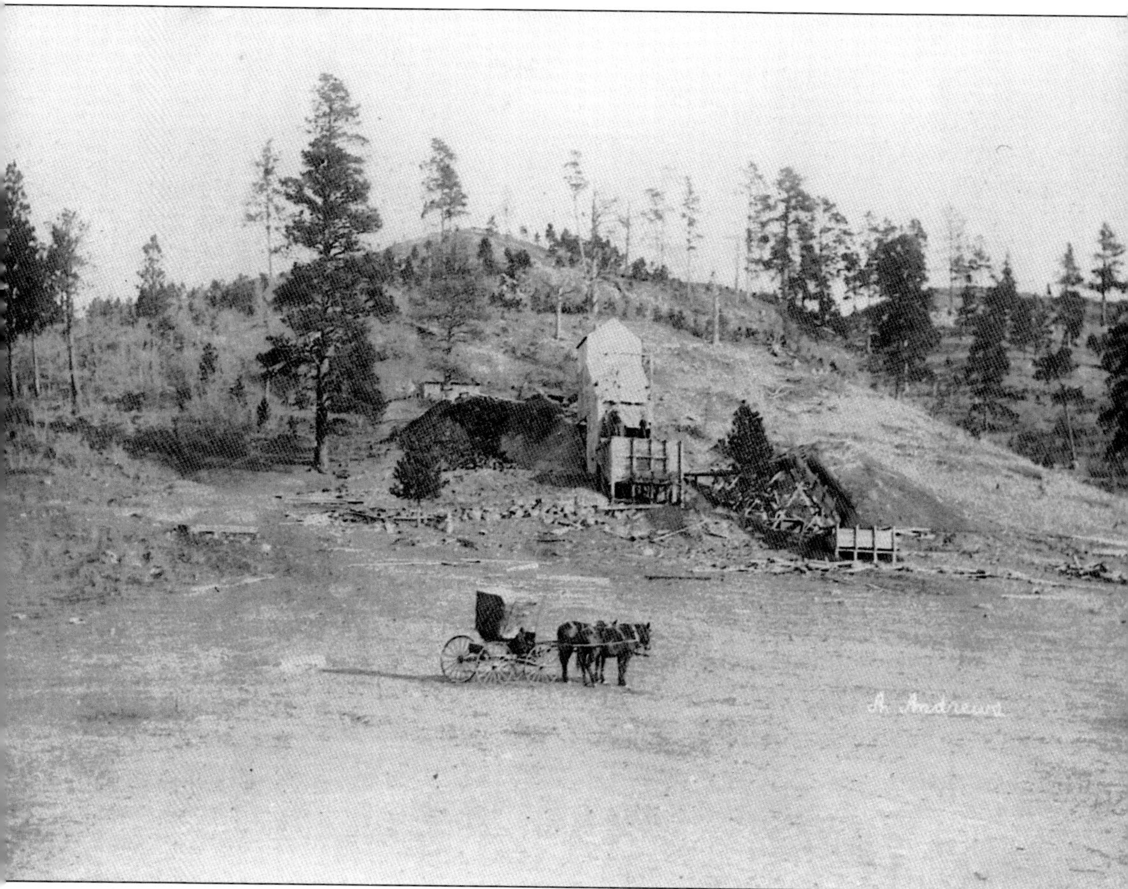

The Bearlodge Mining District was situated a few miles north of Sundance. The advertising for Sundance stated, "The same geological formations prevailed in this country as occurs across the state line into South Dakota where the famous Homestake gold mines." Mines supplied surrounding towns with the coal used for heating and for forges. Several metal mines were struck, but the veins were quickly depleted. Suppliers, surveyors, and conveyors were conveniently located in Sundance for miners. The demise of the mines came when the railroad was not run into the Sundance Valley—it made mining impractical. Pictured is the Belche coal mine located northeast of Sundance in the Bear Lodge Mountains.

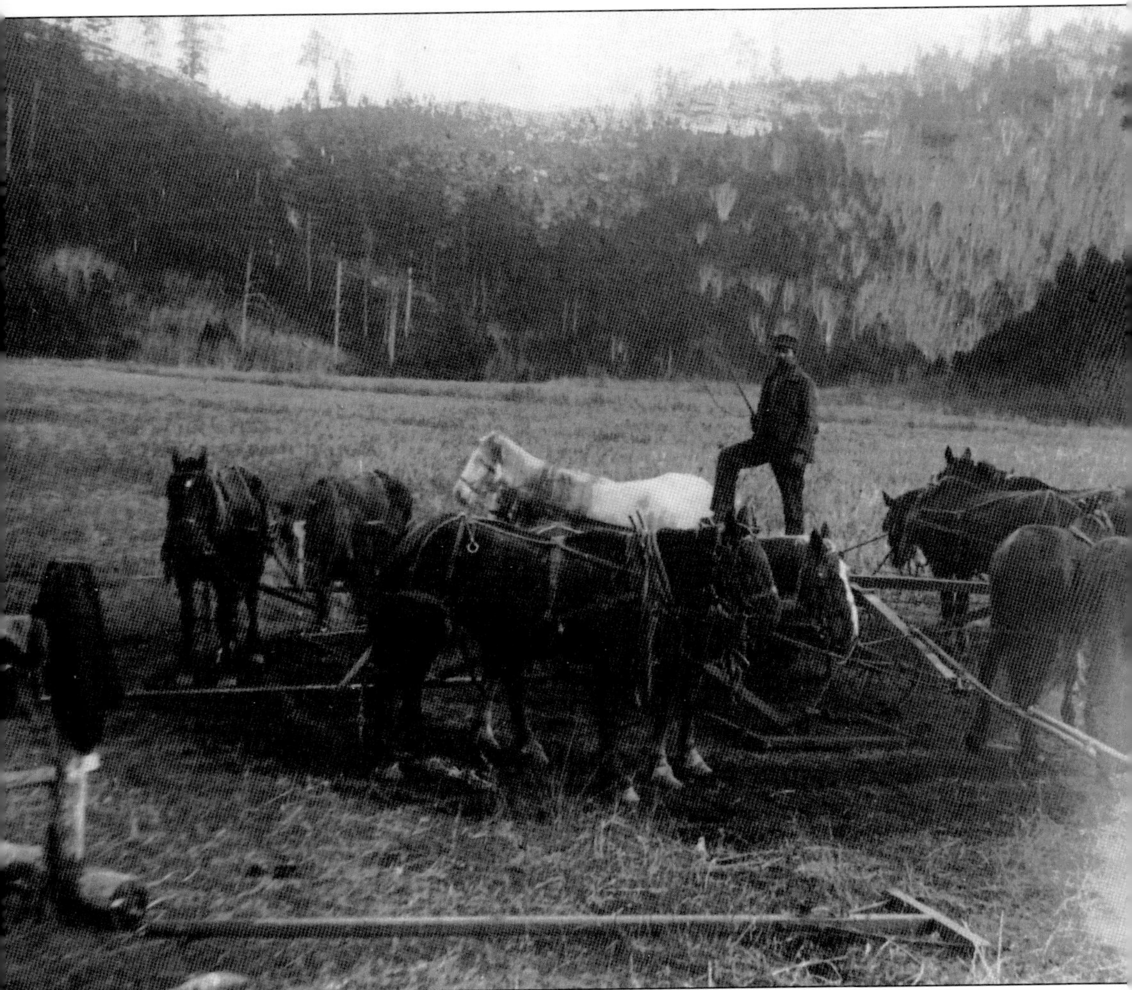

The Enlarged Homestead Act in 1909 doubled the amount of land that could be patented as a homestead. It more than doubled the number of acres filed for entry under any previous homesteading act. At one time, the federal government, railroad companies, and even universities encouraged dry land farming. In early 1900, it was believed that "rain followed the plow." Homesteaders that tried to farm without irrigation planted a number of different crops, including potatoes, but for the most part, dry farming centered on grains such as wheat, oats, and rye. Pictured here is Dan Straight hitching up his team of horses to a threshing machine, just out of the picture, to be able to harvest his field of grain.

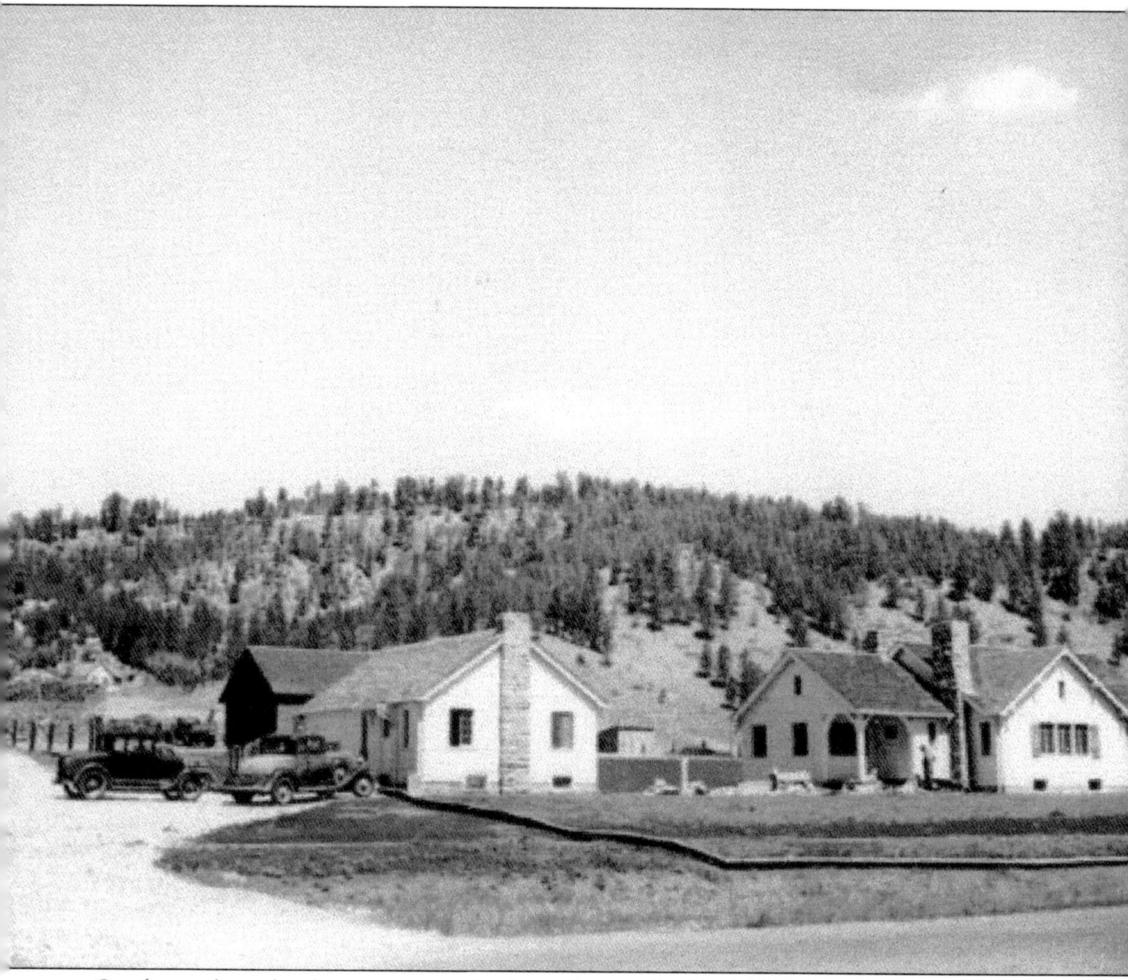

Sundance always has been a community dependent on the Black Hills National Forest for multiple uses of timber, grazing, wildlife, water yield, and recreation. Originally forests were withdrawn from public domain to become the Forest Reserve in 1891. In 1905, Pres. Teddy Roosevelt and Gifford Pinchot created the National Forest System. In 1908, the Sundance National Forest was created. The Bearlodge National Forest was created in 1911. In 1915, both forests were absorbed into the Black Hills National Forest. This photograph shows the Sundance National Forest offices that include, from left to right, a warehouse, the office building, and the Ranger's house.

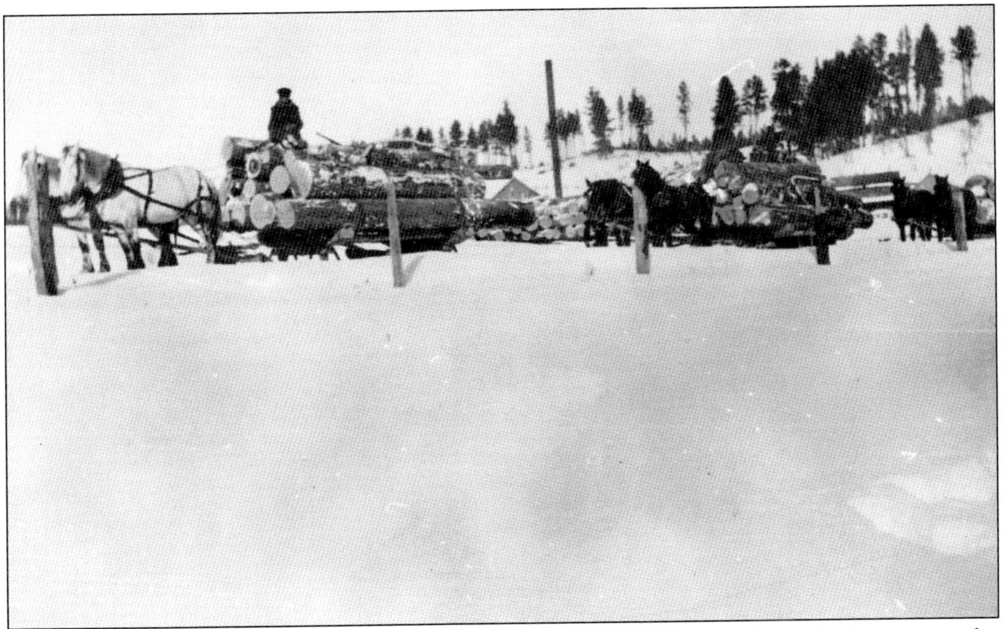

Logs from the U.S. Forest Reserve are being hauled by teams of horses through the snow to the sawmill. At this time, sawmills were located closer to the forests for ease of production.

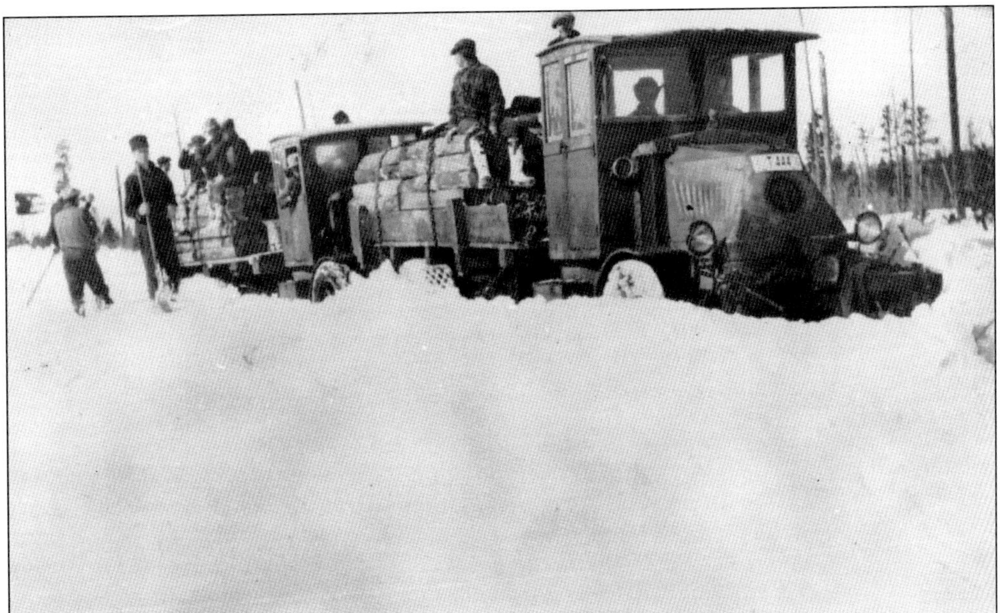

Mine timbers are leaving the sawmill and heading for the gold mines of Lead and Deadwood, South Dakota, using a different kind of horsepower to cut through the deep snow.

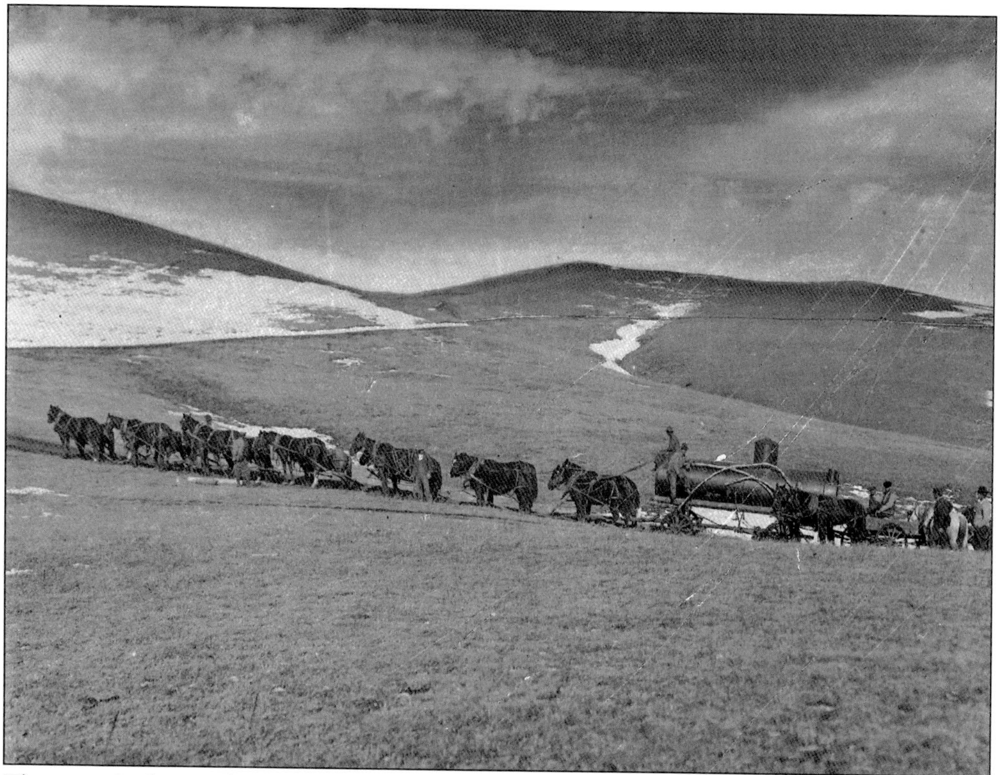

The steam boilers in these pictures came west by train into Spearfish, South Dakota. They were loaded onto wagons and this 14-horse freight team–hauling outfit. The boilers were being hauled up into the Bearlodge Mountains for the Bearlodge Gold Mining Company. Once they arrived on site they would be taken off the wagons and moved into place, where they would be part of the smelting process.

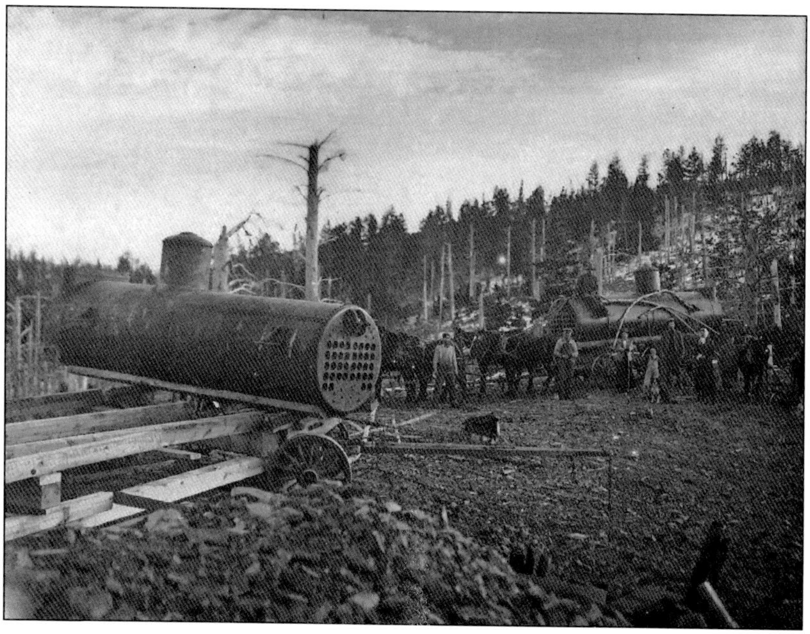

Five

The Town They Built

It is fairly well authenticated that there was no town, nor hint of a settlement, anywhere near Sundance in 1875 when a legislative enactment created Crook County. It was not until the Custer expedition discovered gold that the settlers and miners began to drift into what would become Crook County. By 1878, a general mercantile business and trading post for ranchers was established at the foot of the Bear Lodge Mountains. This business and the homestead it sat on would become the town site for Sundance. Soon there was a hotel that also functioned as the post office and stage stop. There was a saloon and a café in the same building. Lots were soon being sold for families and businesses. An application for the incorporation of Sundance was presented to the county commissioners on April 8, 1881. At that time, the commissioners felt there were not enough residents to fulfill the requirements, and the petition was rejected. Residents reapplied in October of the same year. On October 5, 1881, after a heated discussion against the application, the city of Sundance was incorporated. It was not too long before the legislature was petitioned for a county courthouse. Lots were donated for the purpose of such a structure. With the buildings came sidewalks, and Sundance soon began to look like a real little town. By 1880–1881, the first schools were opened. In 1884, there was a newspaper or two up and running. The first graveyard had been established, and the first burial had taken place. The first utility provided was a water system. Across the years, Sundance has seen a long line of businesses. Some of these have stayed and grown with the town. Some have been replaced with other businesses. Others have not been replaced but have been left to slide into memory as the needs of society and the needs of Sundance have changed. Among the businesses that the town or progress outgrew would be the creamery, livery, icehouse, the brickworks, blacksmith, and the distillery.

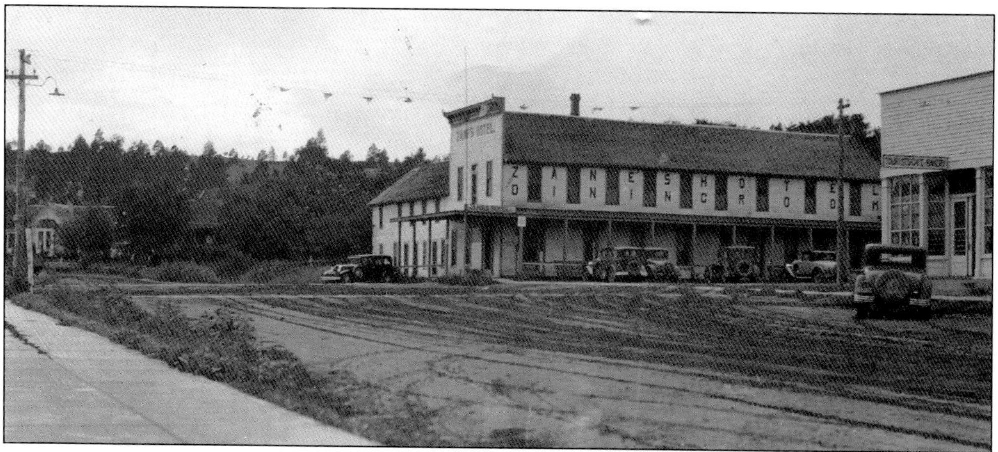

Between 1800 and 1883, Albert Hoge ran the Sundance Hotel on the corner of Main and Second Streets. The hotel functioned as a general store, saloon, café, post office, and stage stop for the Henderson and Smith stage route. The hotel was recognizable by the veranda that ran on the east side of the building. In 1883, he turned the management over to A. J. Meeks and his wife (who was the first Sundance postmistress). They managed it for about six months, and then Mr. Weaver took over. A. L. Ripley bought the hotel and changed the name to the Ripley Hotel. Jim Zane purchased the hotel from Colonel Ripley in 1915 and renamed it the Zane Hotel. Many years later, when Frank Hardy owned this hotel, it burned to the ground, bedbugs and all.

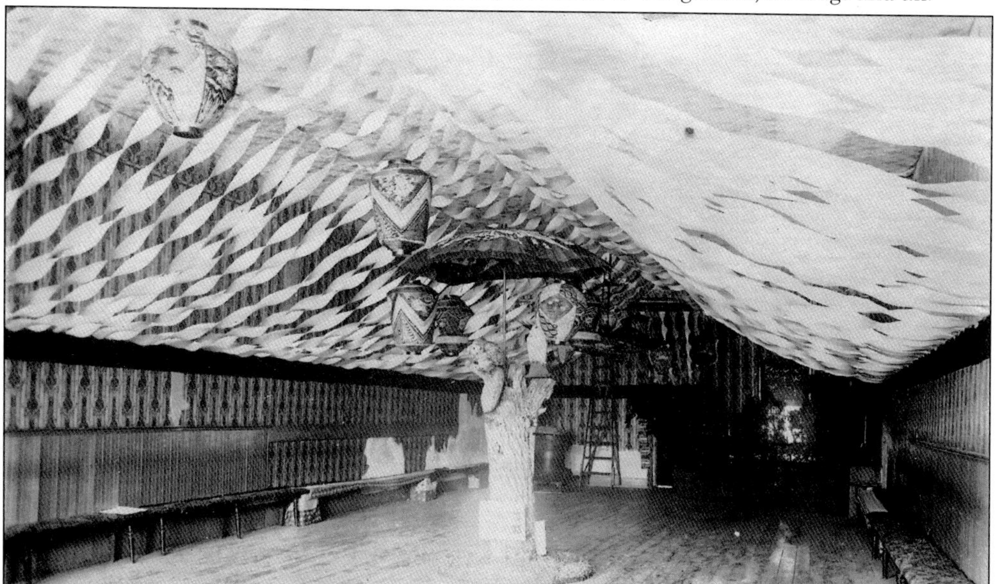

The American House may have been constructed before the Sundance Hotel. It sat on the corner of Fourth and Main Streets just across from the courthouse square. Al Bishop was the first owner. At this time, Mr. and Mrs. Compton managed the hotel. In 1888, Don H. Porter is listed as the proprietor, and Rushaw Bowman was the desk clerk. This hotel had a colorful existence, as at different times it was said to have housed a Chinese laundry, a boardinghouse, the Odd Fellows Lodge, the Owls Lodge, and a bakery. The hotel was built before 1885 and was closed in 1891. It remained closed and was still vacant when Calamity Jane took up residence for a few weeks. This is a picture of an Owl Lodge dance, set up to show off their decorations before the big party begins.

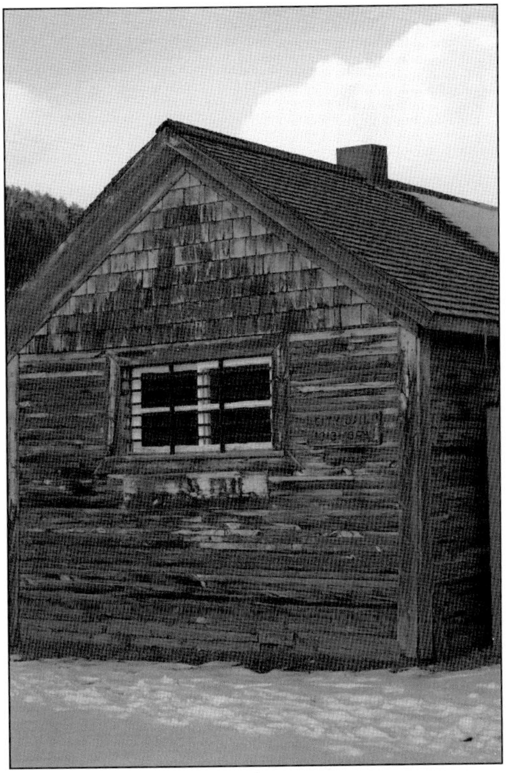

These pictures are of the city jail and cell door. The town of Sundance was using the county jail to hold their vagrants. Sundance was growing rapidly and needed a jail. A. W. McWhortder was awarded the bid for construction of the jail. The 1913 contract stated the builder agrees to furnish, construct, and do any and all work on the jail in a good and workman-like manner. The 14-by-18-foot structure consists of stacked two-by-four walls, floor, and ceiling. They are spiked every foot with 30 penny spikes. Two trap doors, two-feet square, were also constructed in the floor and ceiling. The jail was built behind the city hall and used for 51 years to house prisoners.

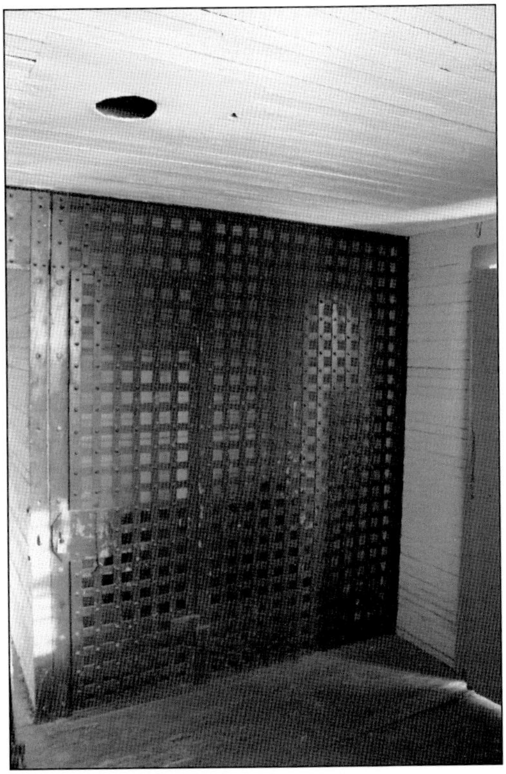

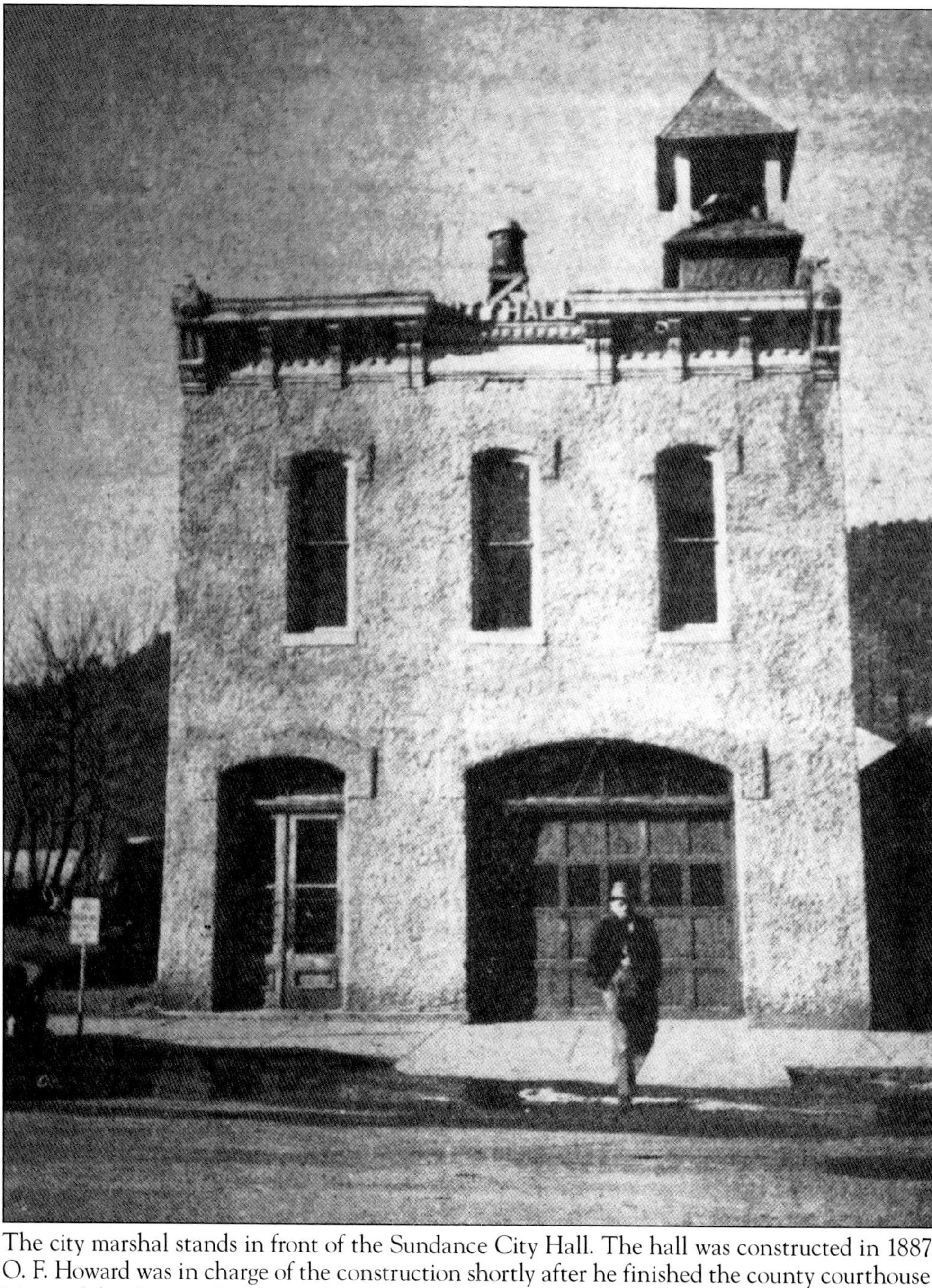

The city marshal stands in front of the Sundance City Hall. The hall was constructed in 1887. O. F. Howard was in charge of the construction shortly after he finished the county courthouse. Material for the city hall came from a brick kiln that was operating in the city. At different times, the Owls, Oddfellows, and the Masons all held meeting in the hall. There were dances and boxing matches in the upstairs.

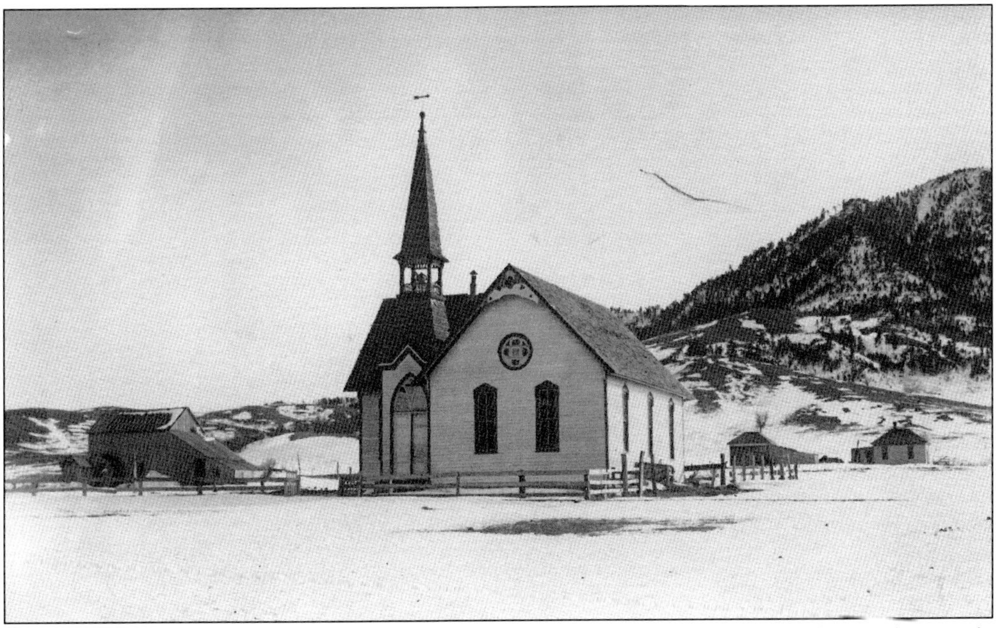

This Methodist church was built in 1886–1887. In this picture, it is setting on the northeast side of Sundance Mountain. W. M. Dudley was the first minister to serve in the new church and given the credit with instituting its construction. When this church was constructed, it had a bell in its spire. After being sold, the church was moved across town. It is now on the northwest side of the mountain, on the west end on Main Street. It went on to become the Wesleyan-Methodist Church and today is a private residence.

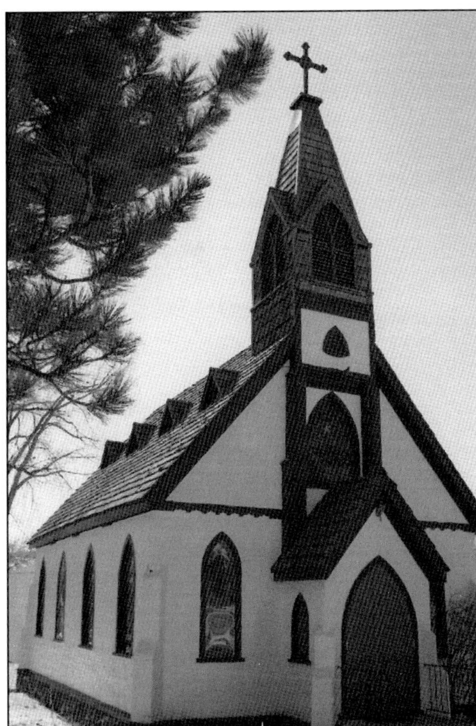

The first Episcopal services were held in 1888. The Right Reverend Ethelbert Talbat, bishop of Wyoming, presided on his first visit to Sundance. In July 1889, he purchased a lot for $100 to build a church. In September 1890, the work began on the foundation. On October 8, 1890, the cornerstone was laid by Sundance Lodge No. 9 Ancient Free and Accepted Masons (A.F. & A.M.) when the church was named the Church of the Good Shepherd. The first services were held on January 11, 1891, and three adults and five children were baptized that day. This church is still alive and active.

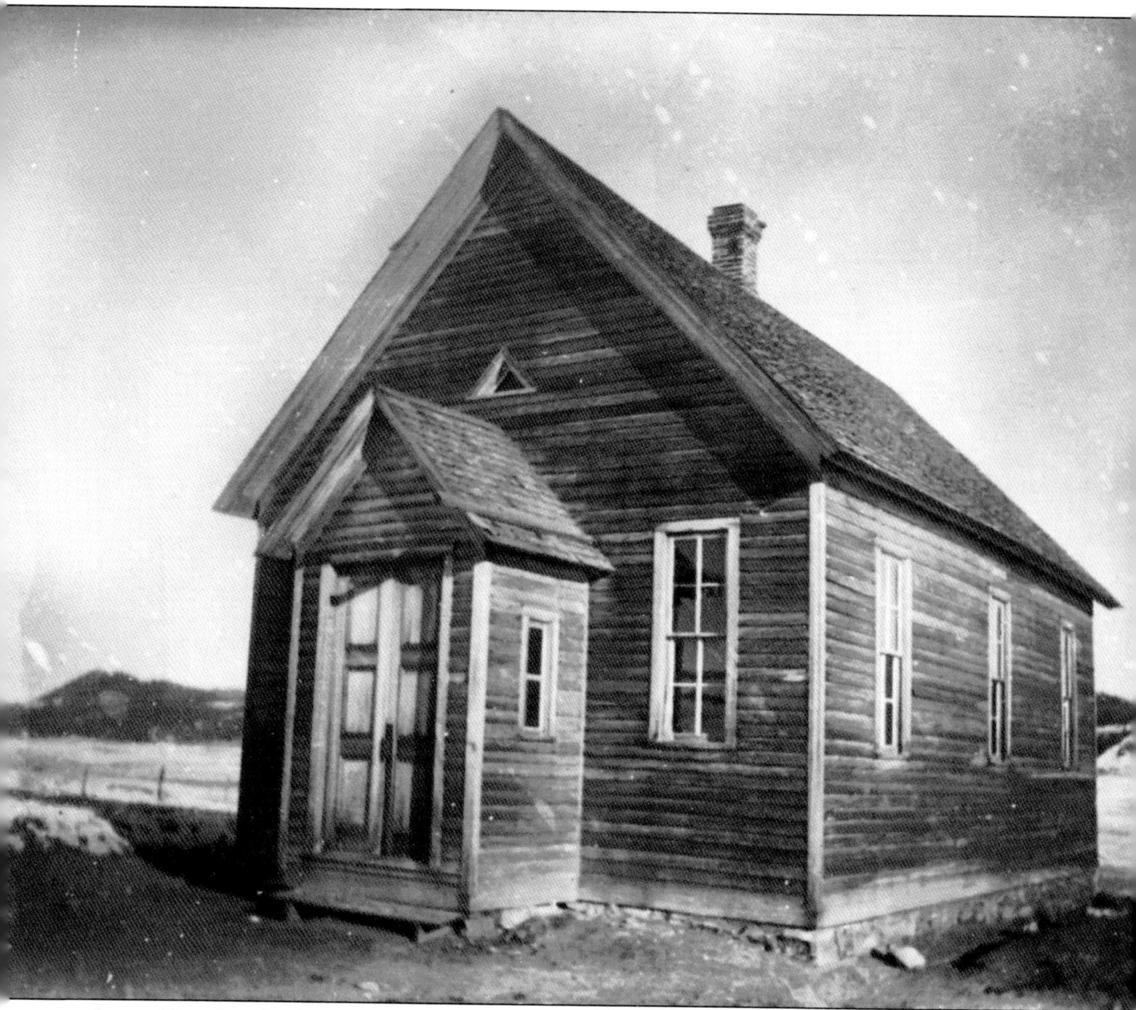

Inyan Kara Methodist Church was built in 1891 on a site north of Inyan Kara Mountain when Rev. O. B. Chassell rode the Sundance circuit. The congregation paid for the lumber by hauling the logs into the mill and the lumber out, and they did the construction themselves—church records show in June 1892 it was completed and free of debt. It was known as the first country church in Wyoming. Because of a changing population and the difficulty getting to the church, it was abandoned for several years. In the winter of 1910–1911, it was moved to government land a mile and half southeast of the original location. The church stood on this site for nearly 40 years before it fell into disuse. It was later sold and moved to the corner of Sewell and Seventh Streets in Sundance and remodeled as a family home.

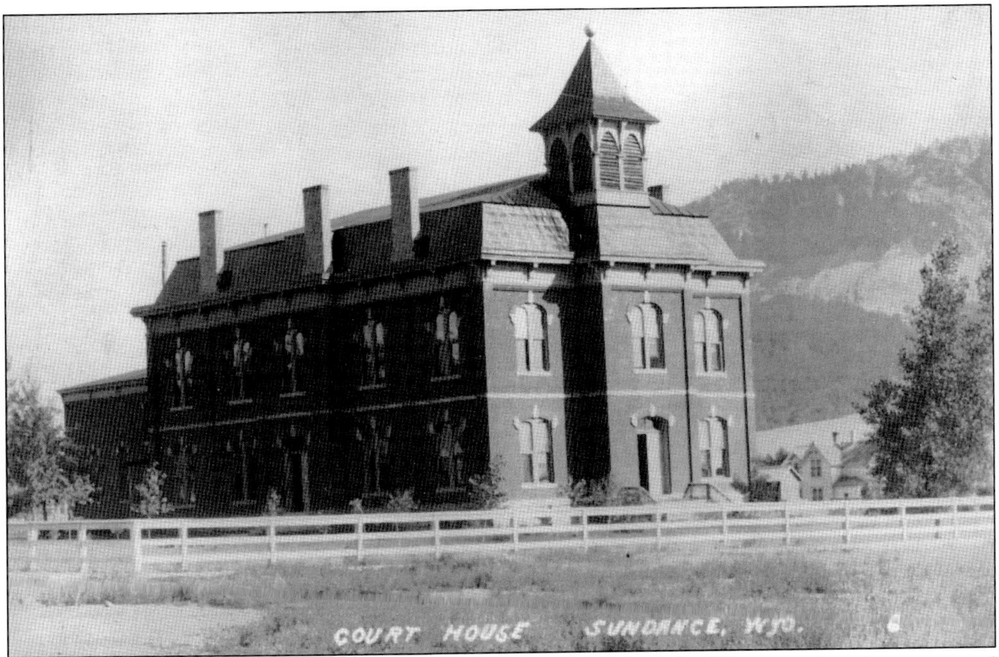

On February 13, 1886, the Sundance newspapers reported that the Wyoming legislature passed the bill concerning the building of a courthouse. A week later, an amendment calling for a special election in early spring for Crook County passed. Not having to wait for a fall election would speed up the process of constructing a courthouse. It was the custom to hold a celebration at the time of the opening of a huge endeavor, such as the building of the first courthouse for a county. These celebrations usually included a dance held inside the new structure. In December 1887, in answer to a citizen's request to use the courthouse for a dance, the county commissioners decided that they did not have the authority to grant such a privilege. And so, Crook County commissioners passed a resolution that there would be no dancing inside the courthouse property. This resolution remains on the books.

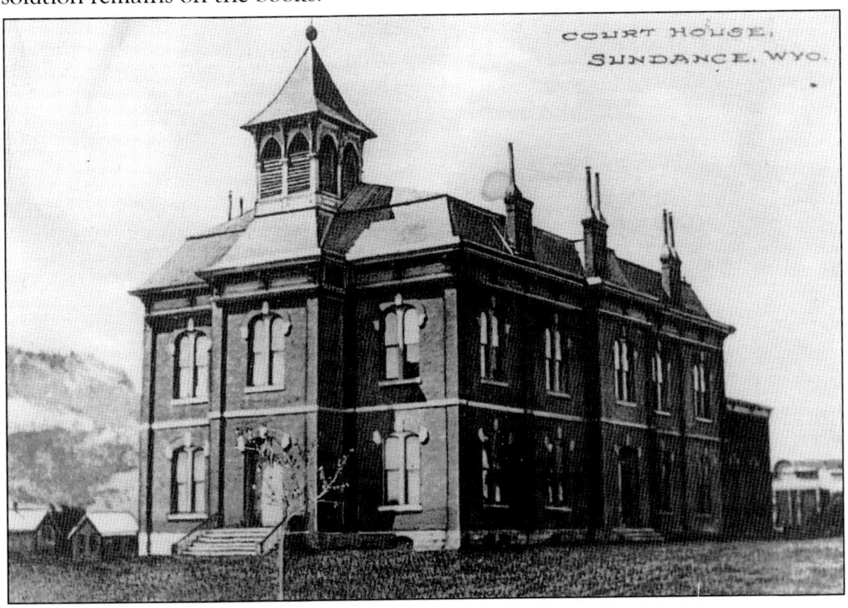

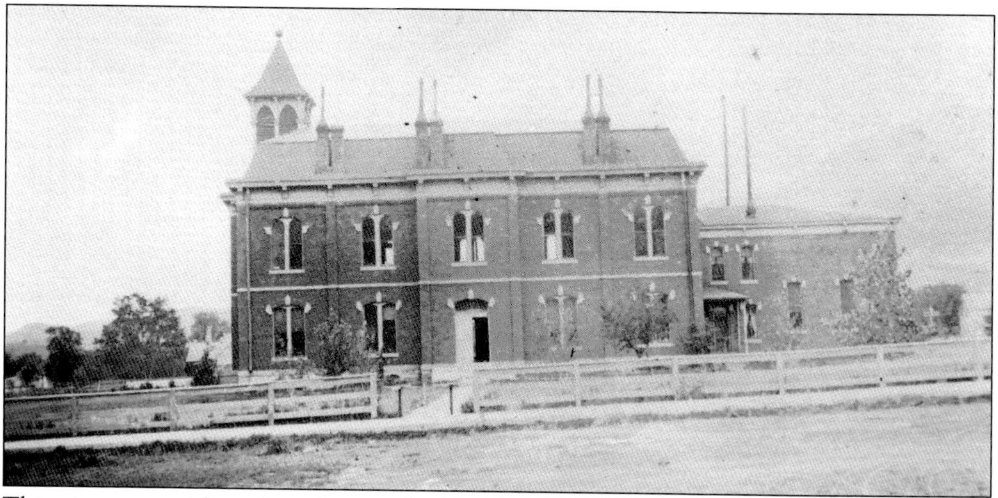

This picture was taken when the courthouse was still empty. You can see straight through the windows. Many of the bricks the courthouse was made from came from a local kiln and were found to be crumbly in later years. Square nails were used in the construction. All the rooms had high ceilings, and the courtroom had a domed ceiling. There were beautiful wood railings up the staircase leading to the second floor and the courtroom. A bandstand was added to the west side of the square in the late 1800s.

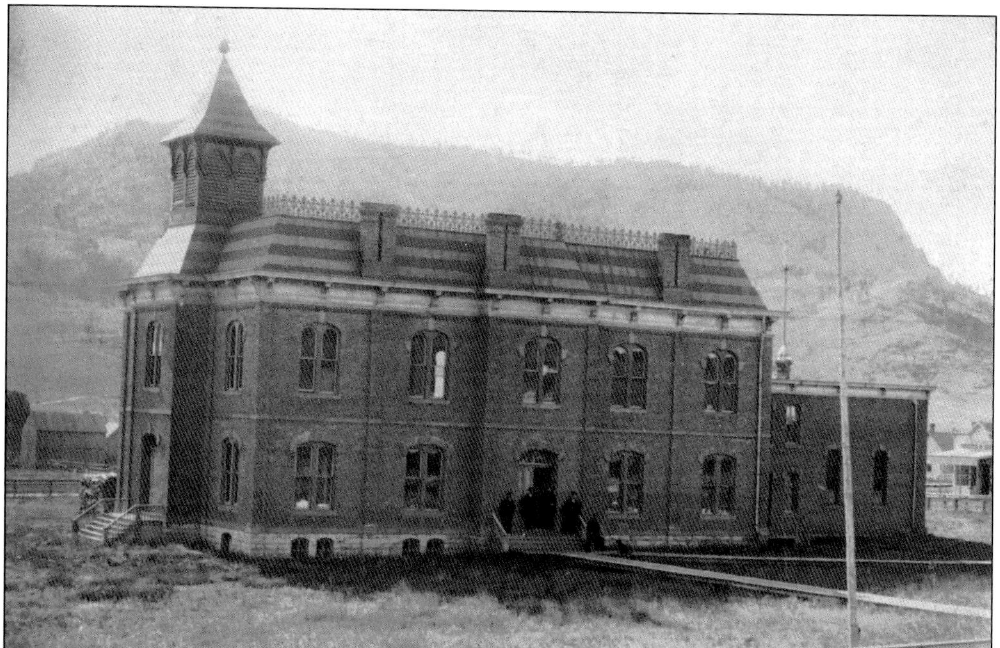

When the Crook County Courthouse was built in 1887–1888, it had a cast iron fence encircling the roof. This was known as a "Widow's Walk." It was removed after about 10 years. In 1907, Captain Young came into possession of portions of the fence. His family used what they needed to fence their yard south of town and stored the unused part in the barn, where Nels Smith found them when he bought the Young ranch. The Smith family created a bed frame out of part of the fence, and smaller pieces were used for trash can covers. A piece that has been saved is on display at the Crook County Museum.

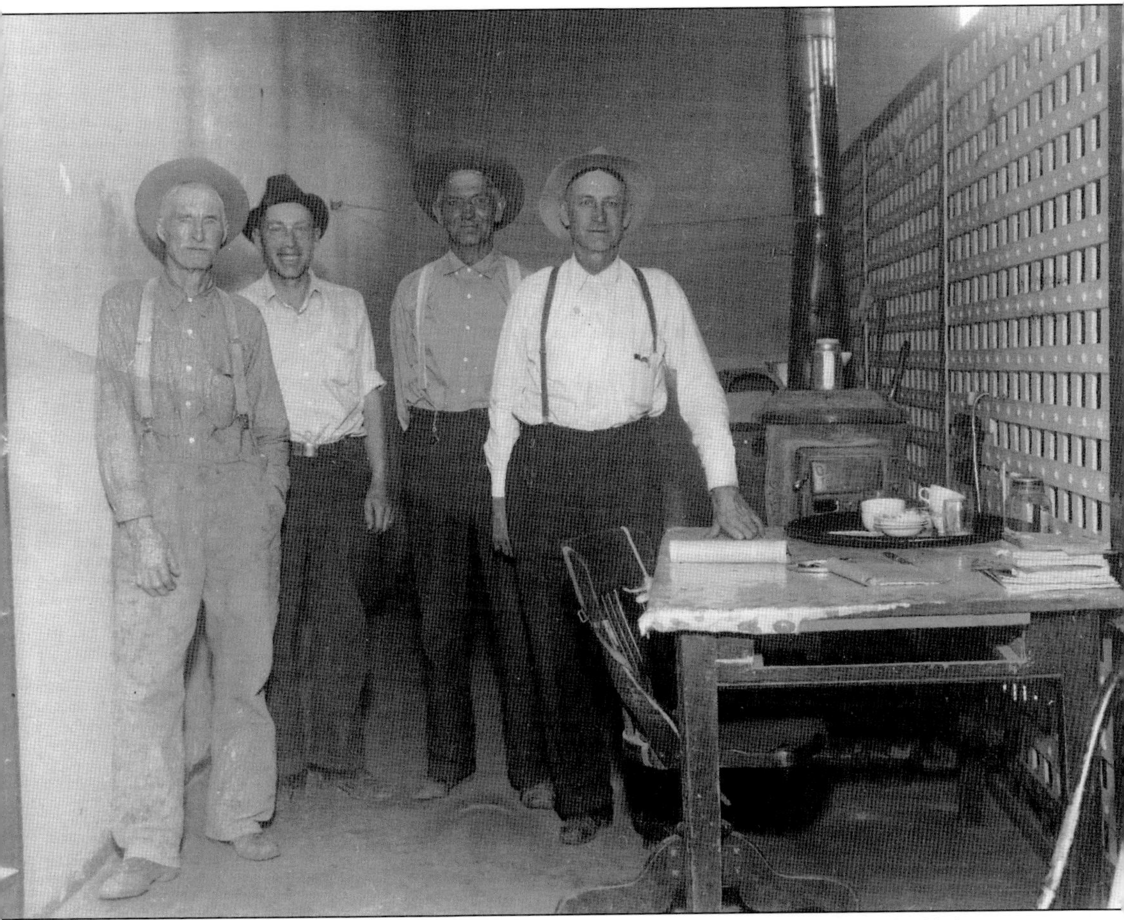

The jail had been built in the rear of the courthouse. There were cells and cages to hold the most desperate bad guy. It was in this jail that Harry Longbaugh spent 18 months trying to think up ways to escape. James Ryan was the first sheriff of Crook County. William Blakeman served the longest term of 24 years. The registry kept by each of the sheriffs contains some very interesting names: George Currie and William McArthur, a horse thief. McArthur escaped from Sheriff Ryan in Nebraska. The first name entered in the registry was a George Tucker, arrested July 5, 1885, for disturbing the peace. He was fined $5 and costs. Pictured in the jail from left to right are an unidentified worker, an unidentified deputy sheriff, an unidentified furnace maintenance worker, and Crook County sheriff Hank Oudin.

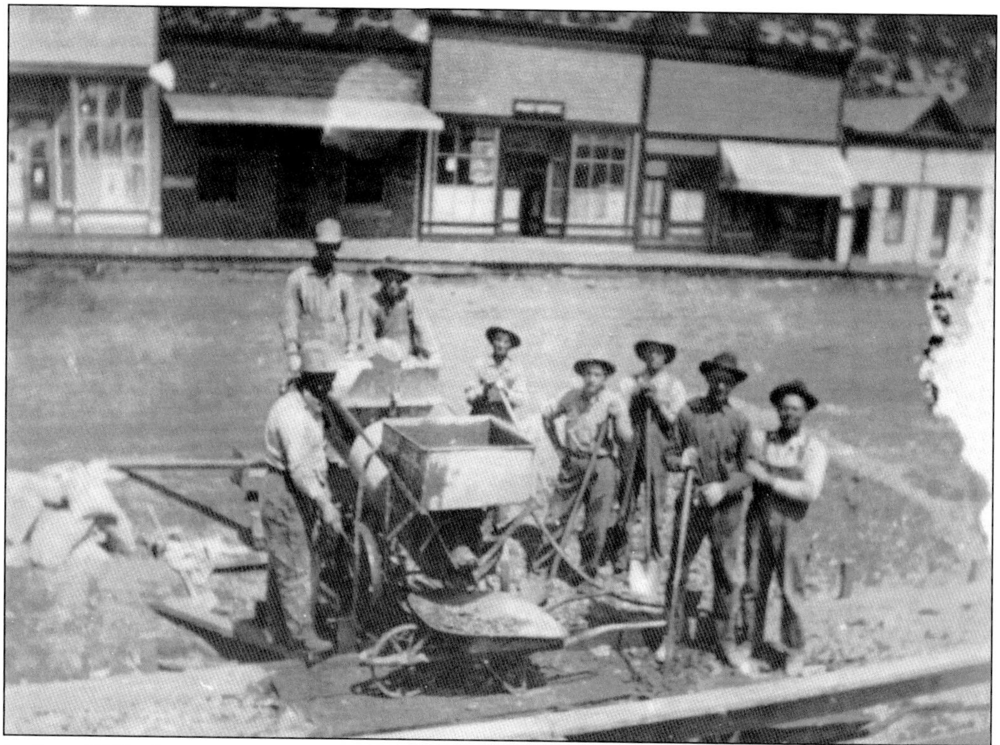

In June 1911, the county commissioners advertised for bid on a 7-foot concrete sidewalk for the north side of the courthouse square. The bid of 30¢ a square foot was made by the Leeman brothers, George and Lee. Their bid was accepted July 5, 1911. Pictures show the construction of the sidewalks on the north side and west side of the courthouse square. Main Street shows the buildings across the street. From left to right are the commercial hall; Security and Title, the security and land title office; post office; unidentified offices; and lawyers' offices. George Leeman is in the back of this group of workers.

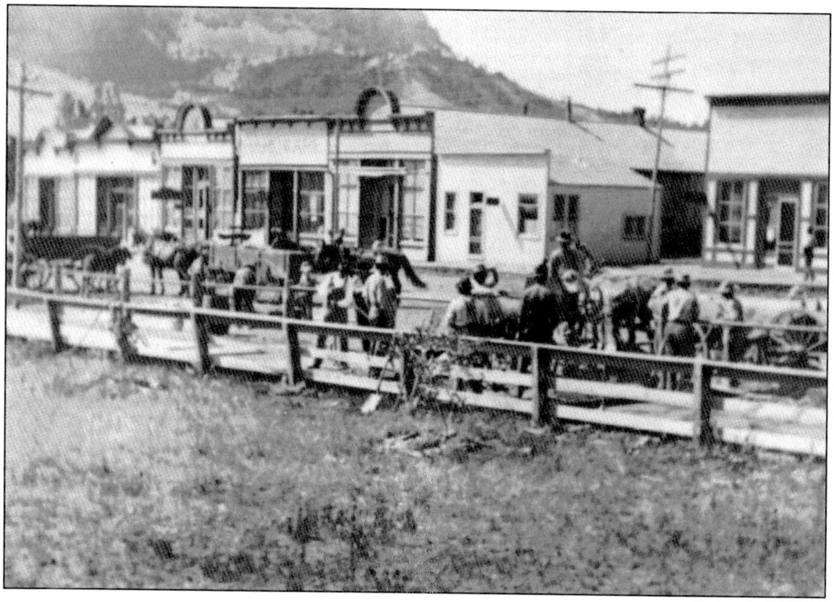

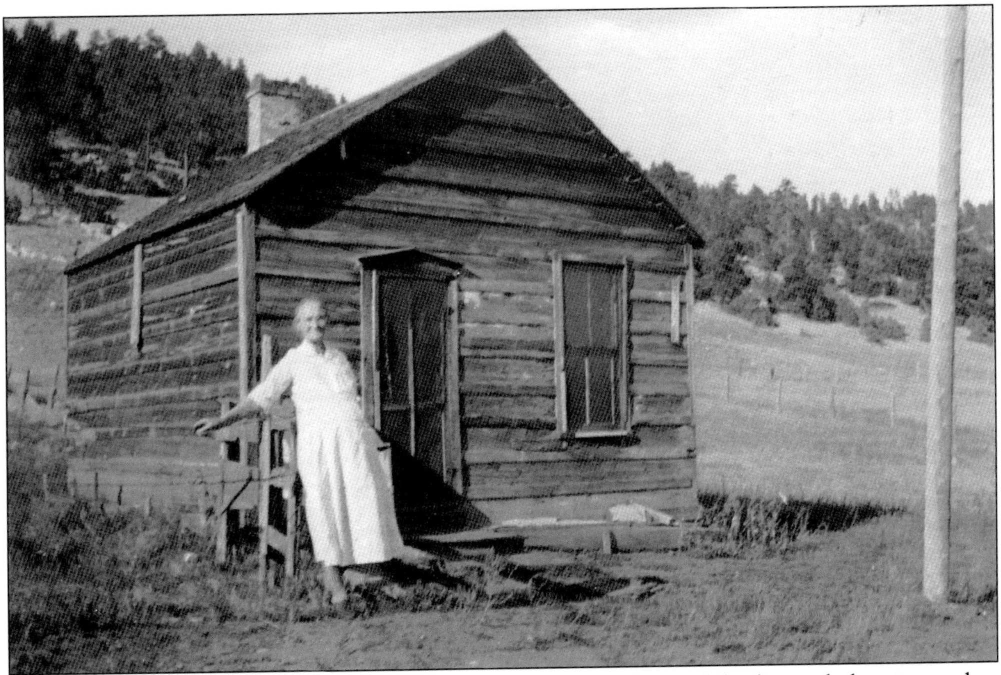

This picture is of Isabel Mills Straight. She is standing in front of the house belonging to her brother Anthony "Rush" Mills. Rush lived in this house from the 1890s until about 1923 or 1924, when the city tore down the old building. Rush had his nose bitten off during an attack by a bear, so he wore an artificial nose made out of clay and held on with black shoestrings, but only during the day. Gov. Nellie T. Ross asked Rush to send her the story of his fight with the bear. He was 75 years old and physically unable to write, so Isabel did the writing for him.

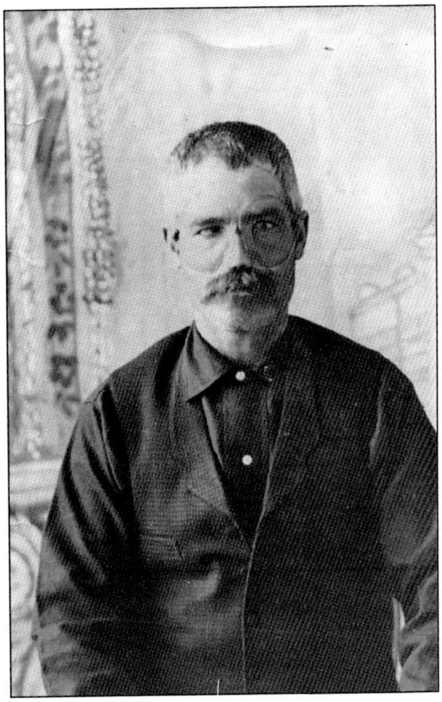

This is Rush Mills and his abridged story: "In November 1900 I went deer hunting about 20 miles from Sundance. I saw a bear. I saw its nose under a rock. The bear took after me. I was too close to aim. It came at me. I kicked it. It bit my toes and leg. I slipped and fell. He bit my nose off. I got my knife. I cut both jugular veins. Then he left. I crawled to camp. I was very week. I held snow to my face. It stopped the blood. I shot a signal for help. My brother thought I was shootin' at deer. He was surprised when he saw me. They brought me to town. The doctor put 14 stitches in my face. That hurt worse than the bear. My brother went and got the bear. I sold his old hide in Spearfish for $30."

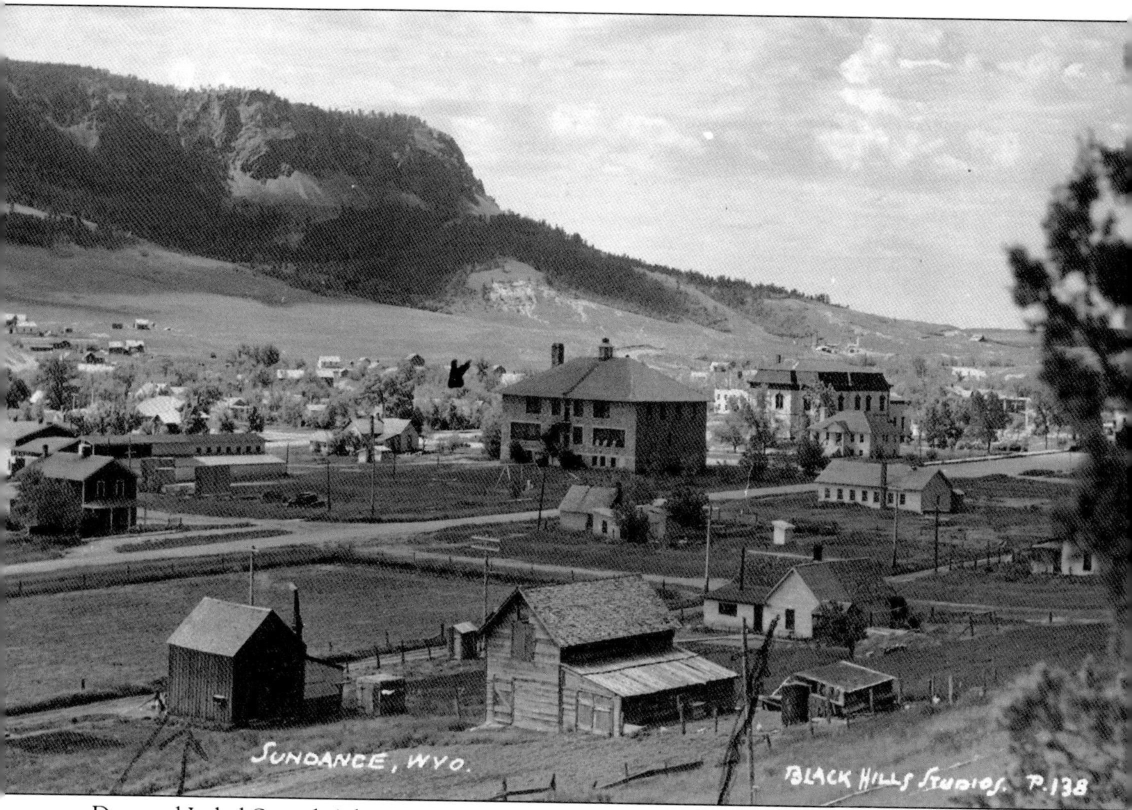

Dan and Isabel Straight's home is in the center foreground. Dan moved this house himself from across town in about 1908. He moved many houses and barns in the area from one place to another where they could be put to better use. There were three garden areas where the Straights grew and sold vegetables. The building to the left of the Straight house, with smoke rising from its chimney, was the last home of Rush Mills. In his later years, from this house, Rush Mills was known to race out and try to scare passing children.

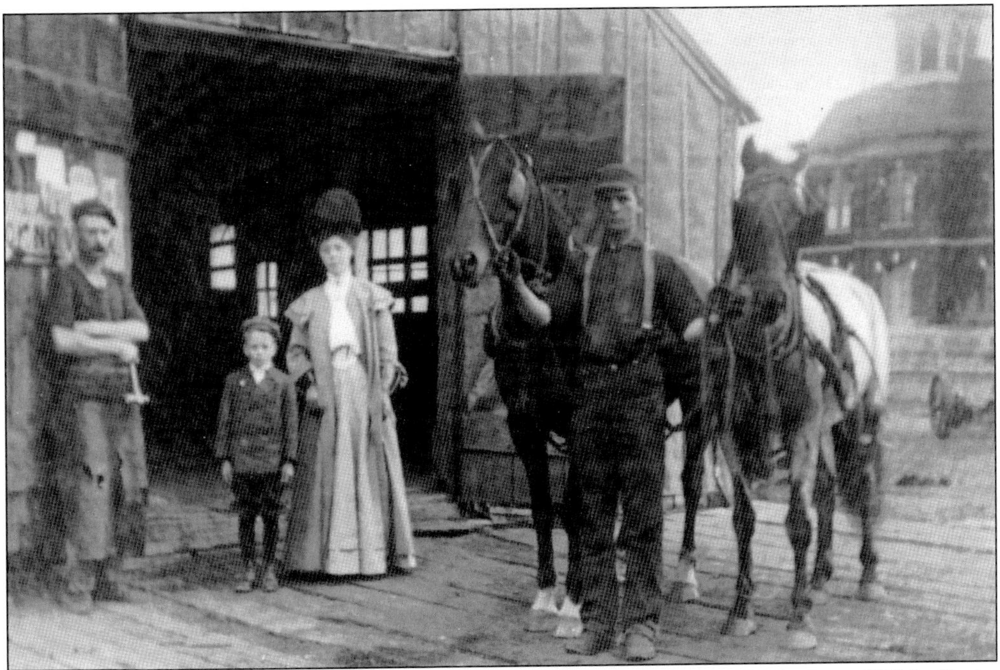

From left to right are Lawrence Mauch, blacksmith; unidentified; Kate Hawken; and Ed Loffer in front of the Mauch livery and blacksmith shop on north Main Street. Lawrence Mauch arrived in Sundance in 1886 with a covered wagon, his tinsmith tools, and $400. He set up his shop on Fourth Street and sold hardware supplies while doing his tinsmith work. In January 1936, he caught a severe cold. With his advanced age and weakened heart, he could not recover, and three months before his 82nd birthday, he passed away. It was said that there was never a whisper of greed that ever stained his name.

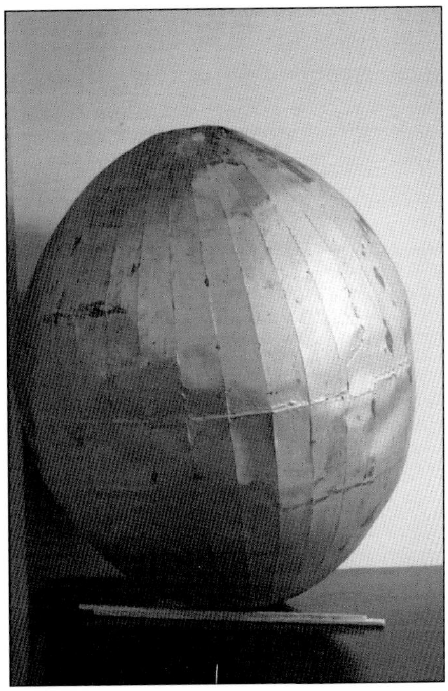

In 1887, when the courthouse was being constructed, Lawrence Mauch fashioned a 22-by-26-inch ball out of metal strips tightly fitted together and soldered. He used a square and compass to determine the exact measurements of each section. There are 35 sections, each 2 inches across at the middle. The 26-inch ends are neatly bound with sturdy steel fixtures, so that a rod may be inserted to hold the ball in place atop the cupola of the courthouse. This ball stood at the highest point on the courthouse roof, until it was declared old-fashioned and removed. Lawrence Mauch took his ball and went home.

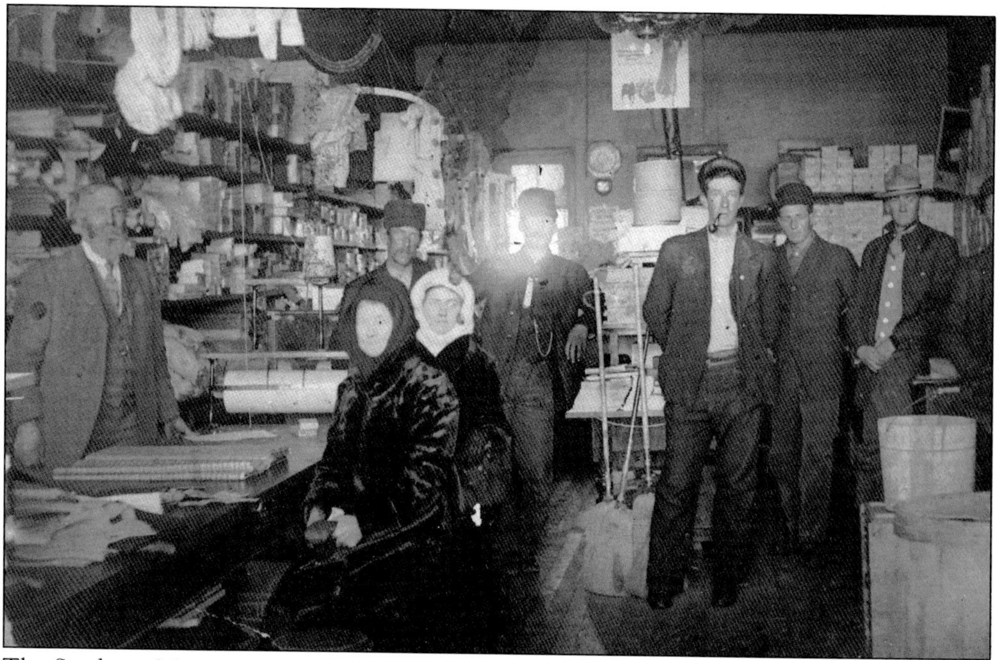

The *Sundance Monitor* reported on November 11, 1917, that owners of the Partlow Store were hoping that everyone would go in to have their measurements taken for winter suits. It also said that the groceries at Partlows were the freshest all the time. Robert O. Partlow said, "I will pay eight cents a pound in trade for your live chickens at the RO Partlow Cheap Cash Store." It is interesting to note that the same price for poultry was paid in 1914. Pictured inside Partlow's store are, from left to right, Robert Partlow, Mrs. Richardson, three unidentified, Ross Butts, York Richardson, and Lewis Ewing.

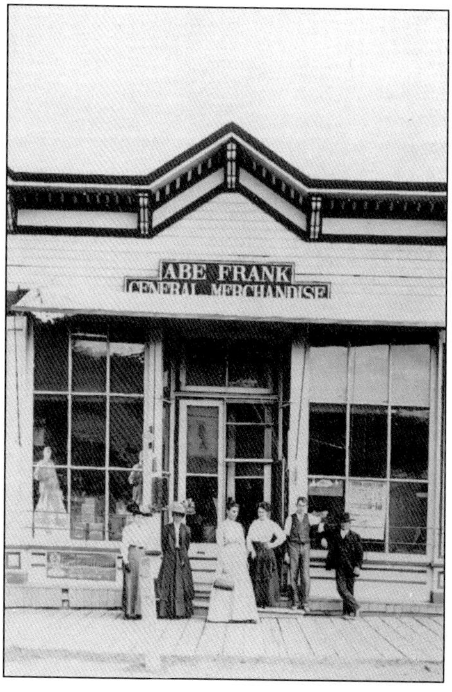

Standing in front of the Frank Store in Sundance are, from left to right, unidentified, Flosie Folden, unidentified, Florence Frank, Elmer Frank, and Vernie Taylor. Abe's brother, Meyer Frank, bought the first lot sold in the town site of what would become Sundance. He developed the first two business blocks. Meyer and Abe had established the Frank Brothers by the time the town was incorporated. The sign on the front of the store read "Abe Frank—General Merchandise." After the 1886 fire, the store was reorganized to be called Frank and Company. While Meyer was still a partner, Abe always ran the Sundance store, and Meyer managed a store and a bank in Newcastle.

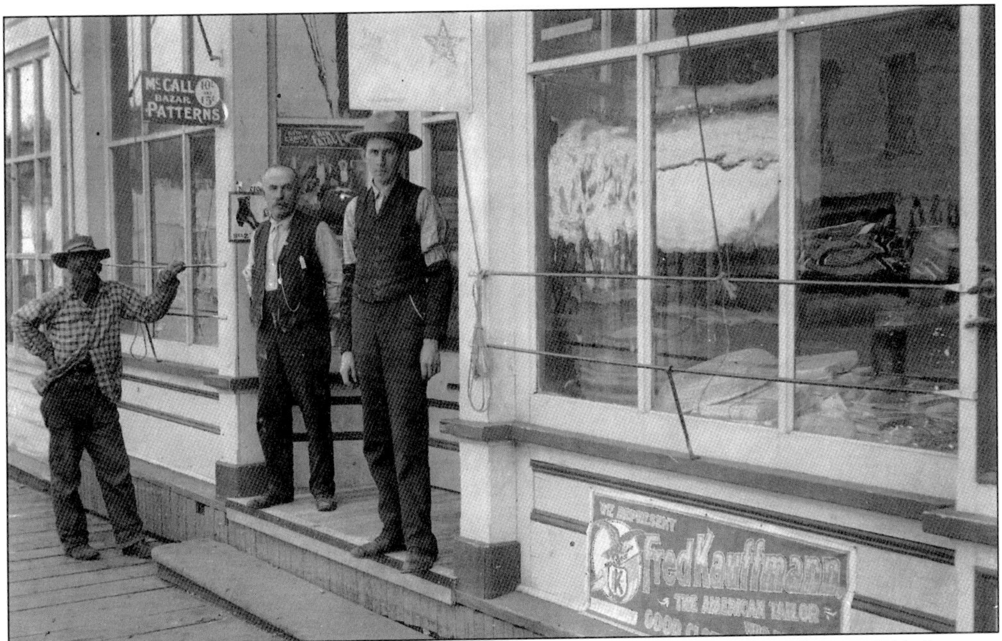

Standing from left to right are unidentified, Abe Frank, and Elmer Frank in front of Abe's store. There was a rumor that Elmer was in love with a girl that worked in the Frank home. However, his mother did not approve, and the affair came to an end. Elmer never married. He was friendly and enjoyed visiting when he was in town but never invited friends to the Frank home. He did, however, help raise several young men who had become wards of the court. As Elmer grew older, he gave up the conveniences of the modern age and took up using a chamber pot like he had as a child. He emptied the chamber pot into the alley, a habit that was not popular with the neighbors.

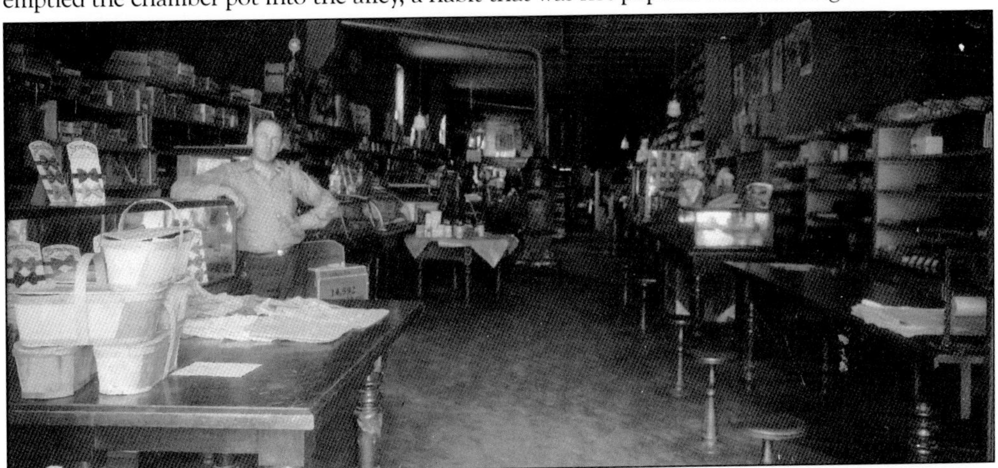

The Frank Brothers store sold general merchandise and groceries. In later years, the first telephone switchboard was located in the back of this store. Anna Hamilton Brockett recalled that when they brought the switchboard it only had 15 "drops" for the entire town. Anna worked from 7 a.m. until 9 p.m. and received the handsome salary of $15 per month. Elmer Frank is seen leaning against a case of bow ties. There were stools for the lady customers to sit as they chose their purchases. Elmer was Abe's only son; he went to work in the store as a young boy and continued working there as long as his father lived. After his father's death, Elmer closed the store and never worked again.

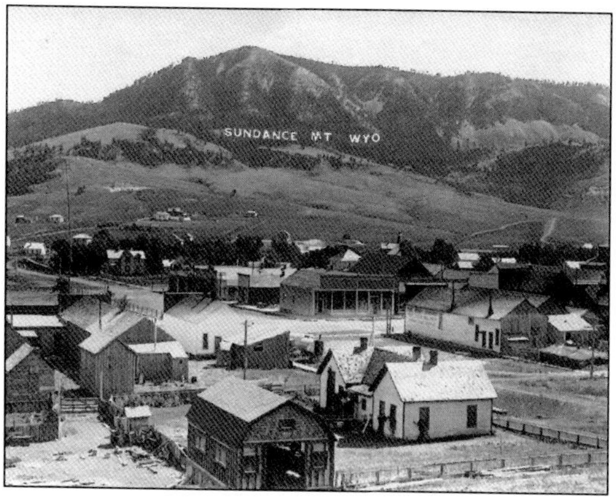

The first banker in Sundance recalled that it was easy to start a bank here. He simply put out a sign that said "BANK." Soon a fellow walked in and gave him $100 for safekeeping. A short time later, another fellow walked in and wanted to place $200 in his bank. After that, the enterprising man felt confident to put up $75 of his own. The Citizens Bank was located on the corner of Third and Main Streets until it was consolidated with Sundance State Bank in 1922. The Citizens Bank is the third building on the right-hand side of the street.

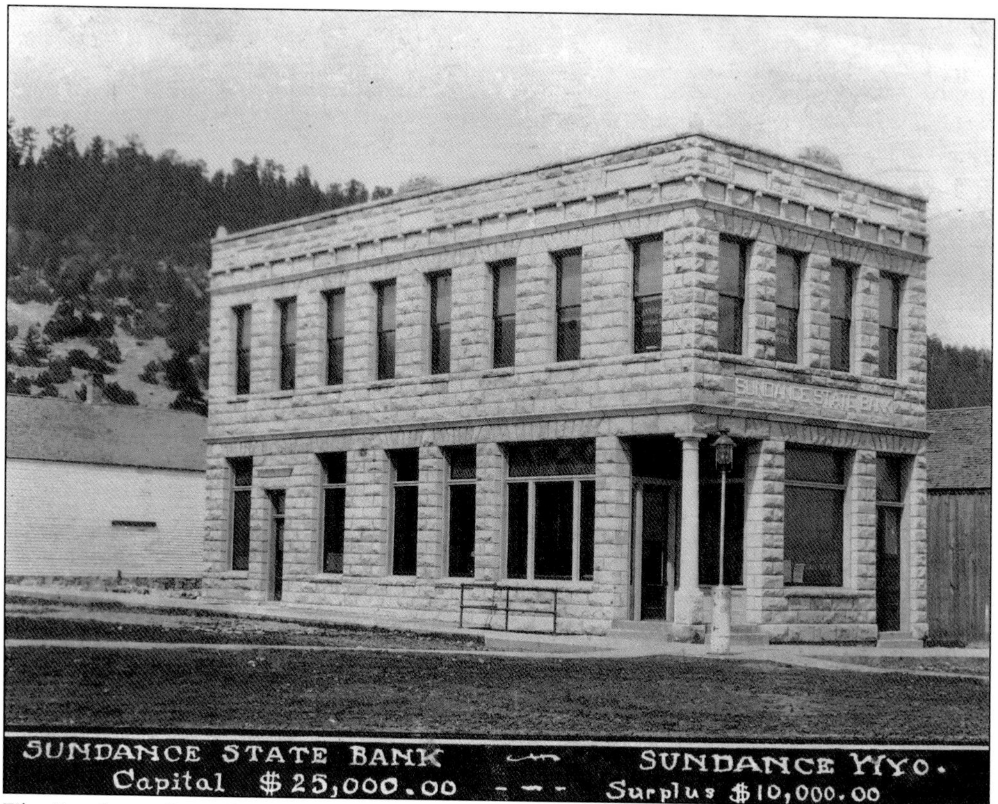

The Sundance State Bank has the second-oldest charter for a bank in Wyoming. During the Great Depression, the Sundance bank was able to keep their doors open. This bank was originally housed in a white frame structure until 1914, when a new stone building was constructed on 301 Main Street. Stone cut for the bank was quarried in Reuter Canyon, located in the Bear Lodge Mountains. The bank operated out of this stone structure until a new modern bank was constructed. The gracious old building housed other businesses and some apartments for a while but has sat empty for years.

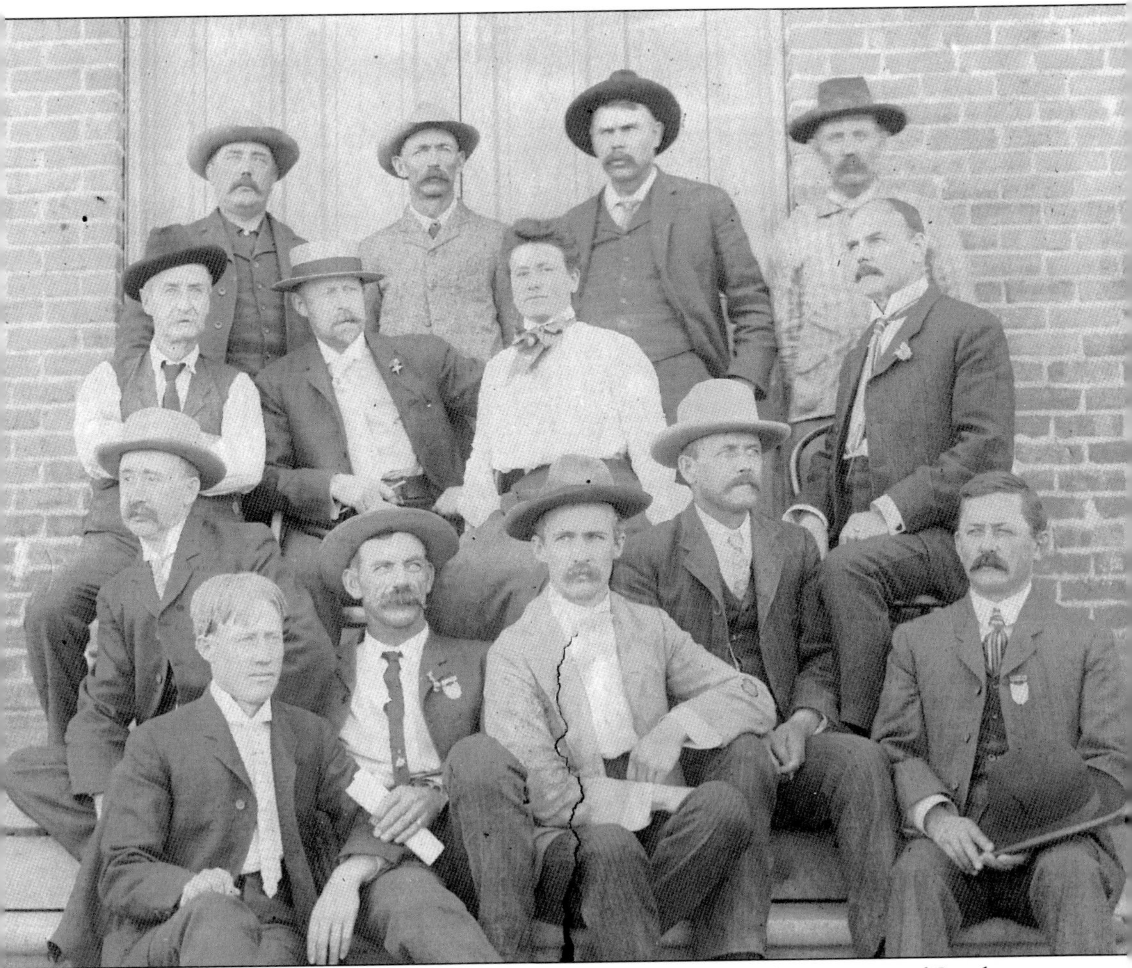

Gathered on the front steps of the courthouse is a group of upstanding citizens of Sundance and the county. From left to right are (first row) Walter Nettlehorst, district court clerk in 1897 and 1898 and county clerk from 1894 to 1899; J. L. Probst, county sheriff from 1903 to 1905; ? Woodcock; Ezekial A. Crewdson, county treasurer from 1901 to 1904; Murray Gordon; and Tom Dunn, district court clerk from 1901 to 1904; (second row) L. R. Davis, Walter Brammel, Bess Moody, and A. E. Hoyt; (third row) Alex Woodcock; Cecil Calvert, district court clerk from 1899 to 1900 and county clerk from 1894 until 1899; Swan Pearson, county commissioner from 1901 to 1905; and Charley Mullholland.

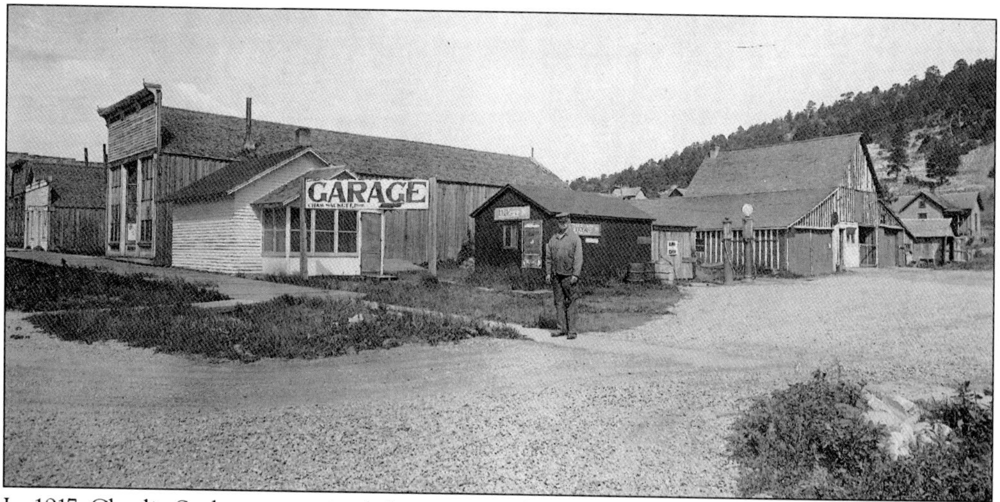

In 1917, Charlie Sackett recognized the coming of Prohibition and sold the saloon. He opened the Sundance Garage, pictured above behind an unknown man. On July 4, 1937, Charlie Sackett and Doc Clarenbach went fishing on Sand Creek. After a good morning and a fine catch, they sat for lunch. On the opposite side of the creek, a South Dakota municipal judge and a former South Dakota sheriff were target-shooting or hunting. A shot came close to the fishermen. Doc yelled at the men just as another shot came across the creek. Charlie's last words were, "Doc, I'm shot." His service was held at the Commercial Theater; he was 78 years old.

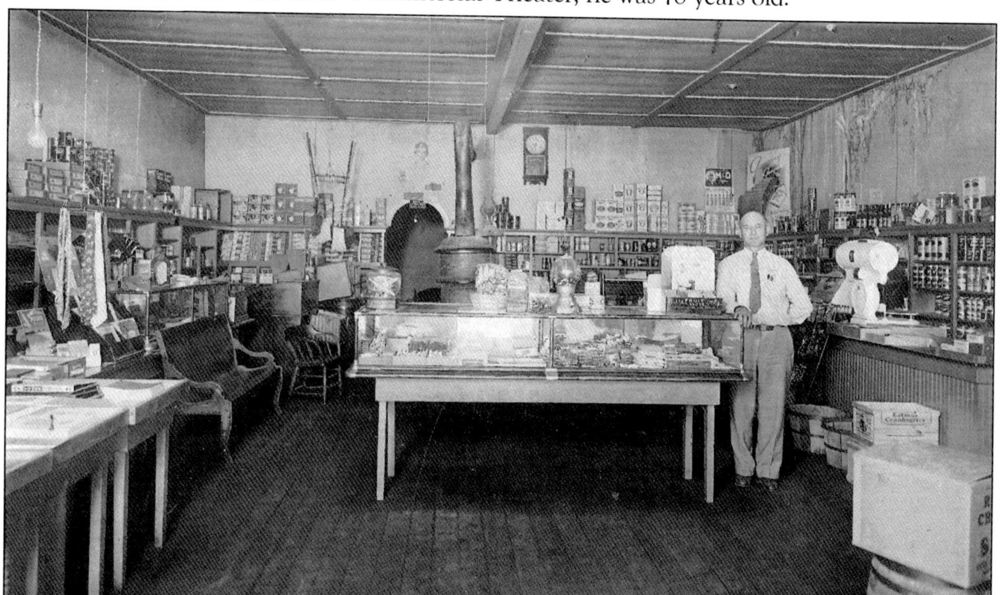

This is the inside of the Model Grocery Store as it was in 1934. John Binney is standing in the middle of the store. John Binney sold the grocery to Clay Massie and his partner, Robert Partlow, in 1934. Clay and his family moved to Sundance in 1925 when he was elected county clerk. He and his wife, Hazel, ran the store. Their stationery read, "Massie Mercantile Company, Staple and Fancy Groceries, Fresh and Cured Meat, Fresh Fruits—Green Vegetables—Baked Goods." By 1939, Clay and Hazel had sold their interest in the Model Grocery store to Dean Bryan and moved to Oregon. Hazel had to remain behind for a while to collect money owed to them on unpaid grocery bills.

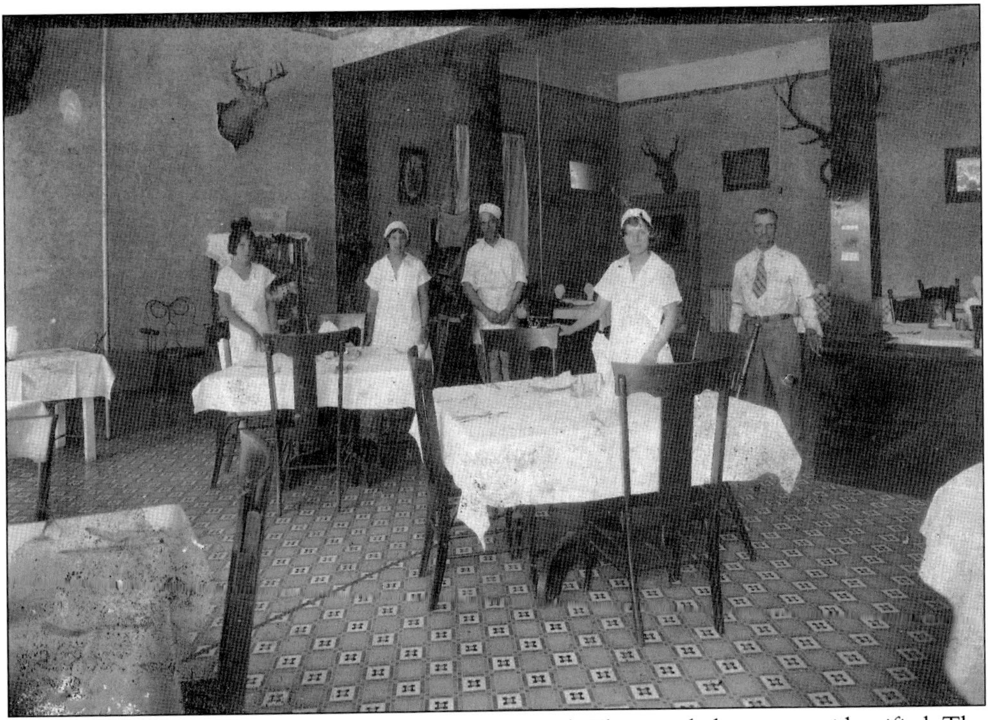

This is a picture of the dining room of the Zane Hotel. The people here are unidentified. The hotel changed owners and names often, but to the people of Sundance it was always the Zane Hotel. The hotel advertised that there was always hot, delicious food ready for the weary traveler. There was said to have been plain and fancy food. The floor was carpeted. The staff was cheerful and welcoming. A hot meal and a warm bed was all a stranger could need or ask for.

Fred Schloredt is pictured in front of his dry goods store. This notice appeared in the July 6, 1900, *Crook County Monitor*, "That is a whale of a name. If you did not know the fellow you would swear he was a German. If you ever do know him, real well, you may swear worse. Fred Schloredt is the man referred to. He has got a lot of ready-made suits with which he desires to fix up 200 men and boys so they can make a presentable appearance on the fourth of July. It is only 365 days and nights from now. Ladies and girls summer clothing of every description. You had better look at the shirtwaists!"

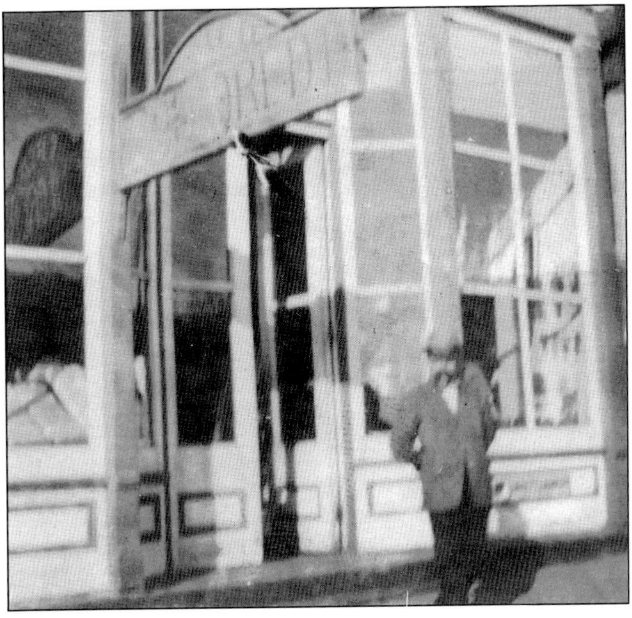

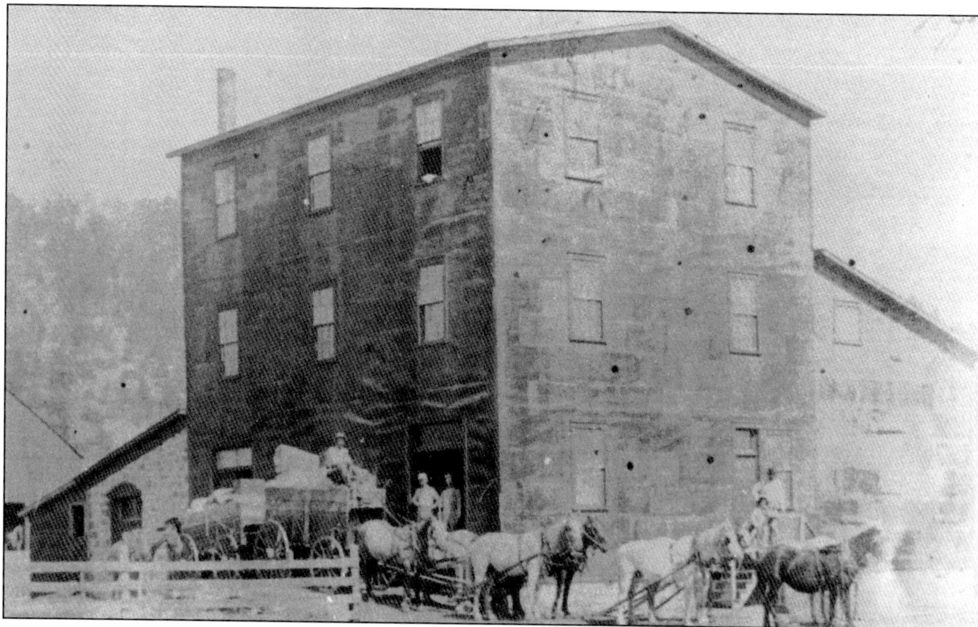

The Sundance Flour Mill was built in 1896. The mill's noontime whistle announced the lunch hour in Sundance for over 30 years. Farmers brought their grain into the mill, pictured here, to be cleaned and marketed.

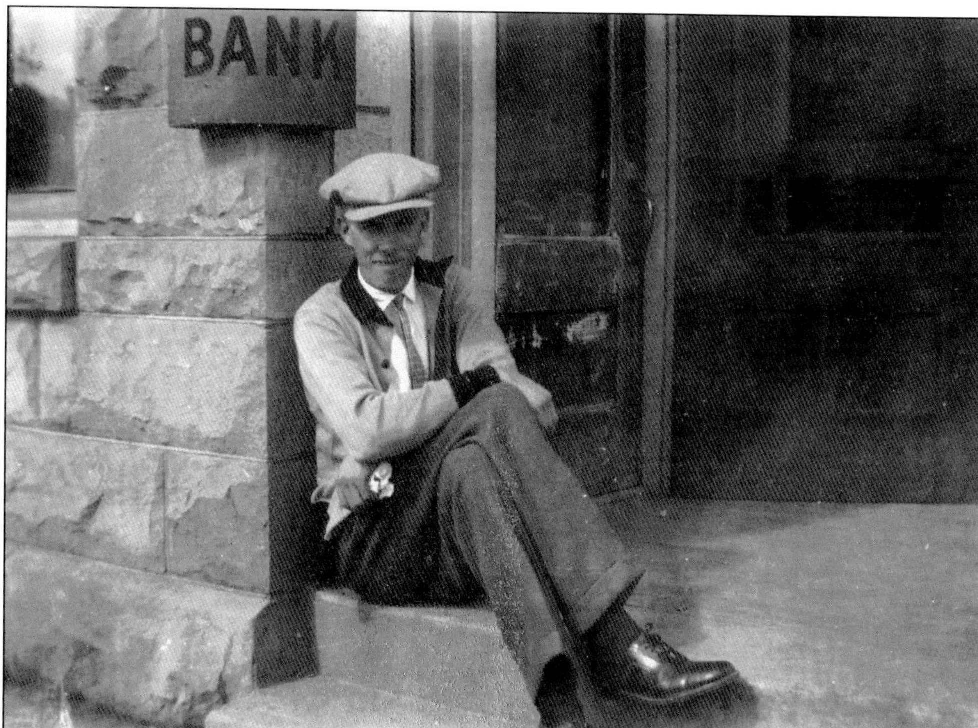

In 1934, Clyde D. "Scotchy" Roberts, pictured here relaxing on the steps of the Sundance State Bank, would form the C. D. Roberts milling company. He sold his flour under the trade name of Mountain Gold Flour.

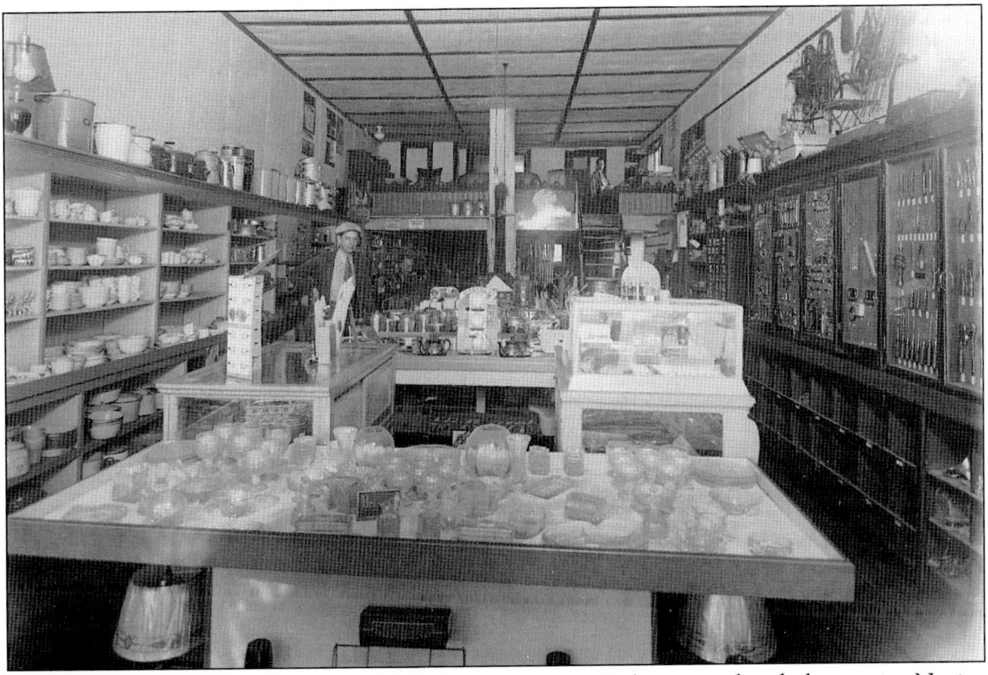

Dick Hooper stands inside Roberts Hardware Store. C. D. Roberts is at his desk upstairs. Notice the wood stove with its chimney up the wall.

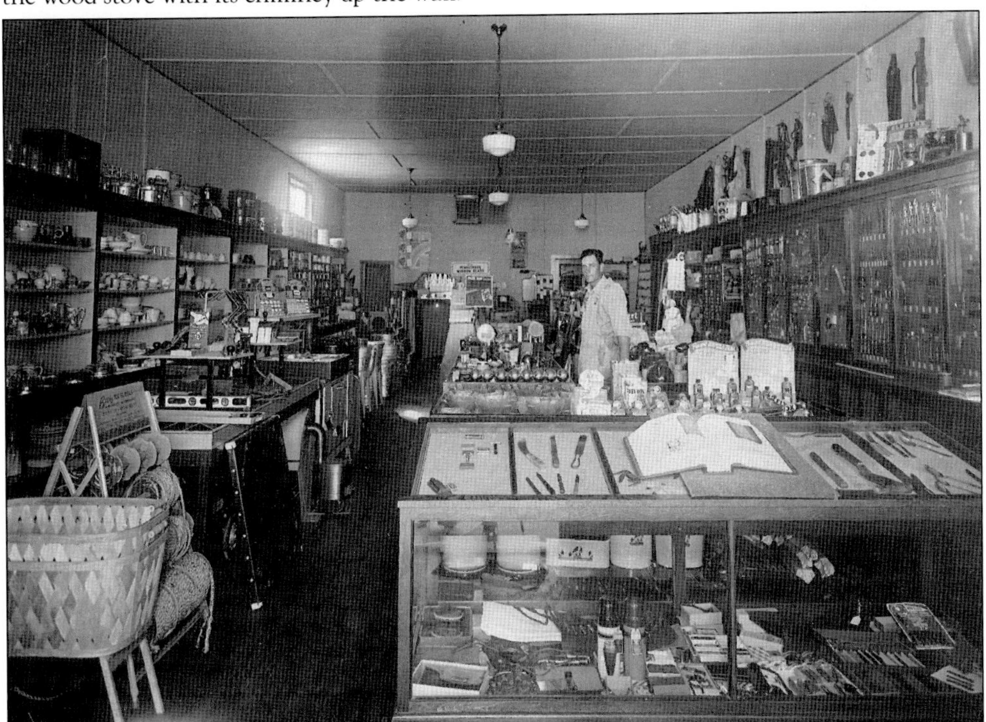

Wilber Dillavou is behind the counter in the same Roberts Hardware Store. Notice that the ceiling has been lowered, the office loft has been removed, and a modern heating unit has replaced the wood stove.

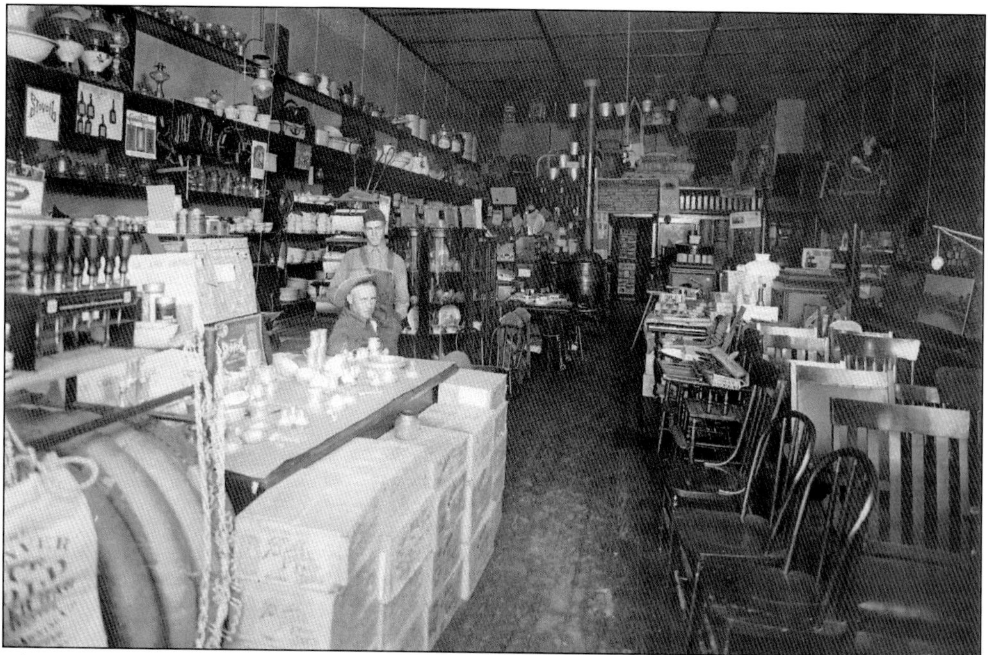

This is the inside of the Roberts Hardware and Furniture Store in May 1924. The gentleman standing is C. D. Roberts. Keith Taylor is sitting in one of the many chairs in the store. The left-hand corner shows a car water bag. These were hung from the radiator cap to provide water in an emergency. Notice the tires and chains, which were and still are needed around Sundance.

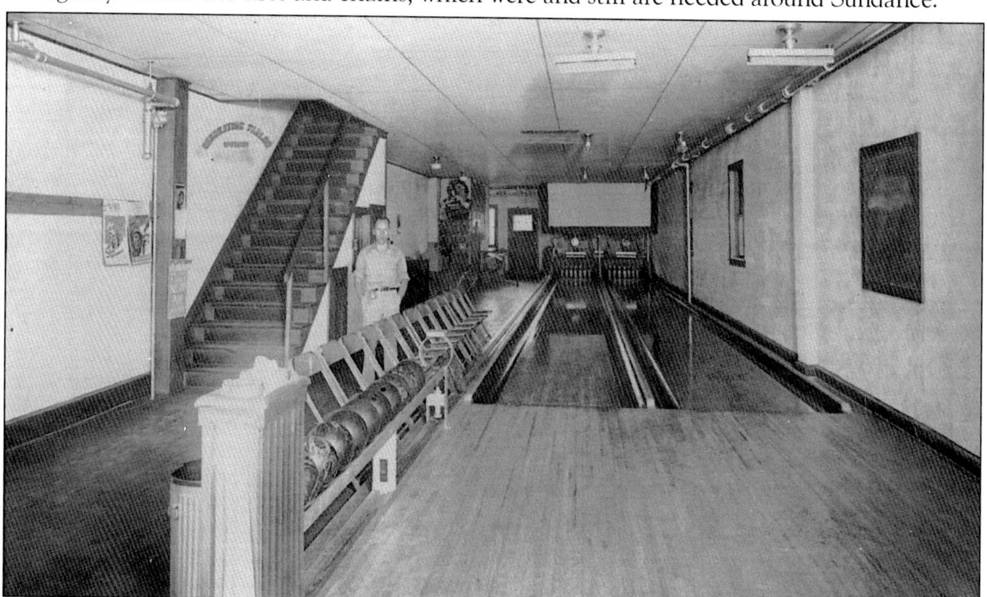

Jess Straight is standing in the Sundance bowling alley. Sundance has had a bowling alley off and on since the late 1880s. The old building that housed C. D. Roberts's hardware store on Third Street was torn down in 1929, and a new structure was put up to hold the modern bowling equipment. The upstairs held a pool table, card tables, and a boxing ring. The Agricultural Stabilization Conservation Service office took over the front part of the upstairs. Pauline Knode remembers working in the office at age 14. A wall was put up to protect the pool players from Pauline.

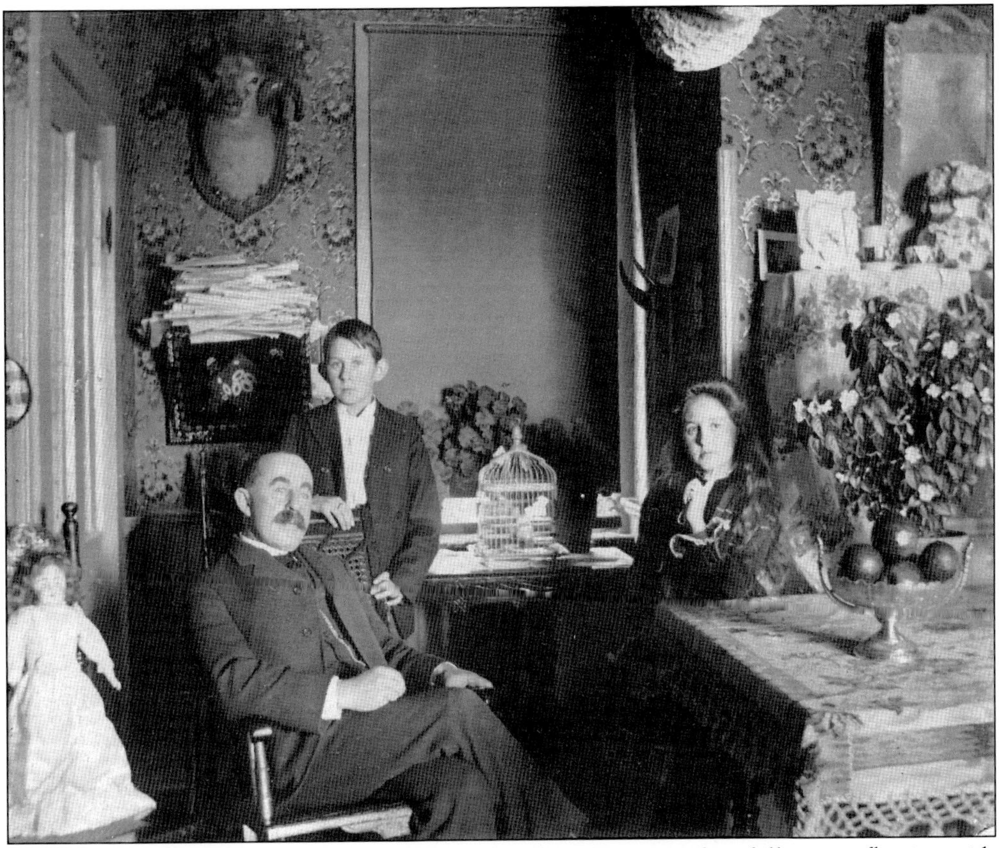

Living and dining rooms of the late 1800s and early 1900s were often full to overflowing with what would be considered very odd items today. In a world before Technicolor, wallpaper was often used to brighten a room and to add character to the entire house. The living room of Abe Frank and his children, Elmer and Florence, shows much of their stylish lives. While the busy dining room of the W. E. Brockett home shows the practical side with the hot water heater that can be seen through the kitchen door. Both homes display the love of wildlife with ducks, deer, and Rambouillet sheep decorating the rooms.

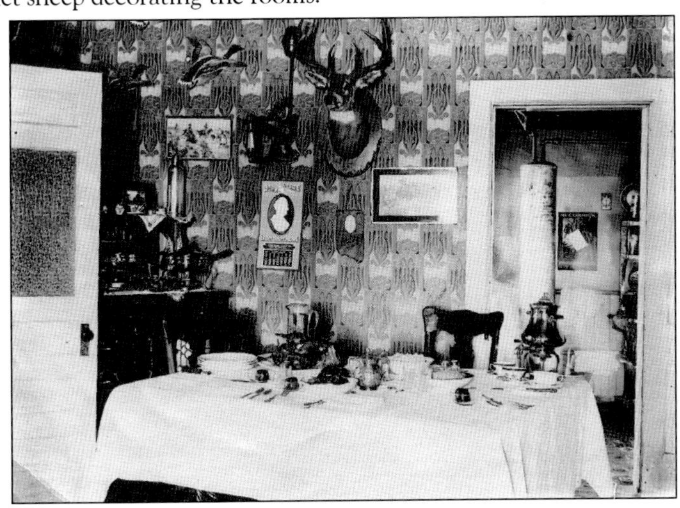

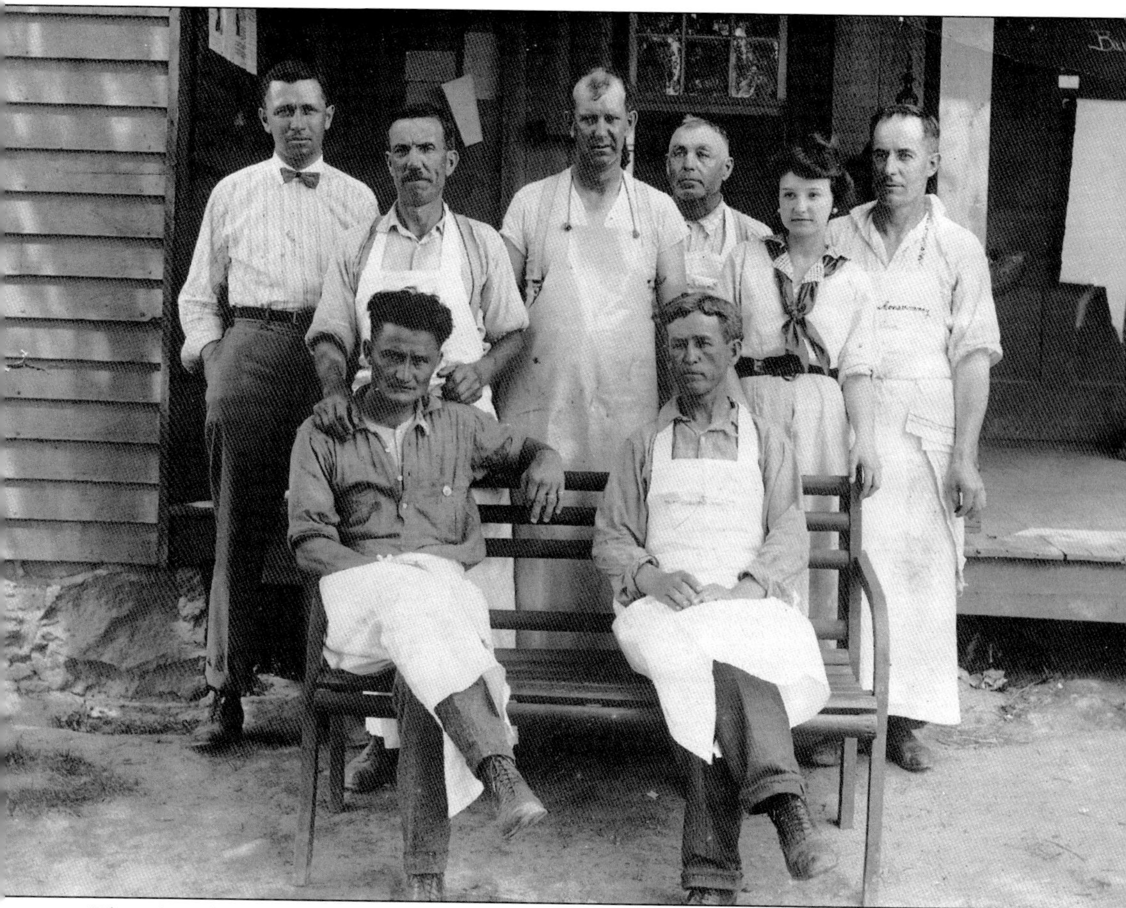

There have been a couple of meat markets in Sundance over the years. This group of unidentified people was part of one of these businesses. In an advertisement in the *Crook County Monitor* on Friday April 8, 1910, the City Meat Market writes that they want your beef and pork. Other newspaper columns comment on the friendly, clean service that could be had from the local meat markets. One editor went on to say how fortunate the people of Sundance were to have a place to buy the meat and poultry already cut and wrapped.

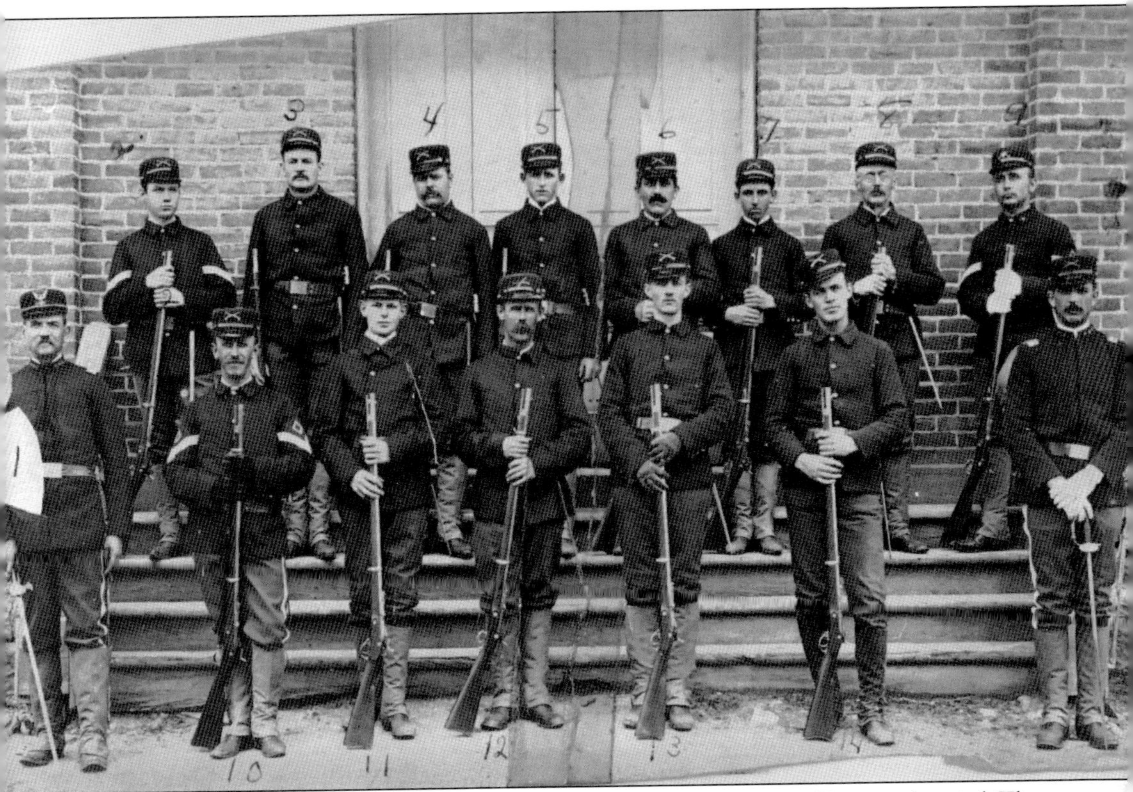

The Wyoming National Guard was established in 1870 during the Wyoming Territorial period. The first federally recognized Wyoming unit was the Laramie Grays in 1888. In 1890, constitutional provisions allowed for the formation of units in the new state of Wyoming. This group picture was taken in the latter part of the 1890s. Pictured are (1) Melvin Nichols, (2) Leroy Salisberry, (3) Dan VanMeter, (4) Ike Joy, (5) Charles Griffin, (6) Alex Wagstaff, (7) Fred Griffin, (8) Wallace Stearns, (9) unknown, (10) Adrian Hewes, (11) Tom Rounds, (12) Oakley Banks, (13) Walter Robinson, (14) Truman Fox, and (15) Horace Nichols.

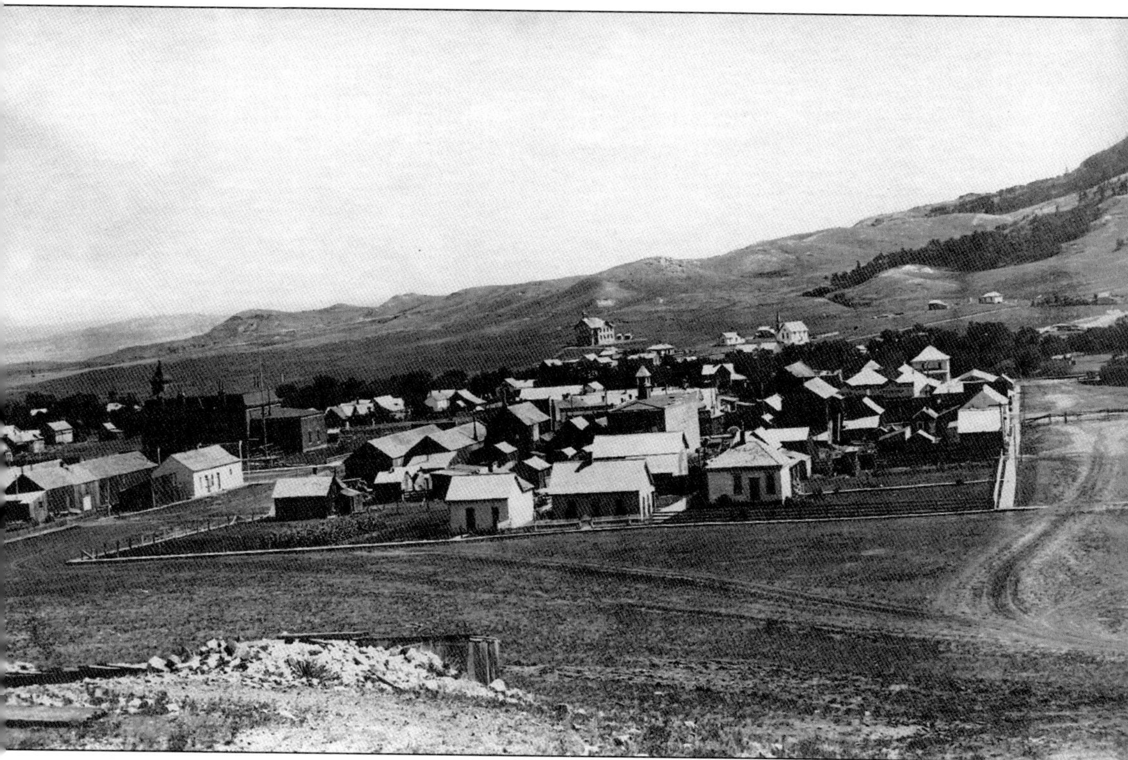

This picture is looking southeast across the town. The courthouse can be seen to the left. The old frame schoolhouse sitting on the hill is in the center. Just a little to the front and right of the school sits the city hall with its bell tower. On the right of town, running through the field, is the town water flume. A town water system was the earliest utility in Sundance. The early water system was made of wood bound with metal bands and was operated by Mose Pettigrew. In 1893, Henry Keets bought it and attained permission from the city council to erect a pumping station. Then in 1896, the city voted $10,000 worth of bonds to buy the system themselves.

Six

Their Children's Schools

The adults of Sundance knew that schools were important for their children and for the growth of their town. Schools started small, as in the beginning there were but a few children of school age. Often these first schools were in someone's home. As more families arrived, the need arose to find larger spaces for schools. The next school in Sundance was a log building. It sat across the creek and was able to provide the proper space for a number of years. When this log building had grown too small, it was time to move out. A bigger one was soon constructed. There was a porch, a fire escape, and large windows. It had all the necessary room and met all the needs of the teachers and of the students. It also had a racetrack as the school yard. Recess went by really fast. In the early 1920s, the need arose once again for a larger building. The school officials began to develop plans for a fine stone school structure. When this school was constructed, it met the school requirements for not only Sundance but the entire county for many years to come. The inside rooms were adjusted as the needs and number of children grew with the town. But eventually, the school became overcrowded. The lower grades were having their classes in the basement of the courthouse. So a new school was erected. Education must march on and leave the stately old stone school building to the mercy of future generations.

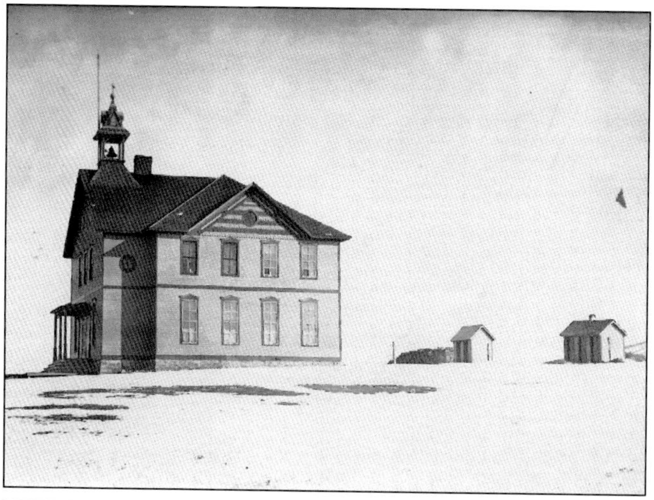

This is the two-story frame school that was constructed to replace the log school. The log building was able to hold about 50 children, and it was holding close to 70 when they decided to construct a larger facility. It was on January 23, 1886, that the school board accepted William Nefsy's plans for a new school building. These plans said that the school would hold 250 to 300 students. The out buildings can be seen behind the school structure.

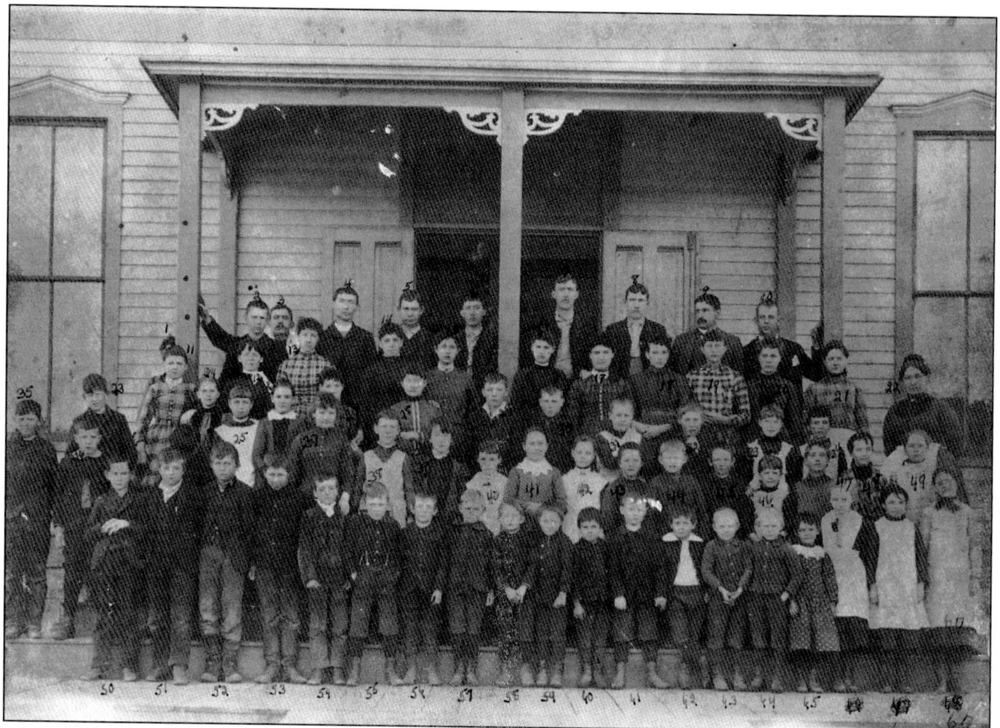

This is the first student body in the new school for 1886–1887. Among those pictured are (first row) Charlie Alden, Van Moore, John Alden, Tom Rounds, Walter Scott, Frank Snivley, Walter Legatt, the McElwain twins, Blanche Kincaid, and Bertha Kincaid; (second row) Ben Best, Georgie Blackwell, Molly Meeks, Florence Williams, Sadie Moore, Bertha Williams, Maud Miller, Clarence Vest, Hazel Baldwin, Dora Lott, and Niaoma Kincaid; (third row) John Vest, Jennie Thain, Nellie Wade, Mary ? , Bertha Nichols, Julia Nefsy, Bert Wade, Herb Stone, Junie Stone, George ?, Edna Rounds, and Edna Pettigrew; (fourth row) Mattie Gird, Sam Enigh, Ermma Round, Emma La Fauntain, Eldora Bruner, Lena Brown, Myrtle Arange, Myrtle Hazelton, Mabel Vest, Maggie Royeter, Sara Emig, and Beulah Sylvester, the primary teacher; (fifth row) Mary ?; Fred Williams; Henry Nevil; John Nefsy; Matt Nefsy; Tom Nefsy; Rev. O. B. Chassell, principal; and Ira Williams.

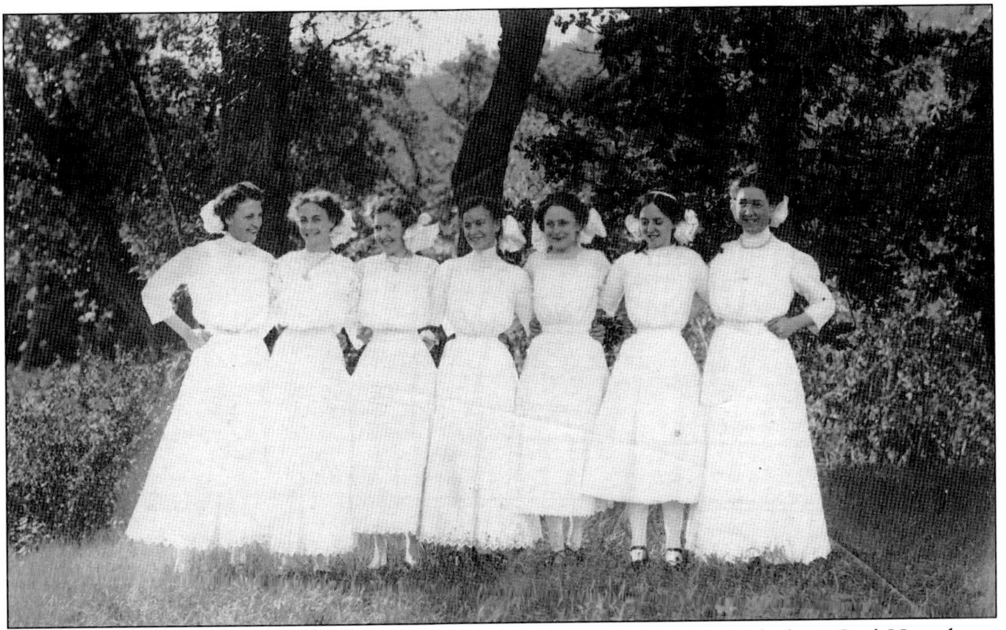

The girls of the graduating class of 1911 are, from left to right, Ava Shober, Gail Hamilton, Florence Nettlehorst, Elizabeth Mauch, Mildred Rounds, Helen Schloredt, and Stella Gage. They are enjoying the day, maybe not breathing deeply, but having fun anyway. They are in dresses that were the style in 1911, all white with lace.

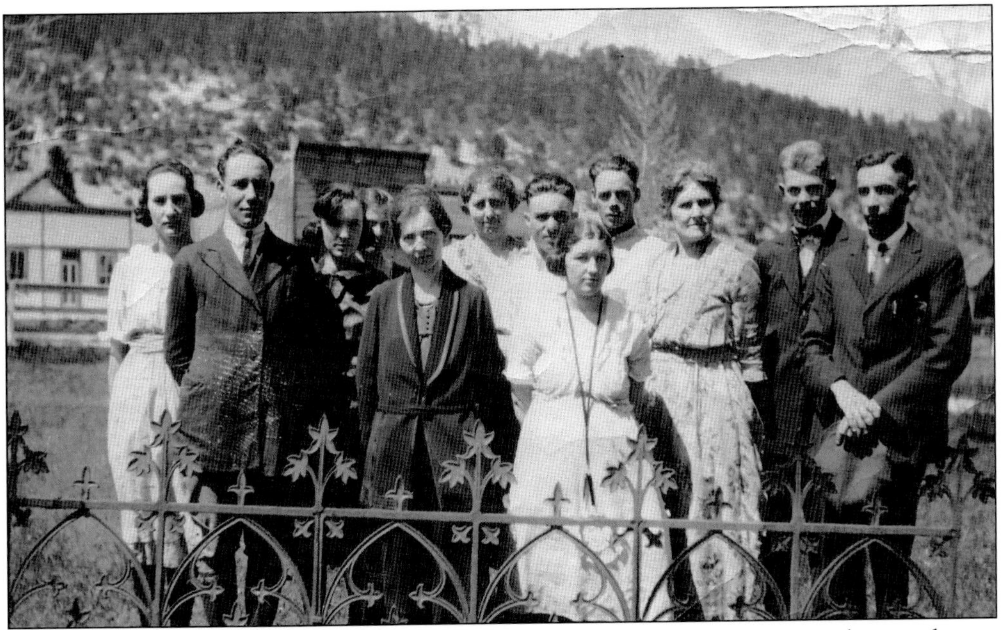

The graduating class of 1922 shows the changes in style—hair was bobbed, more leg was shown, and more color was in the fabric of their dresses. Pictured from left to right are Edna Grandbouche, Walter Williamson, Virginia Mills, Charlotte Carr, Jennie Clarenbach, Carrie Hurtt, Ellis Sluss, Frances Plato, Emmet Williamson, Elizabeth Brandt, Clyde Roberts, and W. R. Mann.

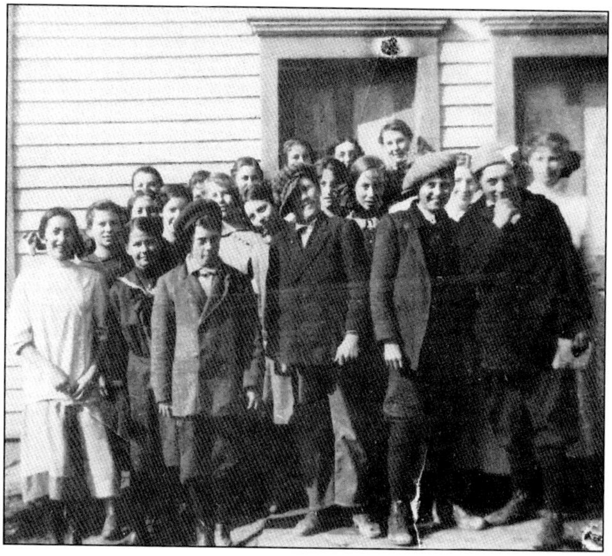

This picture shows students at the old frame school in south Sundance. In the back is the teacher, Anna Bell Lenz. The students in the front row are, from left to right, Leta Brandenberry, Gertrude Storms, Frank "Runt" Farrall, Henry Gage, Mervin Davis, and Merritt Mills. The rest of the students are unidentified. Minnie Cox played the piano at this school for students as they lined up outside the building and marched into their classrooms. She also played for silent movies and at local and country dances. This enterprising woman also worked as a waitress at the Zane Hotel and as a relief telephone operator.

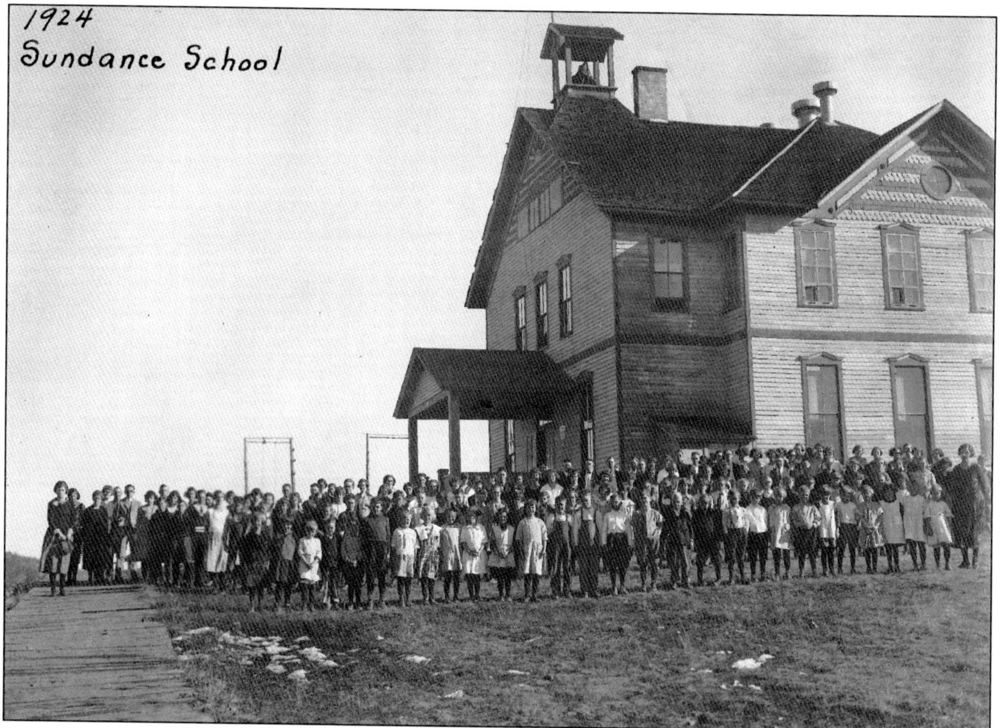

This large picture of the entire school was taken in the early spring of 1924. It was warm enough to be outside for this picture, but there is still snow on the ground. All the grade school children are out to get their pictures taken. The teachers for the lower grades in 1923–1924 were Celia Fawkes, grades 1–3, and Connie Rankin, grades 4–6. Mary Viola Gravelle was the teacher for the seventh and eighth classes. The custodian for the lower grades was Lewis Wayne. The high school superintendent was Elizabeth T. Brandt. The vocational agriculture teacher was Leslie McWethy. Cecil Linch was teaching English in 1923–1924, and Mr. Branden was teaching social studies. This would be the last group of children to attend this school.

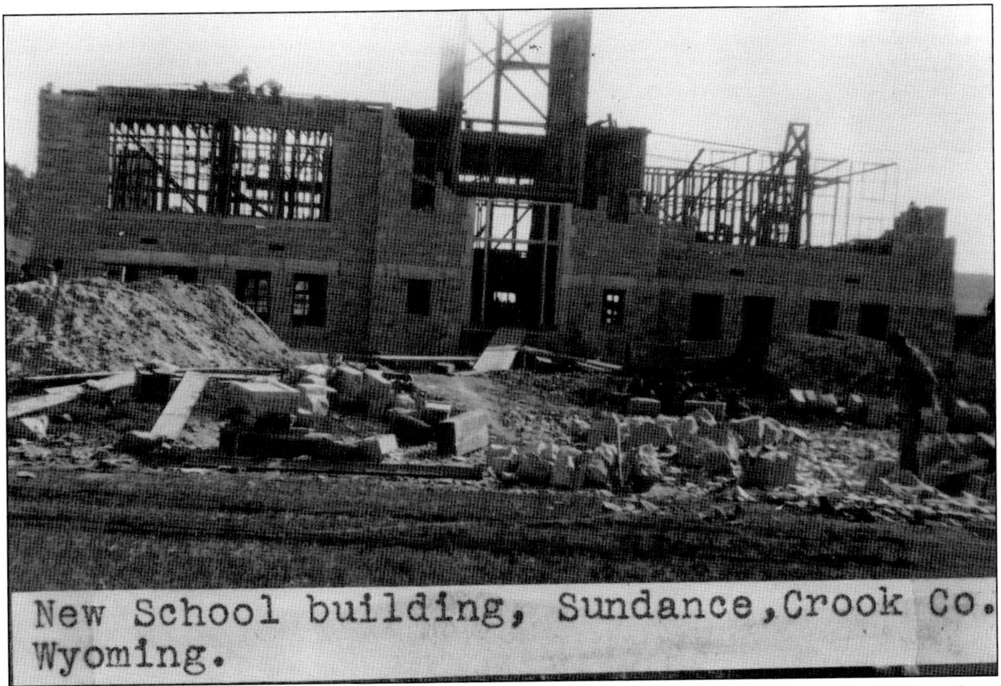

The stone school was constructed in 1923. The new building was constructed of Minnelusa sandstone. The cornerstone was a chunk of flinty basalt taken from the Devils Tower National Monument. The first floor had four classrooms and a library. The second floor had a recitation room, a laboratory, a domestic science room, two commercial rooms, and an auditorium. The basement was laid out as a gymnasium. The floors were maple, and the doors and windows were trimmed in cedar. There was indoor plumbing. This was also the year that a telephone and electric lights were installed in the school. The private power plant supplied electricity for 60 lights. In December 1923, city council approved streetlights to be installed. Power would be supplied from private plants. Nellie Roadifer Humphrey remembered riding with her sister 7 miles to the top of Williams Divide to watch the lights of Sundance. There were four. (Above, courtesy of Wyoming Division of Cultural Resources.)

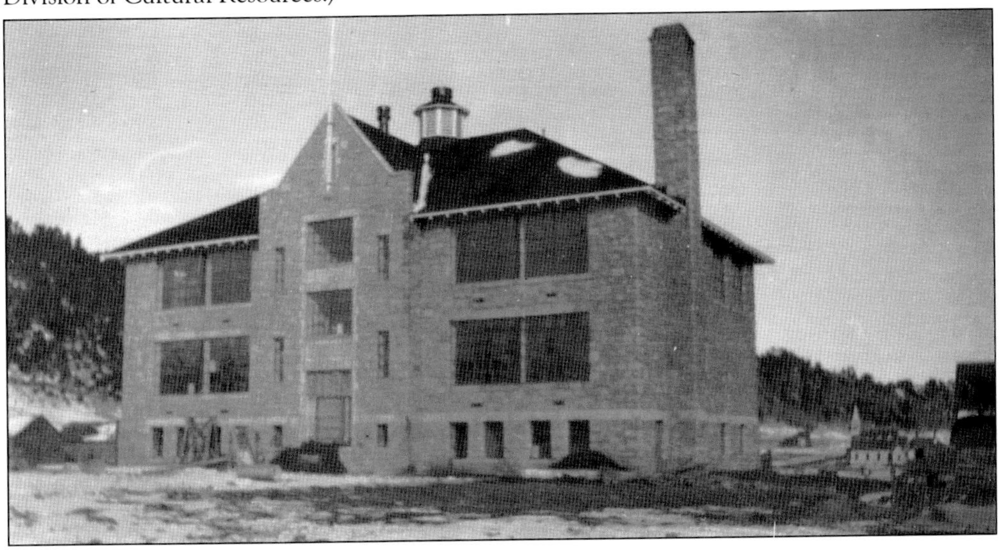

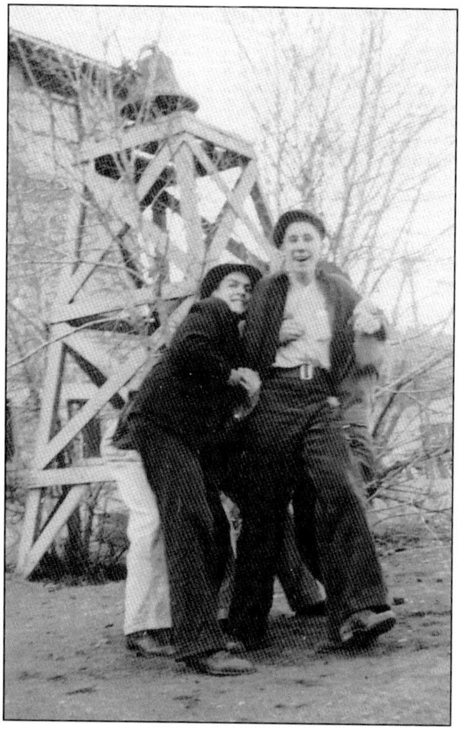

Boys will be boys, no matter what year it is. These five boys did not want their photograph taken, or Dwayne Kaiser, the boy on the right, was up to no good and the others wanted proof that he was there. The Old Stone Schoolhouse was in its prime in 1938 when this picture was taken. But updates and improvements in the school system caused the abandonment of the clanging bell and its wooden tower, which stood on the south side of the building.

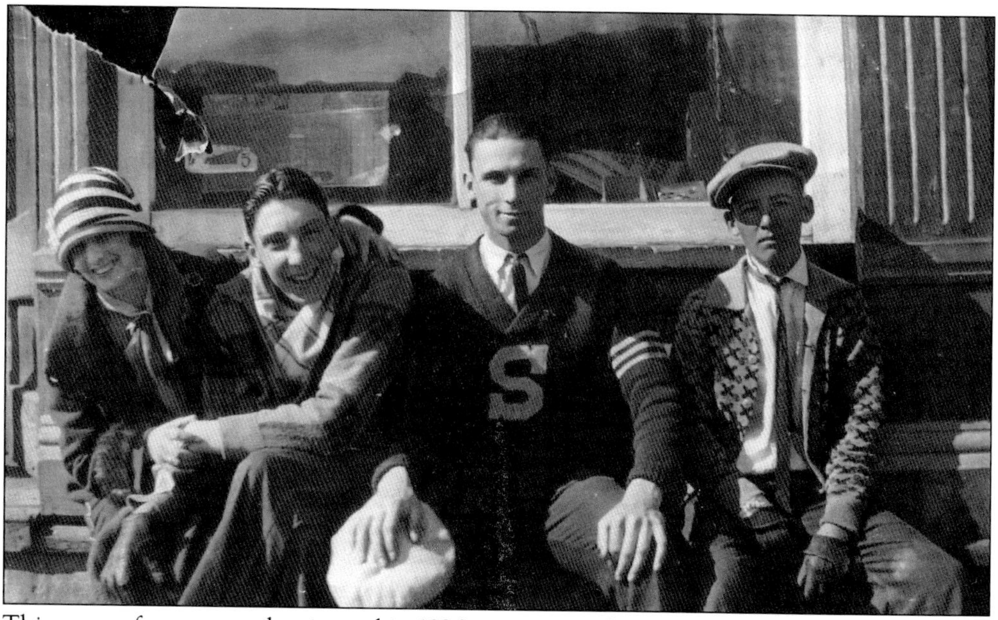

This group of young people, pictured in 1926, is sitting in front of the local drugstore. From left to right are Olive Schelldorf, Bill Thompson, Orville Lincoln, and Raymond Vines. Bill's parents ranched on the Rifle Pit Divide. The road conditions made attending school difficult. Most of the roads were gravel, if there were roads at all. There were several families that opened their homes as boardinghouses for the rural children. The Thompson children mailed their laundry home to be washed and ironed and mailed back. Olive and Bill graduated from Sundance High School in 1927. Orville and Raymond graduated in 1926.

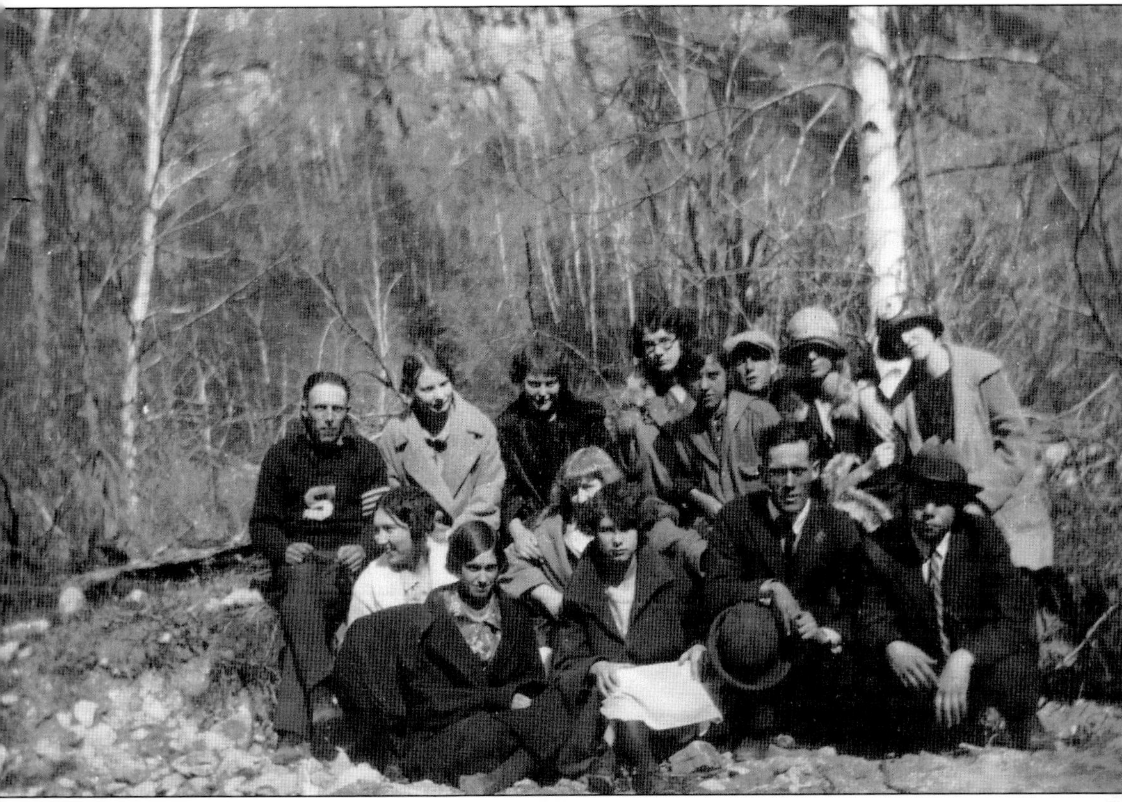

This is senior skip day for the senior class of 1925. It was a nice spring day to take a picnic up Sand Creek Canyon. Most of the class is pictured. Those graduating in this 1925 class were Eleanor Banks, Martha May Booney, Gertrude Roslyn Carr, Lloyd Cole, Robert Davidson, Frank William Farrell, Kathryn M. Frank, Prudence Hawken, Earling W. Mathews, Mary Jean Marr, Alma Mae Riehemann, Grace Alyne Staton, William F. Schloredt, Minnie Straight, Marion Thompson, Elizabeth Ann Waters, Harriet Agnes Waters, and Gaylord A. Zane. Graduation exercises took place Friday, May 29, 1925, at 8:00 p.m. in the auditorium in the Sundance High School.

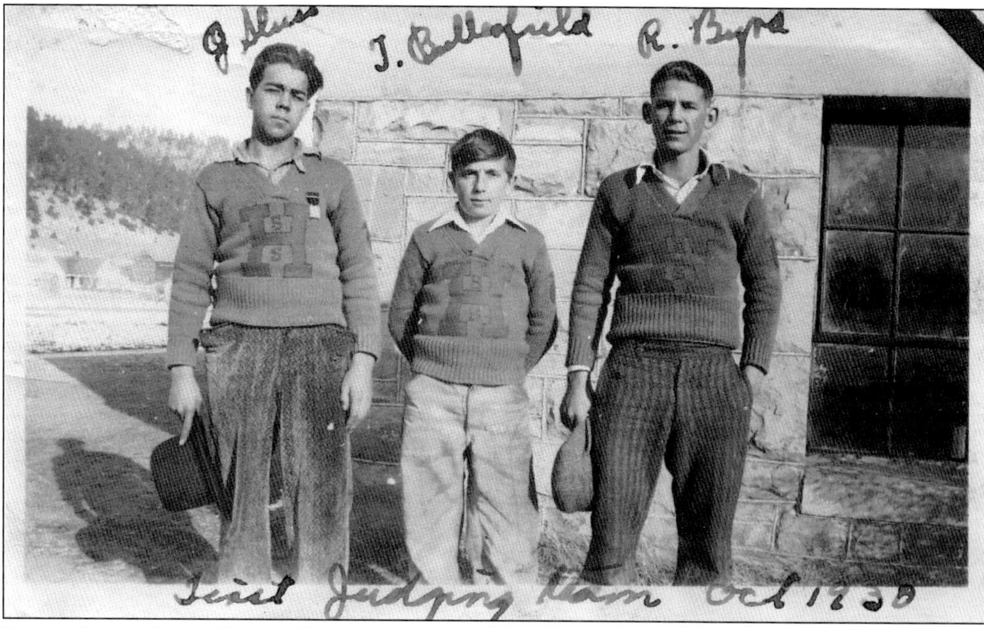

From left to right are Eugene Sluss, Ted Butterfield, and Rex Bird. These boys are the judging team for 1932. In those days, most high schools had agriculture classes for the boys to take. Lessons would be on rotating crops, building terraces, contour plowing, planting wind breaks, the right crops to plant, spotting weeds, and fighting bugs. The judging teams learned to pick out the best animals and explain why. The farm shop class was held across from the school on the corner of Main Street and Fourth Street. These boys learned welding, mechanics, and wood building.

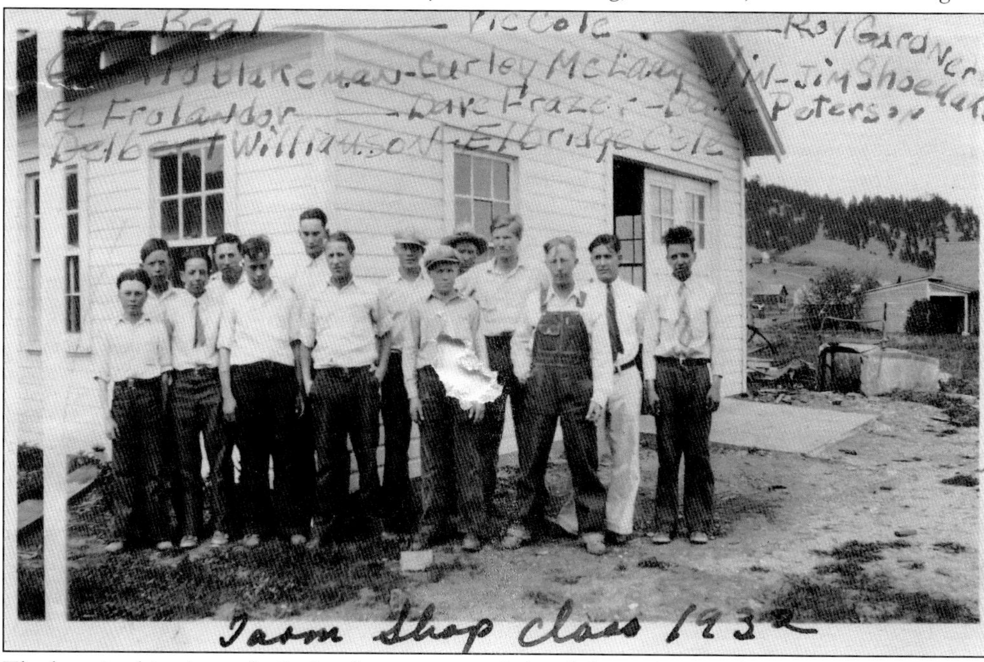

The boys in this picture built the classroom seen behind them. Among them are Joe Beal, Victor Cole, Roy Gardner, Gerald Blakeman, Dan Frazier, Dale Peterson, Delbert Williamson, and Elbridge Cole.

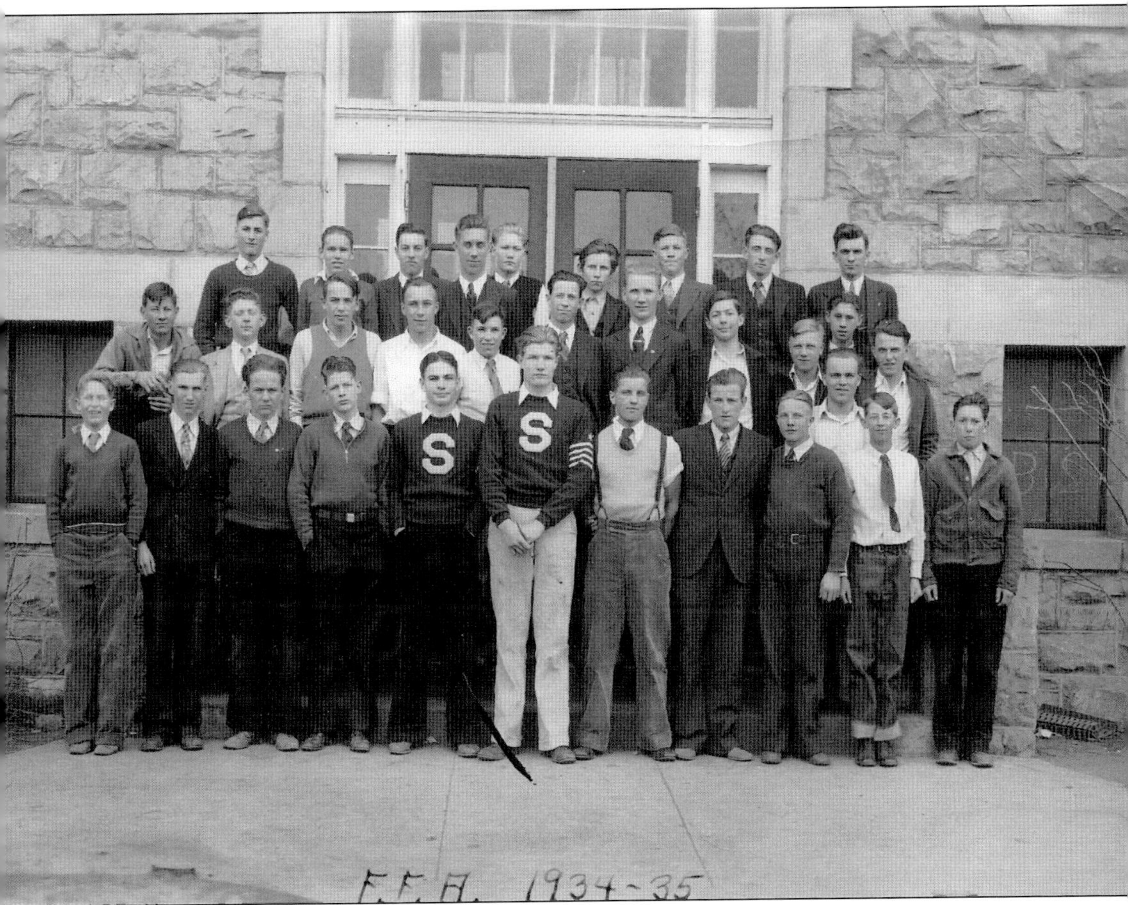

Future Farmers of America (FFA) was organized in 1929 for vocational agriculture students in the high schools of the United States. The idea was to create and nurture a pride in country life. Pictured here are the FFA members in 1939. In the first row are, from left to right, Floyd Erickson, Clinton Kipp, Richard Smith, Ted Rounds, Jess Sipe, David Frasier, Ray Beldon, Hal Oudin, Stanton Reynolds, Edwin Wells, and Jim Bowers. Among those pictured in subsequent rows are, from left to right, (second row) David Well, David Zimmershied, Edgar Partlow, Wes Huckins, Jack Finch, Kenneth Canfield, Lincoln Kaiser, ? Gulford, Gene Reynolds, Kenneth Fitch, and Norman Weaver; (third row) Darrin Soloman, Richard McWethy, Maynard Hayes, Albert Kaiser, and John Wood.

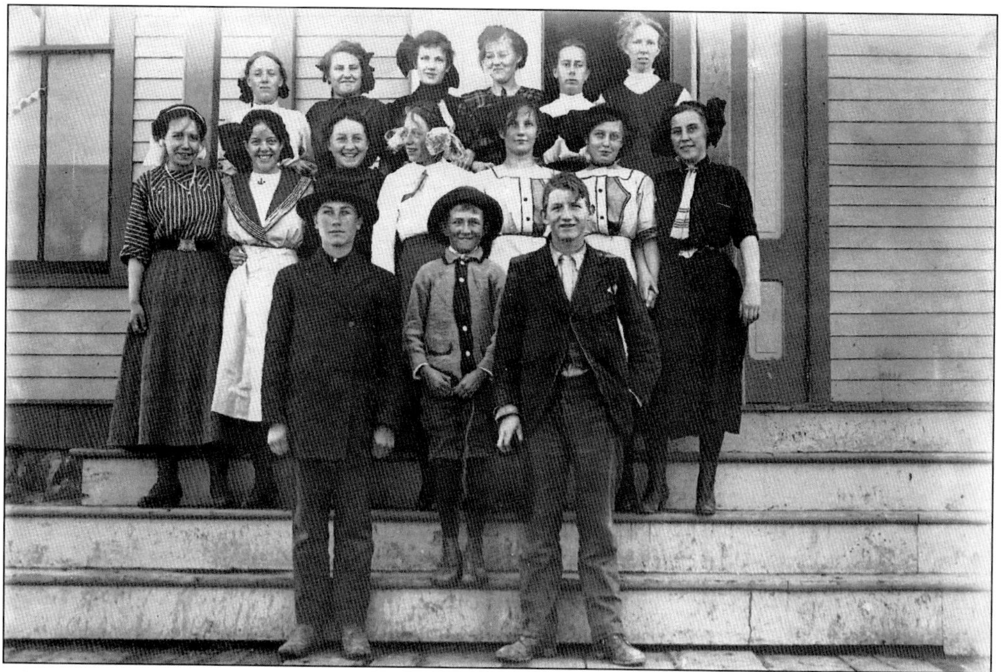

These are happy students standing on the steps of their school. This picture was taken before 1923. In 1924, the new school opened. This school was closed and torn down. From left to right are (first row) Ron Earl Gage, Walter Mulholland, and Raymond Roadifer; (second row) Ethel Williamson, Blanche Lytle, Annetta Gage, Henrietta Liely, Ivy May Nettlehorst, Carinne Nettlehorst, and Marie Morgan; (third row) Elise Mohaffey, Ina Eaton, Florence Good, unidentified, Inez Williamson, and Flora Falden.

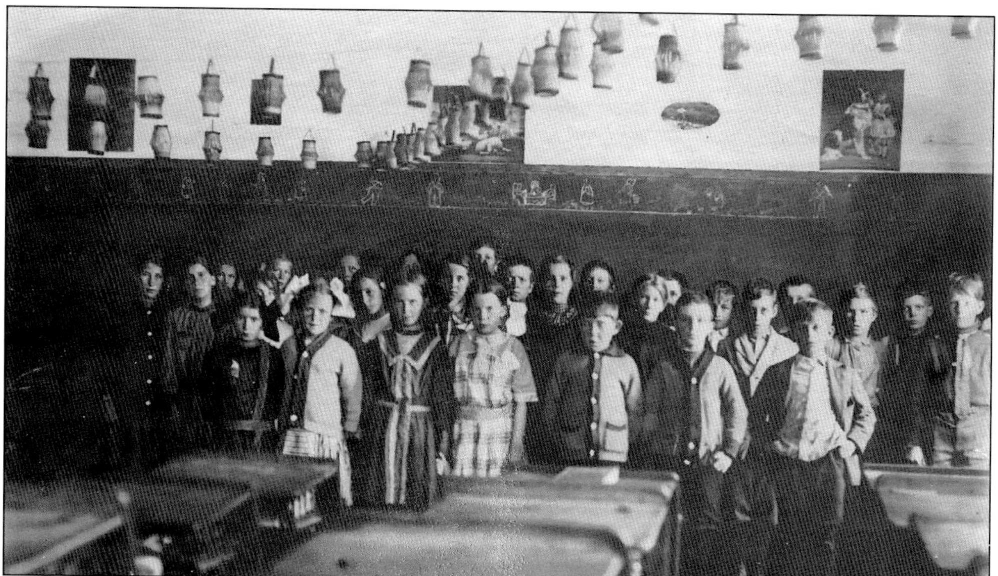

This is a picture of a class in the Sundance grade school, which was in the large frame school on the hill at the south end of town. Those names that are known to belong in the class are Hubert Mulholland, Gretchen Davis, Polly Roberts, Virginia Lytle, Ellis Sluss, Frank Farrell, and Wesley Storm.

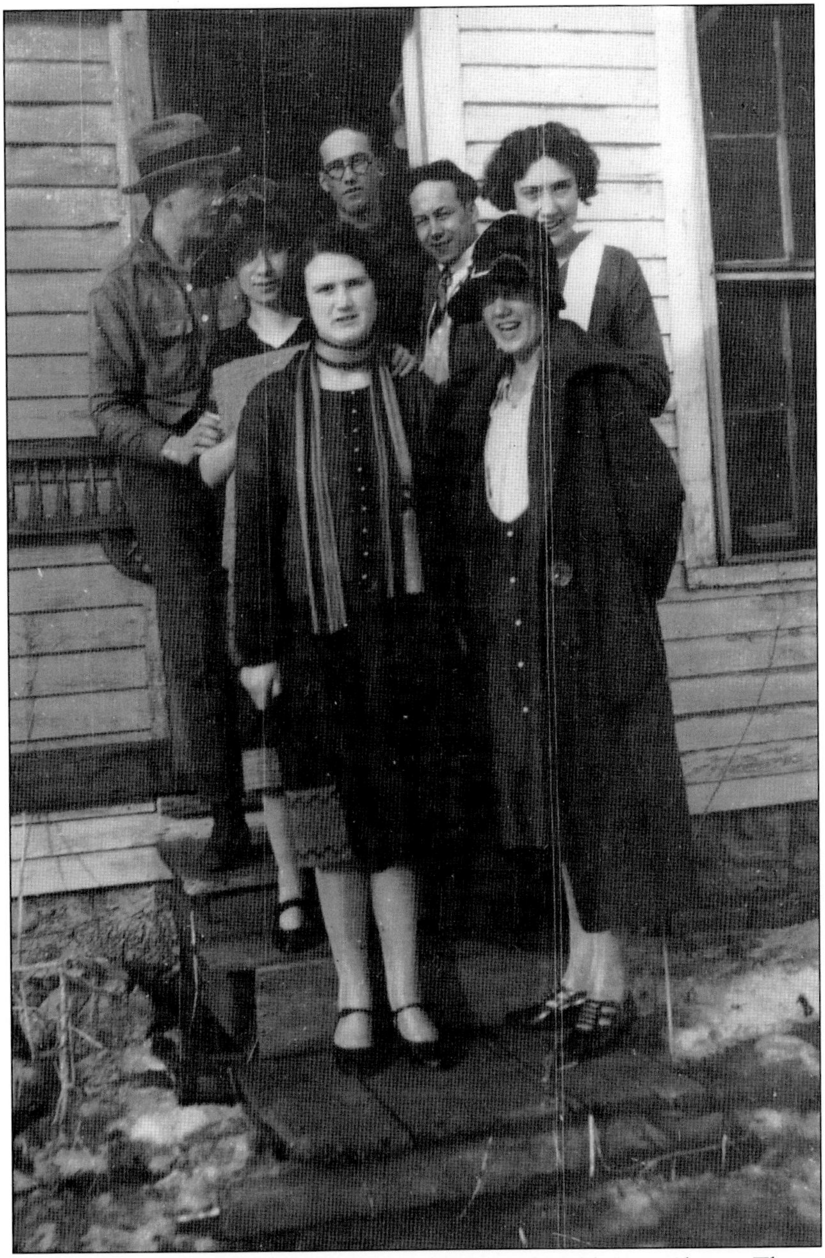

This picture was taken in 1926 on the front steps of Ben and Mable Vines' home. The nicknames are listed in no particular order: Word, Toots, Vines, Smithy, Nibs, and Tommie. Where were those stuck with the nicknames Gas, Shorts, and Tourchy? Vines could be Raymond Vines in the glasses. In the second row on the right is Tommie, also known as Marion Thompson. Marion graduated from Sundance High School in 1925. She attended the Spearfish Normal School and received a teaching certificate. She taught in country schools for several years. She also went to business school, after which she became the deputy county clerk. Her brother's father-in-law was the county clerk at that time. She went to work at the Sundance State Bank in 1934. When she retired, she was vice president. When Marion died, she left a note in her will that explained that, being of sound mind, she had blown it all!

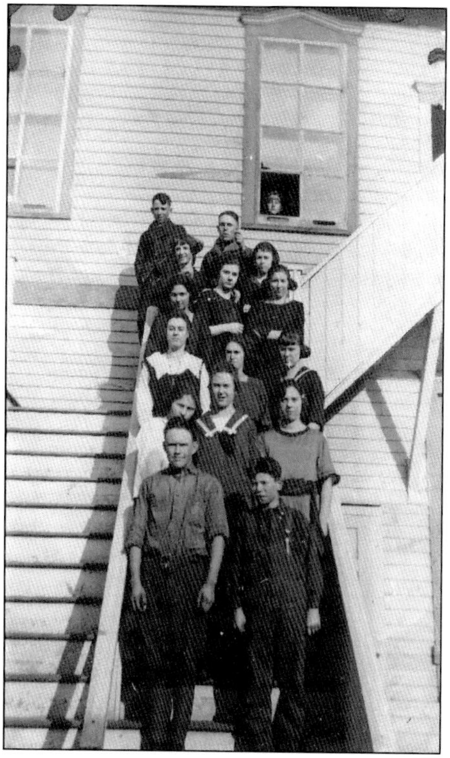

The back of this picture says that this is the sophomore class of 1922–1923 and that they are standing on the fire escape. The 1925 graduation announcement lists 18 graduates. Sixteen of those students are in the picture. Their class flower was the daffodil. The class colors were green and gold, and their motto was "Labor conquers all."

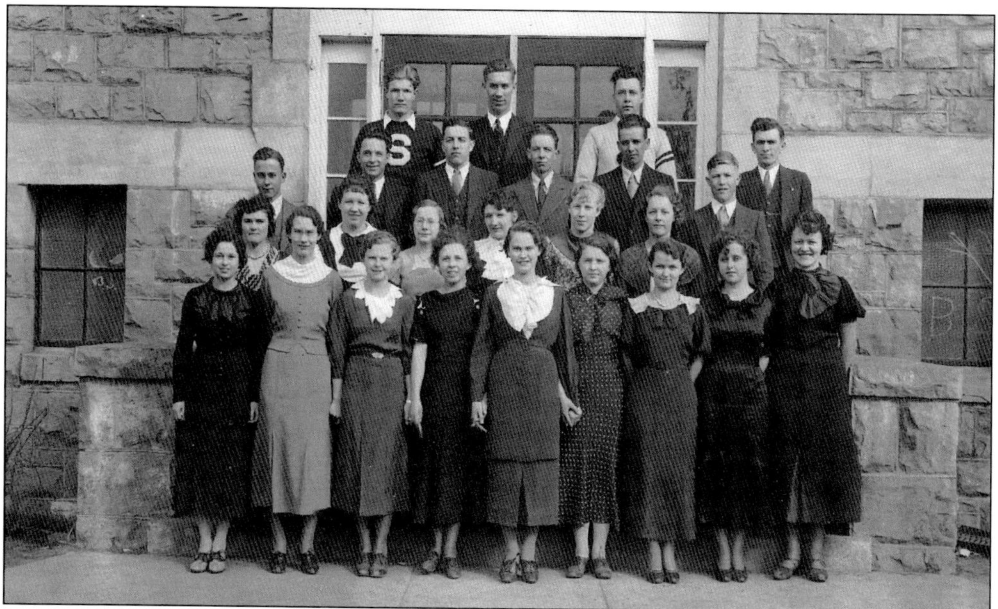

This is the graduating class of 1935. In no particular order, the members of this class are Edith Schloredt, Edna Taylor, Anna Mae Blakeman, Wilma Smith, Elbridge Cole, Victor Cole, Verla Mae Justice, David Fraiser, Edwin Frolaner, Ester Davadison, Dorothy Plumb, Albert Kaiser, Gladyce Liam, Rose Plachy, Ruth Frolander, Dickie Ackerman, Maynard Hayes, Roy Gardner, Thomas Hooper, Ruth Gardner, and Lois Roadifer. The class motto was "Success comes in cans, not in cannots."

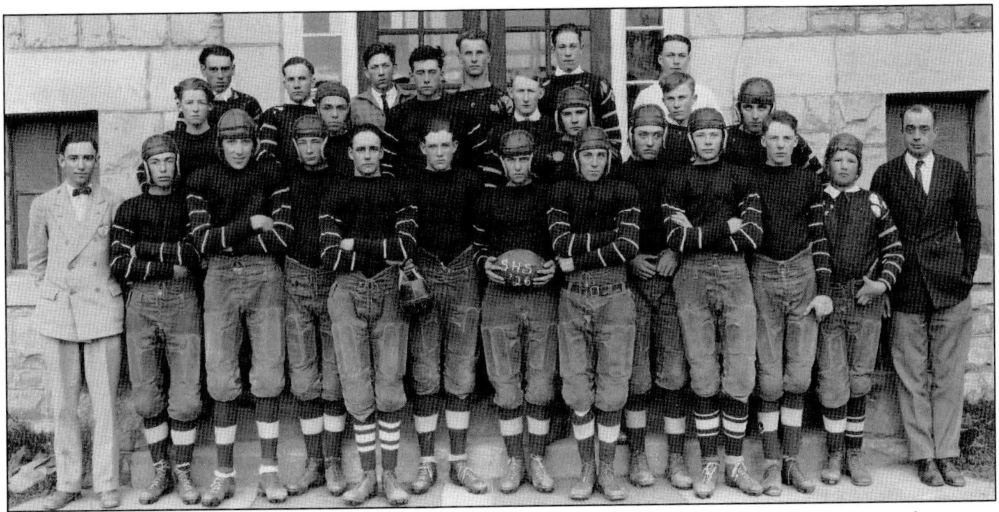

These sullen leatherheads were a fierce group to contend with. The leather headgear the team wears was first introduced in 1896 and consisted of only earpieces and straps to protect the ears. Around 1900, helmets were padded and resembled aviator helmets. This new design cut down on concussions and torn ears. The 1926 Bulldog team colors were crimson and white, with uniforms being a little worse for wear. Coach Teeter, far left, coached football for only a few years. He also held the position of senior class sponsor. In the 1928 class annual, it was written in the class will to "bequeath their sponsor, W. W. Teeter, sheik extraordinary, to the lower classes, charging them to keep him clear of all matrimonial alliances and designing females until he shall have reached the age of responsibility."

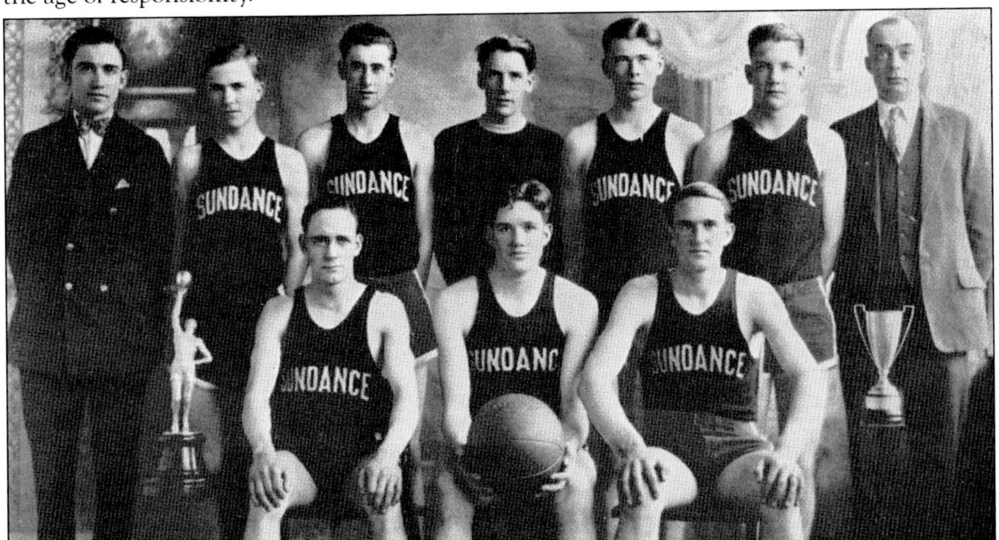

In 1928, the Bulldogs learned they could fly. Coach Teeter's basketball team won all but 4 of 20 games that year and was eligible to play in the regional tournament in Gillette. Sundance High School smelled blood. The week of the tournament arrived with fierce snowstorms. Roads were blocked in all directions. Not to be denied, the school contacted Clyde Ice and chartered his new Eagle Rock airplane. At 10 O'clock Wednesday morning, Clyde circled Sundance and landed in Hooper's field east of town. At regular intervals of one hour and 15 minutes, two team members at a time were flown to the game. The Bulldogs won every game and drove home with the trophy.

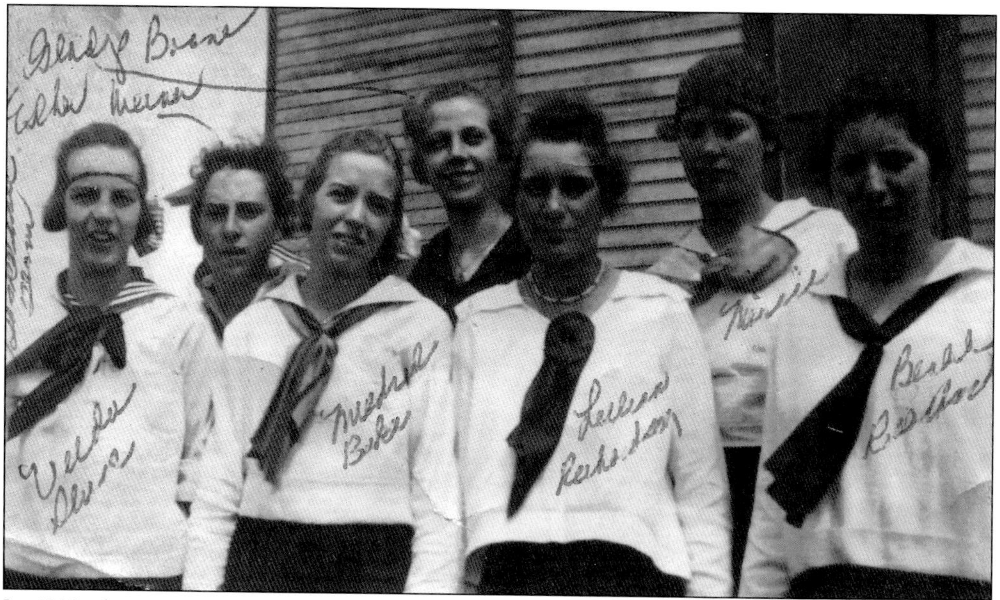

In 1918, there was a shortage of girls who wanted to play basketball, and so the girls practiced against the boys' team. The girls are, from left to right, Velda Sluss, Esther Weaver, Mildred Baker, Gladys Boone, Lillian Richardson, Minnie Straight, and Beulah Richardson. The girls' uniforms sported long-sleeved sailor shirts and probably knee-length split skirts.

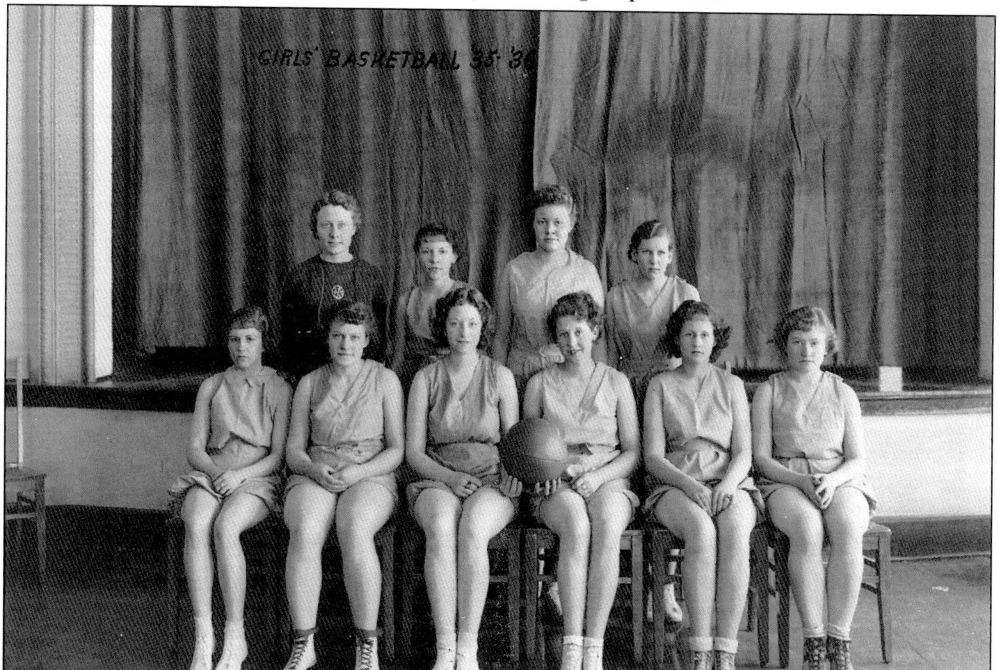

By 1935, the uniforms reflected the changing times with more ease of movement and much more skin showing. From left to right are (first row) June Schloredt, Greta Cleveland, Louise Roark, Leona Canfield, Rachel Canfield, and Fontella Cleveland; (second row) coach Fern Nelson, Ellen Clarenbach, Edna Justice, and Lottie Granham.

Seven

Their Transportation

The modes of transportation for the residents of Sundance have changed with the people, and the country has grown and developed. People traveled on foot years before Custer and his horse soldiers arrived. They knew that sometimes, to get where you wanted to go, you might have to pull your own load or pack it on your shoulders. The first step on any adventure is always the hardest. The horse could travel faster, and it was kinder on people's feet. Horses could be ridden or harnessed to pull a wagon, buggy, or a plow. Children rode an old horse to school and back home again. Boys rode horseback to meet their girls or to a baseball game. Girls were known to ride miles just to see twinkling lights. Donkeys and mules were the transportation of many a prospector because of their ability to haul a heavy load and their sure feet. Automobiles of all makes and models arrived shortly after Ford invented the assembly line. Sundance had Hupmobiles, Dodge Brothers, Internationals, Studebaker cars and wagons, and even a John Deere or two. Just like two feet gave way to four feet, four wheels would give way to two wheels. Sundance found bicycles were a good source of transportation on the streets and sidewalks of town. The trouble was there were not many streets and sidewalks that were paved. A motorcycle might get you where you wanted to go more quickly than an old bicycle, but the neighbors did not take kindly to the noise.

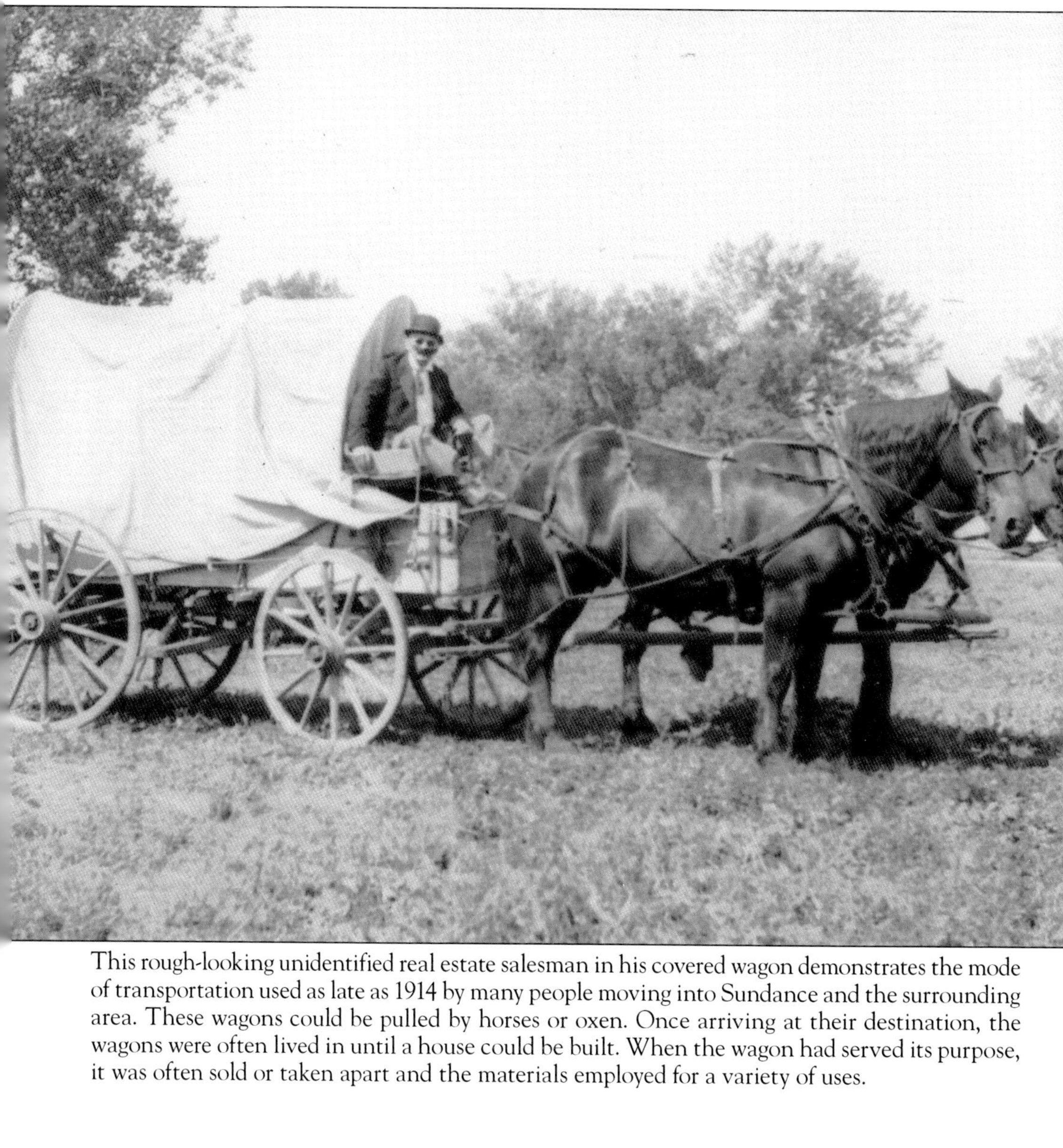

This rough-looking unidentified real estate salesman in his covered wagon demonstrates the mode of transportation used as late as 1914 by many people moving into Sundance and the surrounding area. These wagons could be pulled by horses or oxen. Once arriving at their destination, the wagons were often lived in until a house could be built. When the wagon had served its purpose, it was often sold or taken apart and the materials employed for a variety of uses.

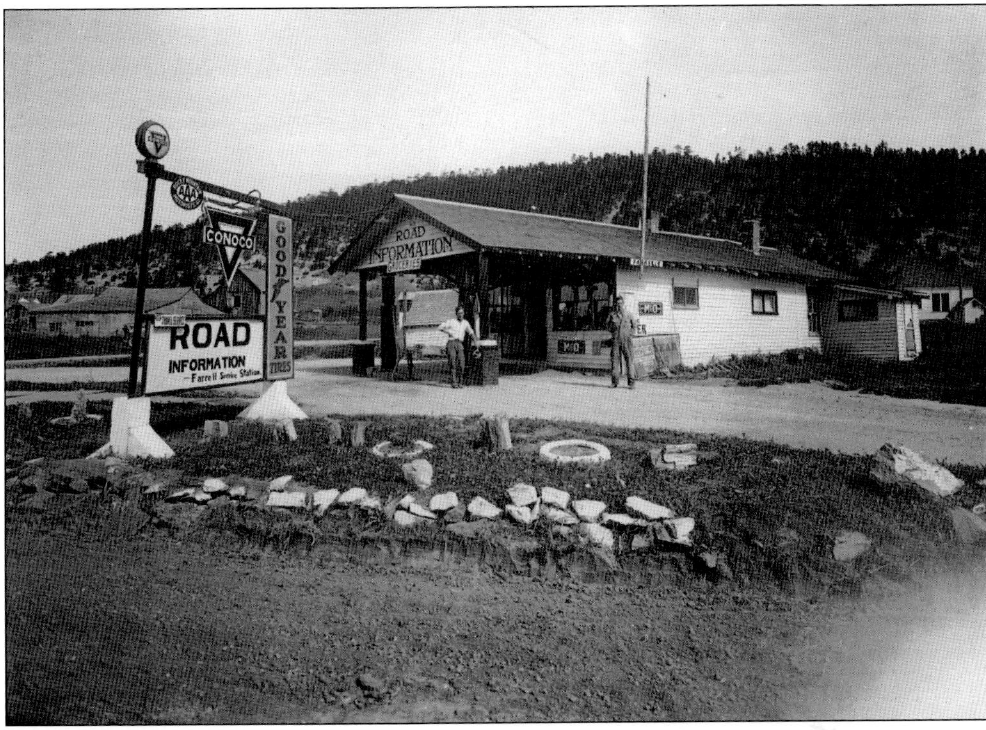

The barn in the background once was used to board horses in town, but the hooves that once incessantly clopped down the streets have now become few and far between. The Farrell Filling Station pictured above was just one station that popped up during the automobile craze. With the automobile came more travel, new roads, and the need for supplies and information for that special trip. Mickey Farrel recognized this opportunity and built his filling station on the Main Street thoroughfare through town on Cleveland Street, catching who he could as they passed by.

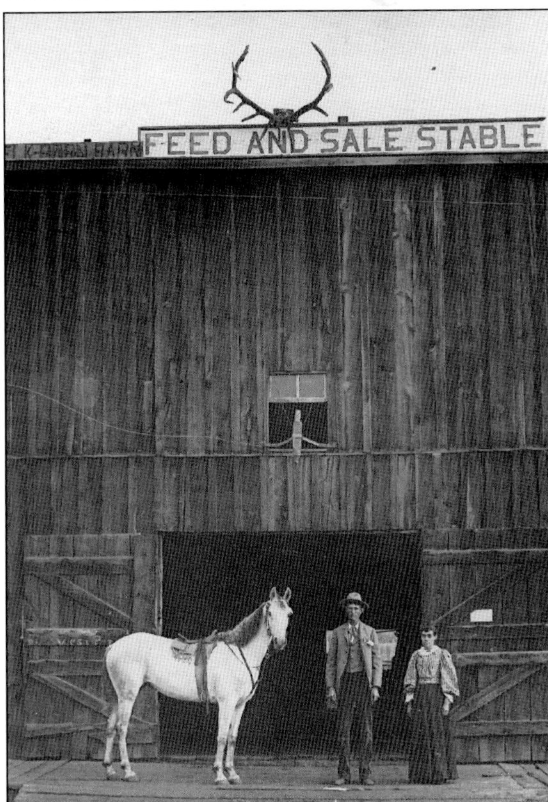

Standing before an open door to the livery barn, a horse waits for his rider to mount. The unidentified couple is interested in who will ride this fine steed. In the very near future, animals like this would be replaced as the main means of transportation.

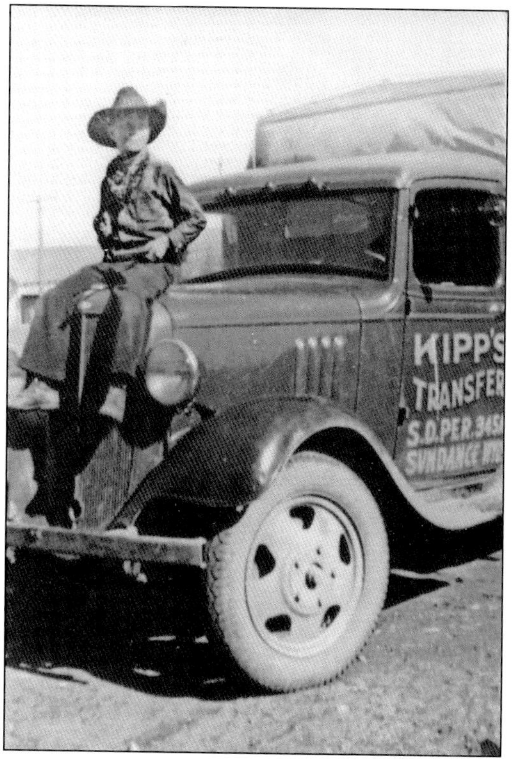

Earl Kipp's son is sitting on the hood of Kipp Transfer Company's first truck. In 1932, Earl began the mail route between Sundance and Spearfish, South Dakota. This mail route continued for over 70 years. He also started to deliver cream from the local farms and ranches to the creamery. Then he added the delivery of bread to the local grocery stores. In 1934, Earl started his freight line, Kipp's Transfer, between Sundance and Deadwood. The freight line brought groceries, tires, toys, clothes, liquor, and other staples to the towns and villages throughout northeast Wyoming.

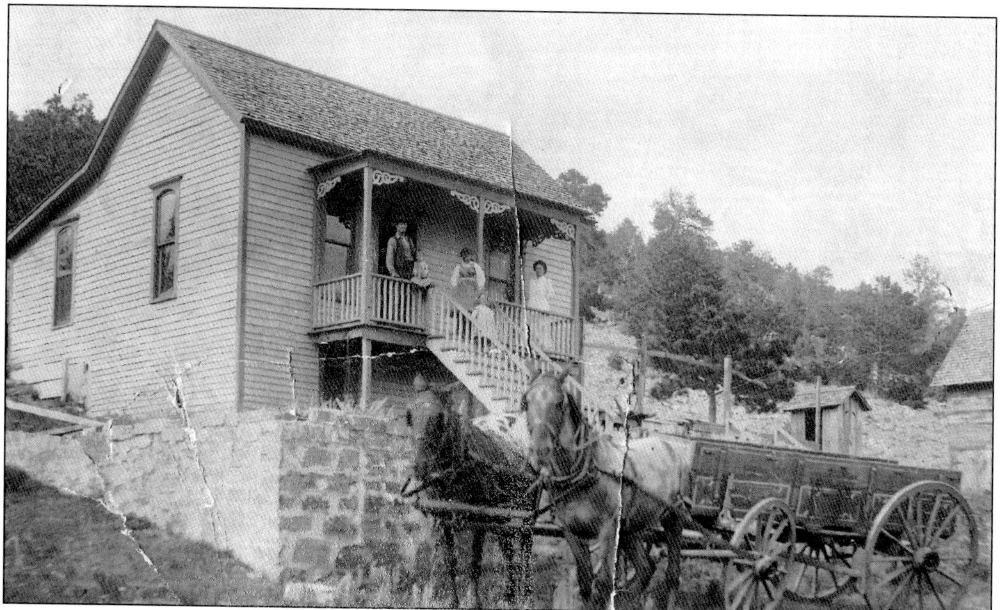

Standing on the porch are, from left to right, Dan, Thomas, Wesley, and Isabel Straight. The little girl in the front is unidentified. Dan used this horse and wagon to haul freight. He would load grain into the wagon and haul it using one or two teams of horses. For many years, Dan hauled beer from the breweries in South Dakota to Sundance for Charlie Sackett's saloon. It took him four days to make the round trip. Sometimes he would haul barrels of whiskey from the mining camps. It cost $5 a barrel to haul the whiskey but $2.50 a gallon to drink it.

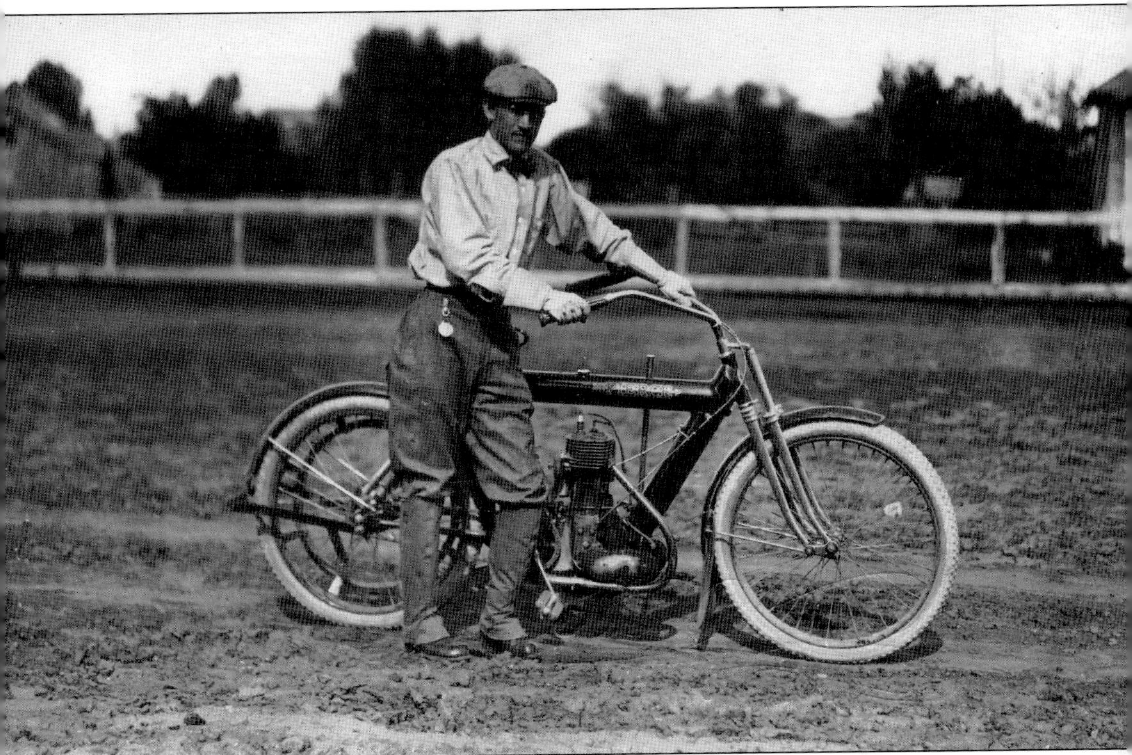

This unidentified Sundance man is proudly showing off his 1911 Pierce Arrow Belt Drive single motorcycle. He had to explain that the upper and rear frame were 18-gauge steel frame tubes and could hold 7 quarts of fuel, while the front tubes carried 5 pints of oil. This could feed the 592 cc single cylinders, which could send its rider to the unbelievable speed of 55 miles per hour. It must have been exciting to go that fast over the dirt streets of Sundance with its ruts and rocks. He must have attracted a lot of attention when he first rode into town.

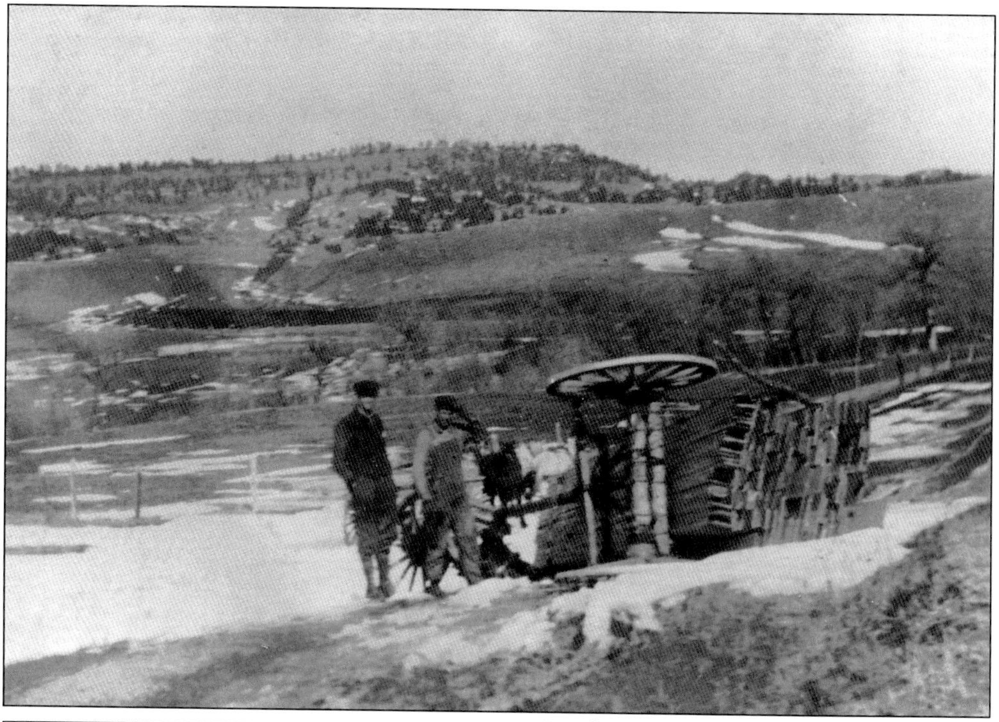

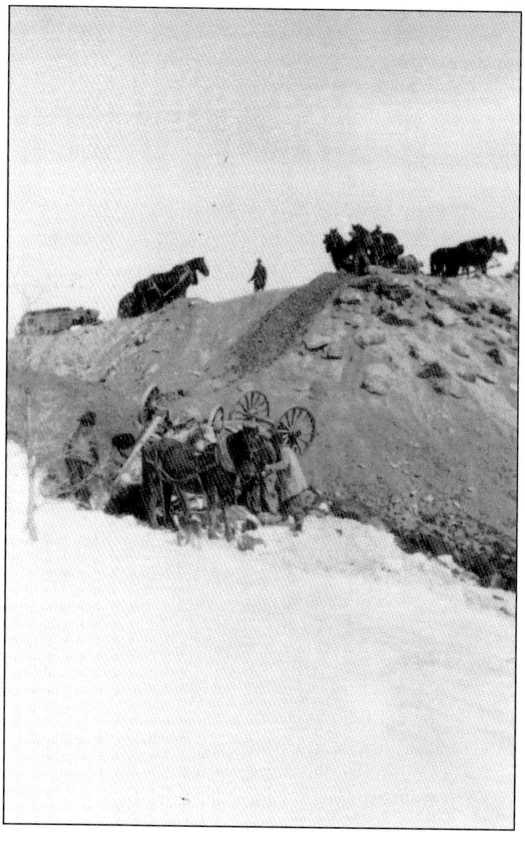

Loading too large of a load on too small of a wagon caused many problems. The roads were mostly a double track trail, which was either dusty or slick and most often rough. Freight wagons were used to haul lumber and supplies to waiting families. If they were lucky enough to live near a sawmill or town, it was not much of a problem. Trying to get back to the homestead with one load, instead of taking two trips, forced them to use their ingenuity, which as seen, sometimes did not work out as planned.

Tons of earth was moved by hand and horses to change the grade of the hills and level the gullies. Accidents were not an everyday occurrence, but they did happen. Too close to an edge that crumbled or the loss of a horse's footing ensured a dramatic end to a mundane day.

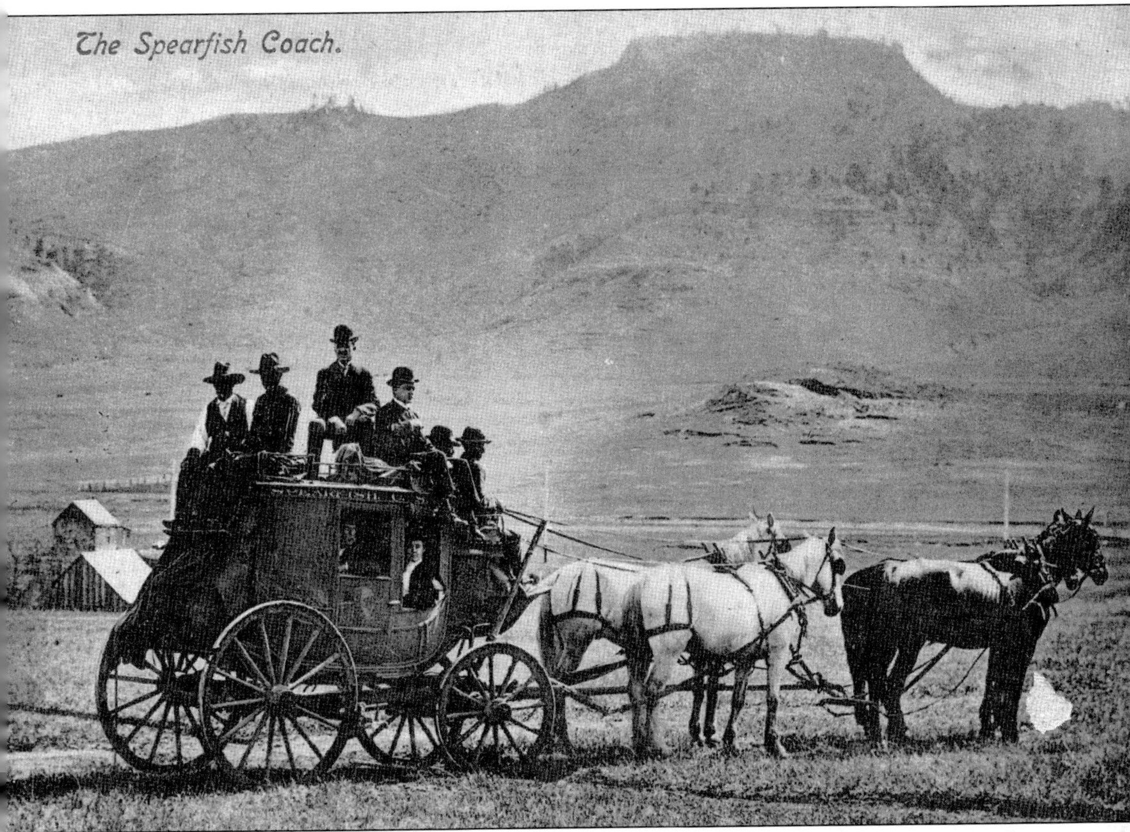

The stage from Spearfish, South Dakota, to Buffalo, Wyoming, was a mode of transportation that stopped daily in Sundance. There were many stage stops along the way, much like a Greyhound bus ride today. Most communities were isolated. Stagecoaches were often the only mail trucks that a community had. We can only speculate on the number of letters lost to rough roads, bad weather, and pure carelessness. There were very few conditions that stopped the stage lines. If the passenger was willing to take the chance and pay the price, the drivers did their best to get them to the next stop.

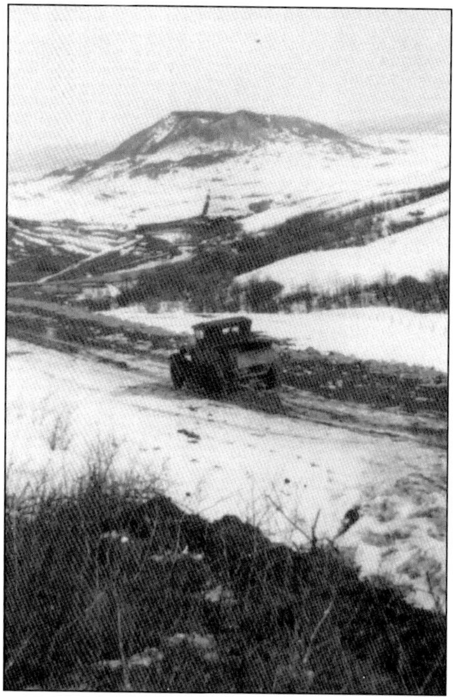

The roads that lead to Sundance had not changed from the trail systems that helped form it. Road improvements would not happen until around 1928. Traveling would take much determination and good luck. The soil would change around every corner. The rocks would tear up a wagon, and the sand would take its toll. Mud could be so slick one would have little control or so sticky it would just collect on the wheels or the hooves. The elevation increase and steep grade has always been a challenge and continues to be.

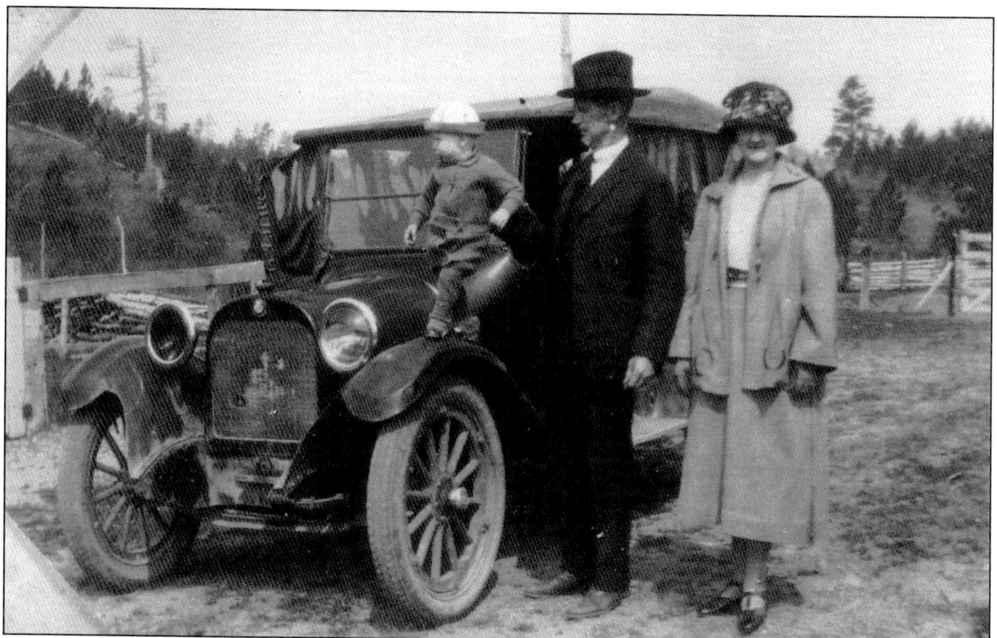

The introduction of the automobile greatly shortened distances. Oscar and Willie Carlson, with their son, Otto, are out visiting friends and family in the Bearlodge Mountains north of Sundance. The automobile was used and abused past its limits. Dr. Julius Clarenbach would chain up his tires in spring and not take them off until mid-summer. The superintendent of schools in Crook County often attached wooden boxes on the fenders of her vehicle to carry more supplies to the schools. The automobile was the cause for the demise of the stage, just as the telegraph was for the pony express.

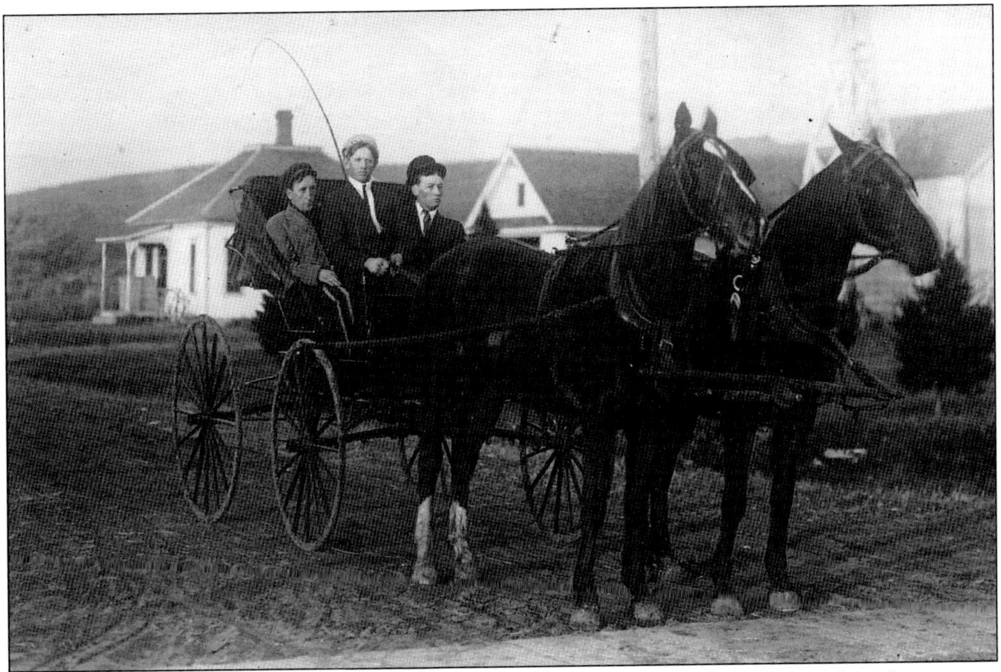

From left to right are Carl Marsh, Floyd Van Cleave, and Earl Hamilton. Floyd has the reins in his hands and is about to take his friends for a ride around town. Carl does not look too sure about the arrangement. With dirt streets in Sundance and the roads of the county, mud was a problem around every corner.

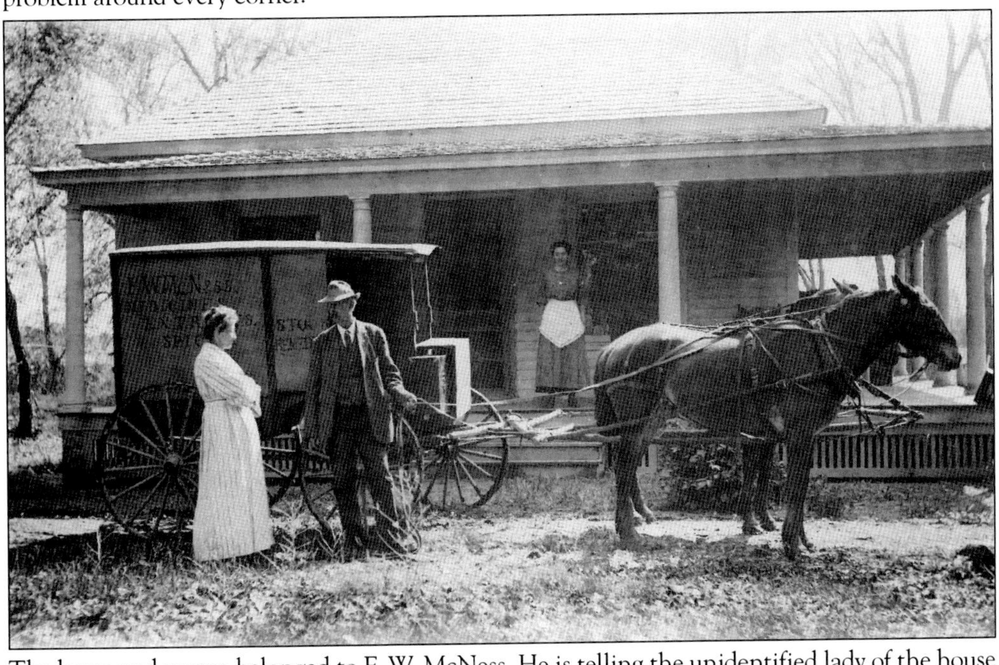

The horse and wagon belonged to F. W. McNess. He is telling the unidentified lady of the house about the wondrous things he can sell her. He had medicine, extracts, and spices. These traveling stores often carried sewing needles and thread as well as peppermint sticks. The unidentified couple on the porch just might be waiting for a candy treat.

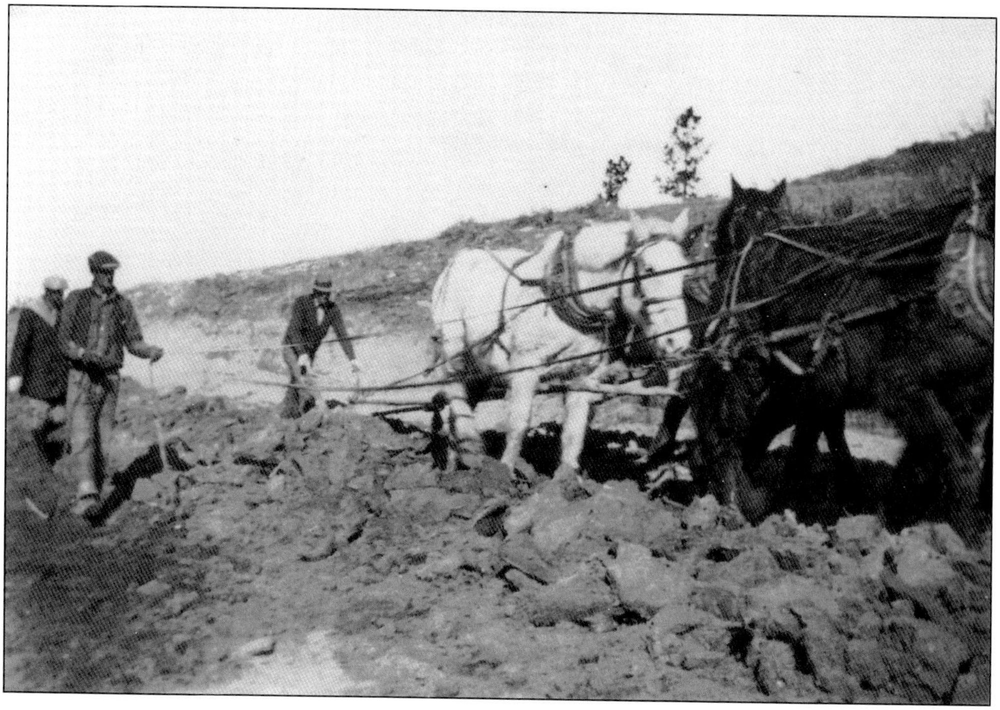

In 1927, the road between Sundance and Carlile was the road project for the construction season. This team of four horses was used to break up the ground with a plow. Earl Pursel of the Sharrock and Pursel Construction Company is on the plow. The other two workers are unidentified. In the 1920s, horses and wagons were still an important part of any job that needed horsepower to be completed. These horses are hauling good old Wyoming dirt. This road project had too much dirt in one place and not enough in another place. It had to be moved.

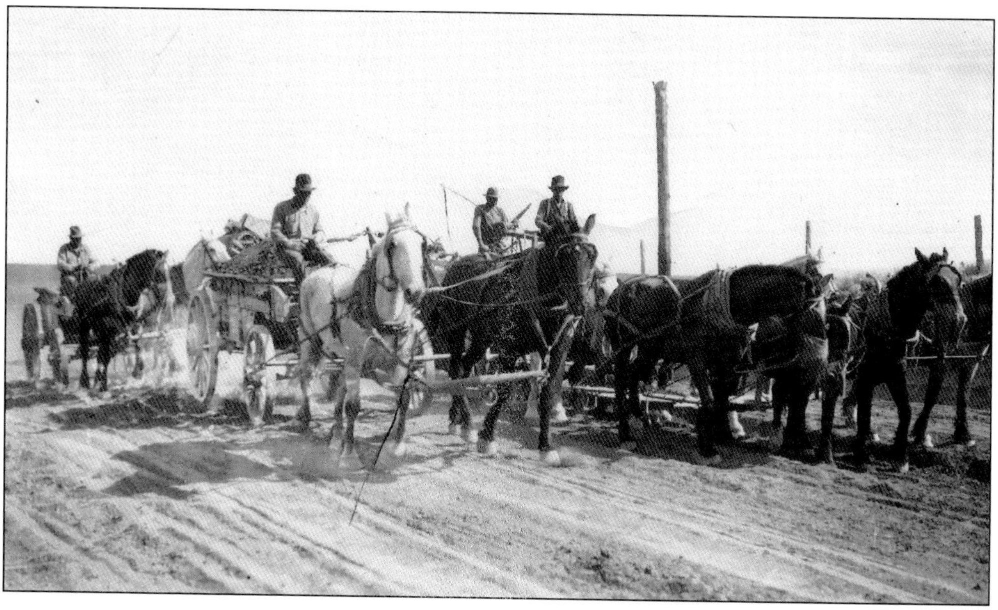

This is Sharrock and Pursel's Osgood Steam Shovel on the road to Hulett and Moorcroft, west of Sundance, in 1928. The driver in the door is an unidentified worker. This machine made the roadwork go much more quickly, as it could dig up and move more dirt than a crew of human beings. A steep hillside was no longer the same daunting obstacle.

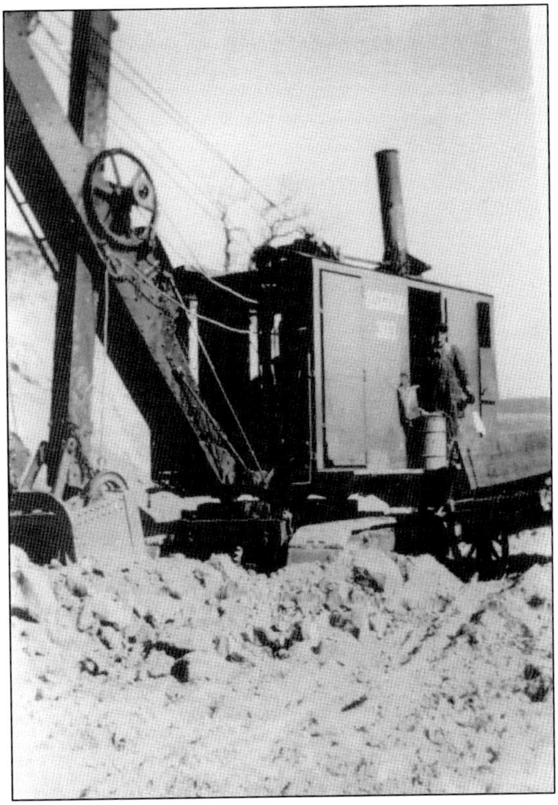

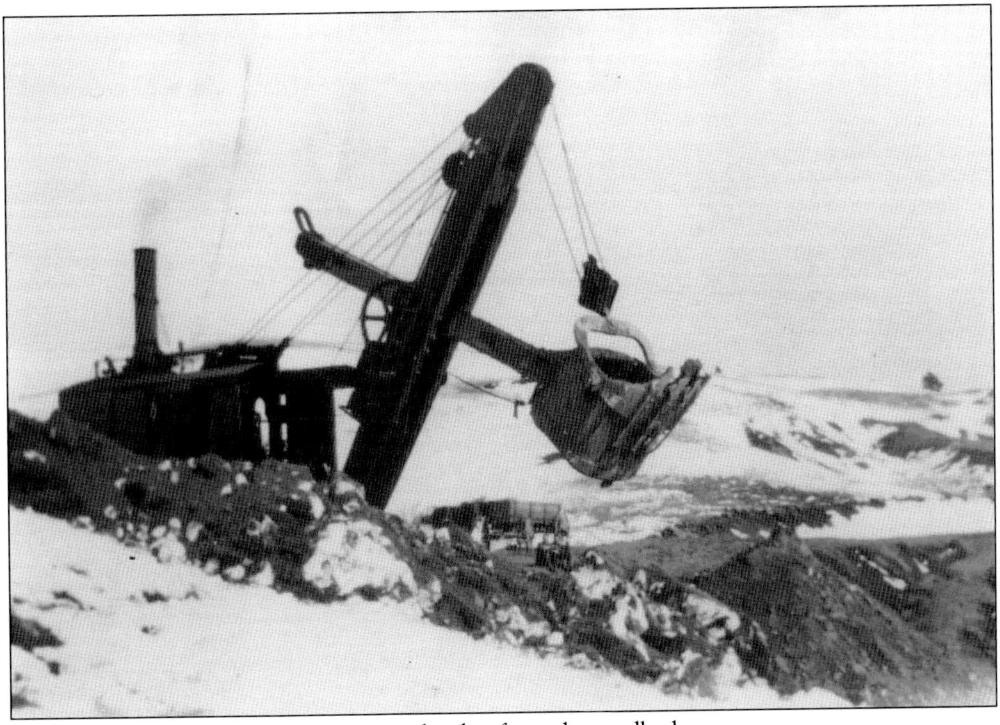

The steam shovel is in action, moving the dirt from the roadbed.

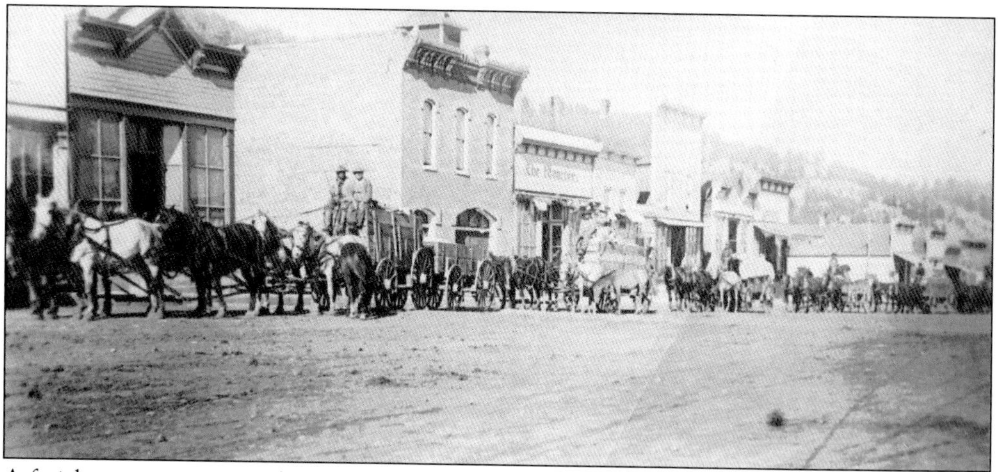

A freight team is coming down Main Street in Sundance. The city hall is in the center of the street with the offices of the Crook County newspaper on the right. Freight would arrive in Sundance and then would be distributed from here to Spearfish, Deadwood, Hulett, Aladdin, and to other small towns.

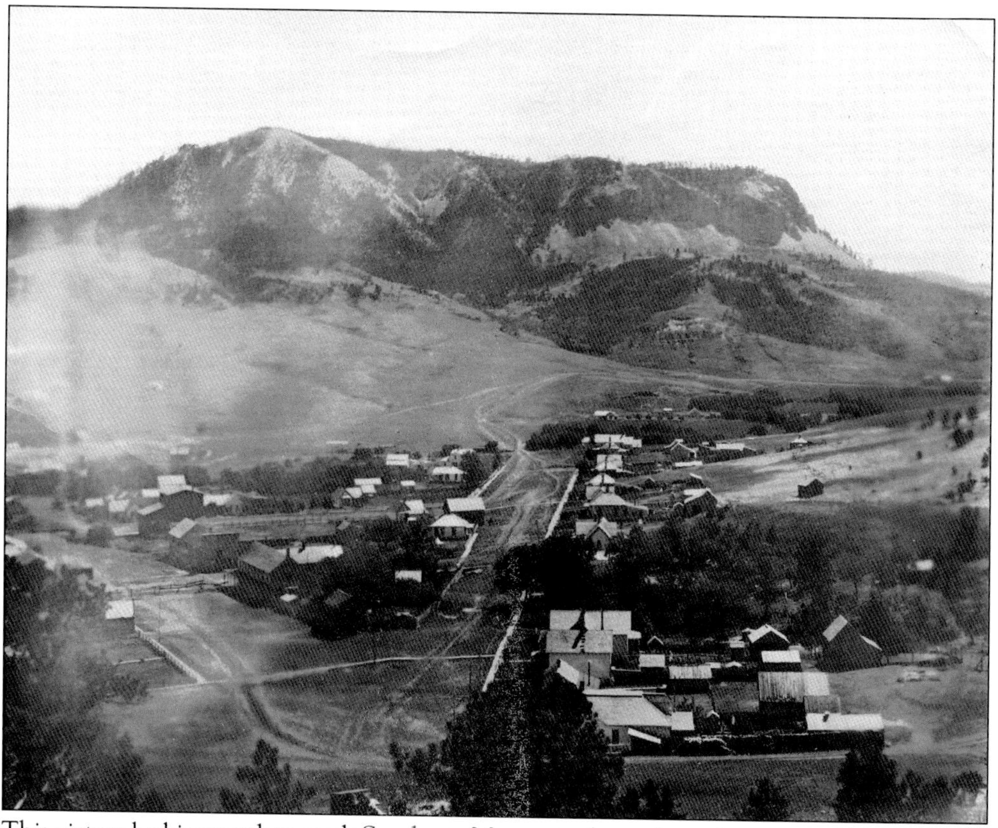

This picture looking south towards Sundance Mountain shows the wide streets of the town. The streets were wide enough to turn a four- or six-team pulling a wagon around in the street. A wagon pulled by four oxen needed plenty of room. They do not make sharp turns.

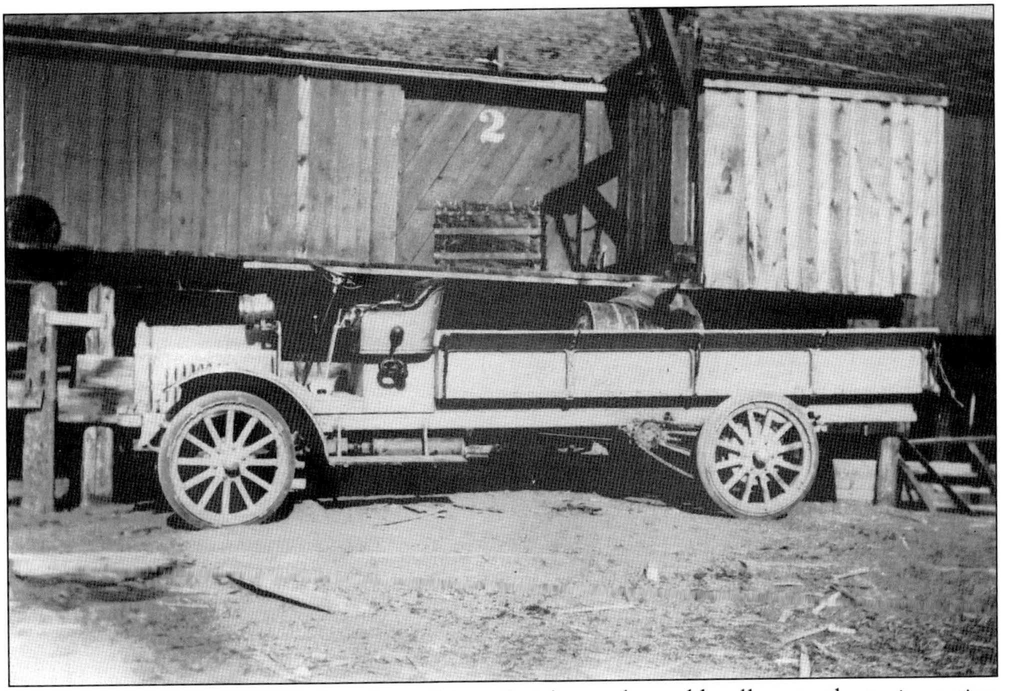

From 1910–1920, trucks like this chain-driven freight truck would pull up to the train station loading dock in Spearfish or Aladdin to pick up whatever was on that day's delivery to Sundance. The delivery pictured includes a barrel of something already in the truck and the camelback trunk waiting to be loaded.

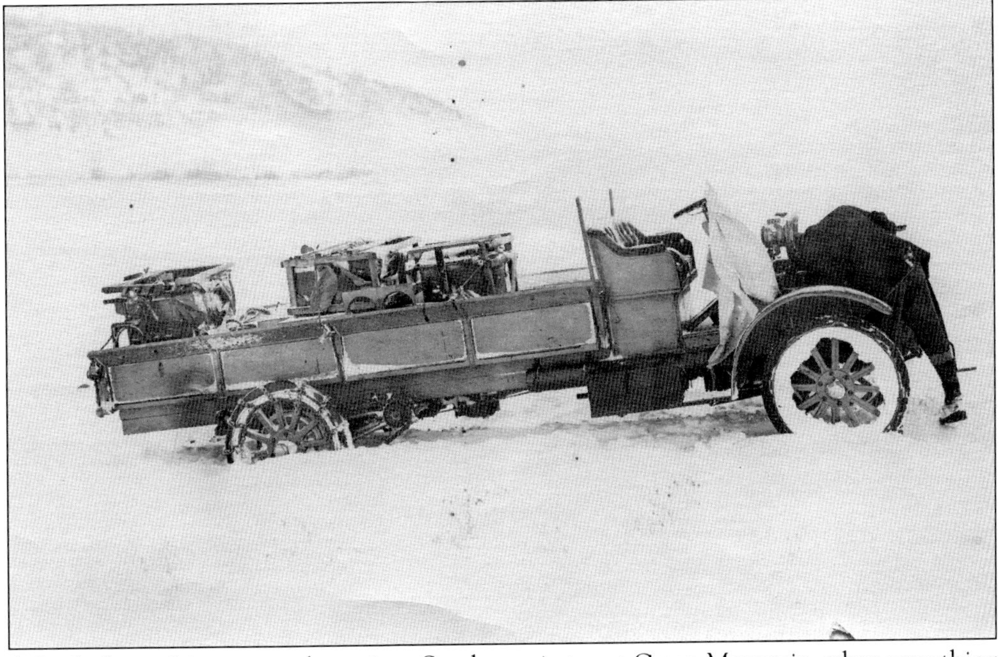

A load of crated items was almost into Sundance, just past Green Mountain, when something went terribly wrong. The chances are high that when he fixes what went wrong under the hood, he will be stuck in the snow.

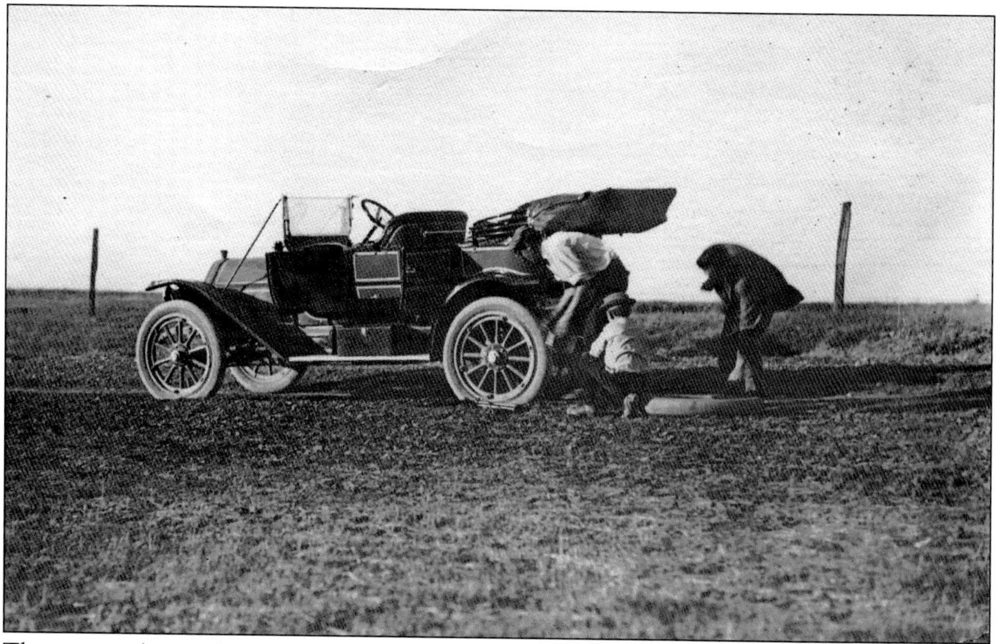

This picture shows what happened all too frequently. Flat tires have not ever been fun to change. These tires were probably the worst. To patch these tires took a lot of work. Like all successful tire changes, this group had one person along to supervise.

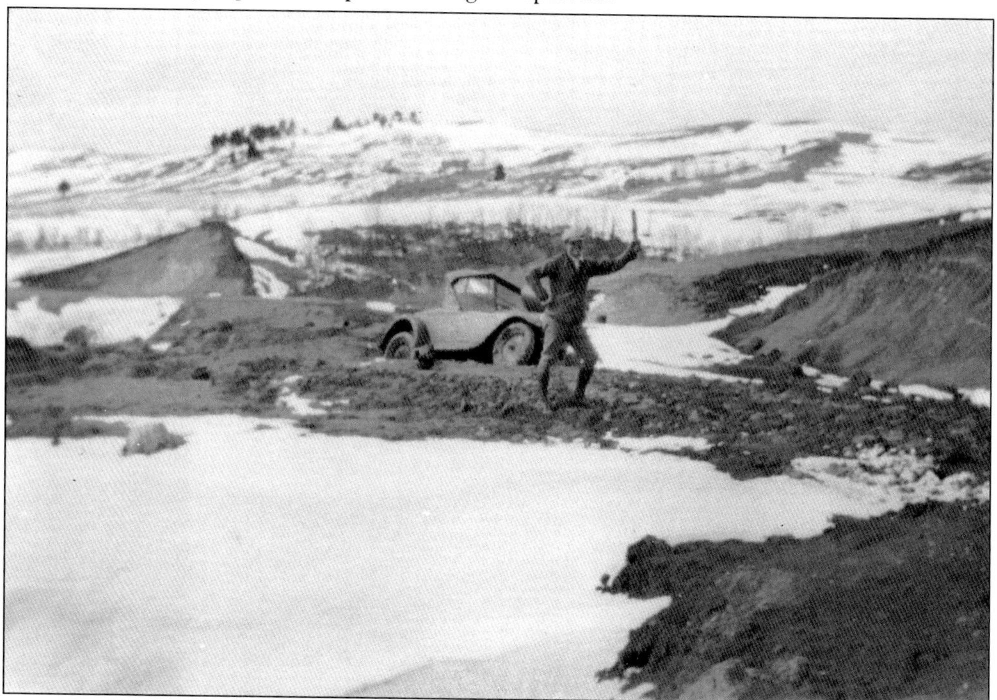

Here is a foolhardy unidentified young man that thought he could take his 1926–1927 Roadster out for a spin on a path that was still under construction. It took horses with plows and big steam engines to construct the roadbed, and this young person thought he could make it all the way to Sundance.

Eight

The Troubles They Had

There is a saying that as a landmass, Wyoming does not take kindly to humans. The hardy people that made Sundance their home had many troubles. They had the elements of wind, rain, water, and fire. The combination of wind and fire was what they worried about the most. A fire would sweep through the town and take out entire blocks. The stores and structures would be built and rebuilt. In 1888, a fire swept through the hills and prairies. And in 1936, fire would strike again. Rain and snow would either dump from the sky or not at all. Crops would either come up stunted and be pulled up in disgust or not grow at all. But the dirt would be shaken off. "Waste not, want not." Other years, the rain would not stop. In the winters, the snow could pile up in the draws and on the flats. In 1886, Montana and Wyoming cattlemen lost entire herds. And then there were the bugs. There were Mormon crickets and grasshoppers that could eat everything they crawled across—the grass, the clothes on the line, and even the line. There were bedbugs that liked to sleep with anyone. There were unwanted animals that caused fear and destruction. The wolves had bounties on them to keep them from eating the sheep, cattle, and small dogs. Prairie dogs could destroy entire pastures and leave a desert behind. The outlaws and horse thieves were always a cause for concern, long after the Native American ceased to be a threat. And still the people of Sundance kept on.

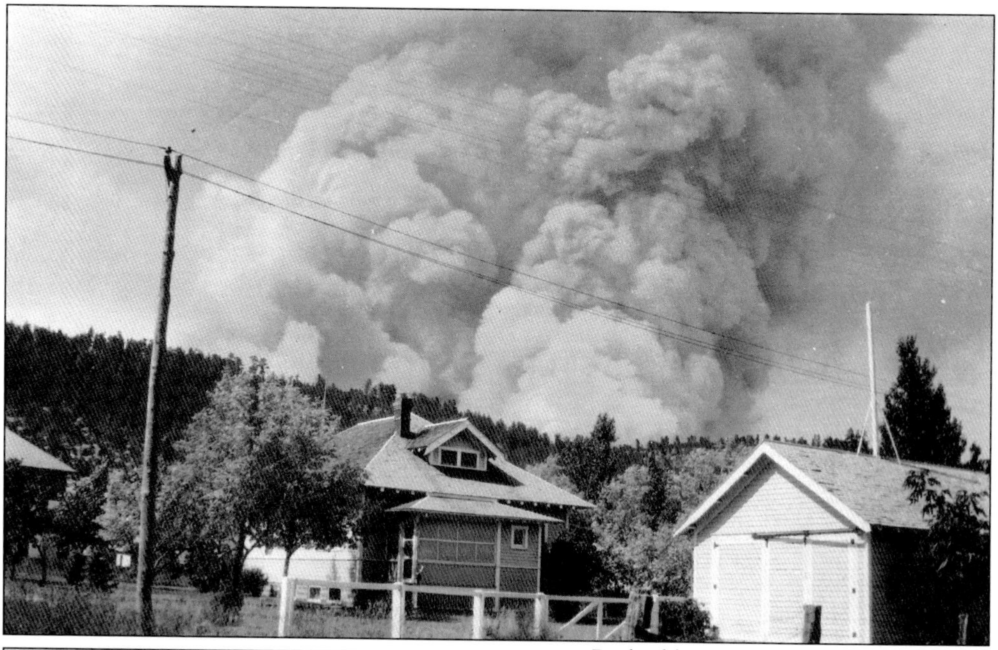

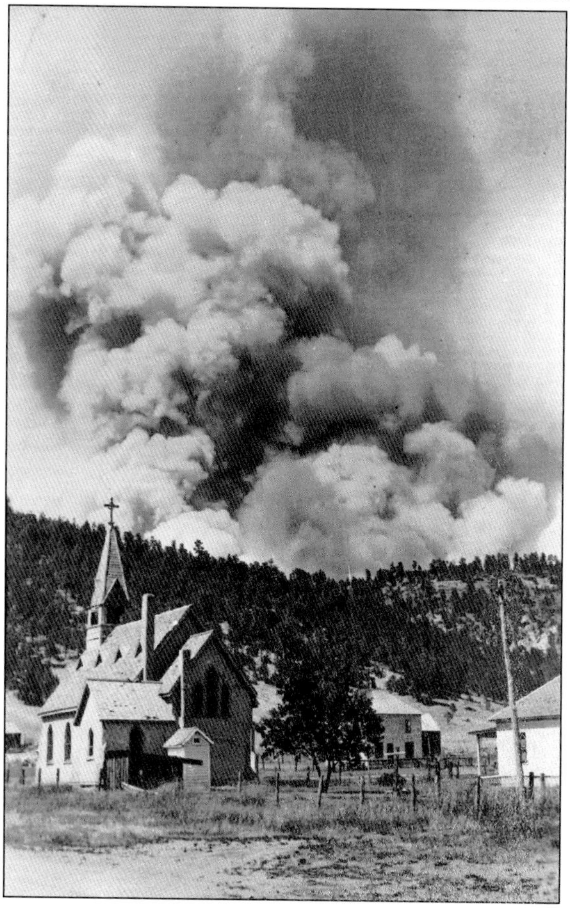

Pushed by a fierce southwest wind, a forest fire swept over a large section of the Bearlodge National Forest for one week in July 1936. Hundreds of people battled the flames day and night. The fire was started by picnickers in the grass and quickly traveled to the scrub oak and into the heavy timber. It traveled at a terrific speed. The *Sundance Times* estimated that it was covering a distance of 3 miles every 15 minutes. Spreading in all directions, it threatened a number of ranches. The Ogden and Cole ranches were the first in danger. A tremendous effort was expended to save both places. Ben Vines' ranch was not so lucky. The house was saved, but the barn and garage were destroyed. The smoke can be seen boiling over the trees behind a home on Cleveland and Fourth Streets and Good Shepherd Episcopal Church.

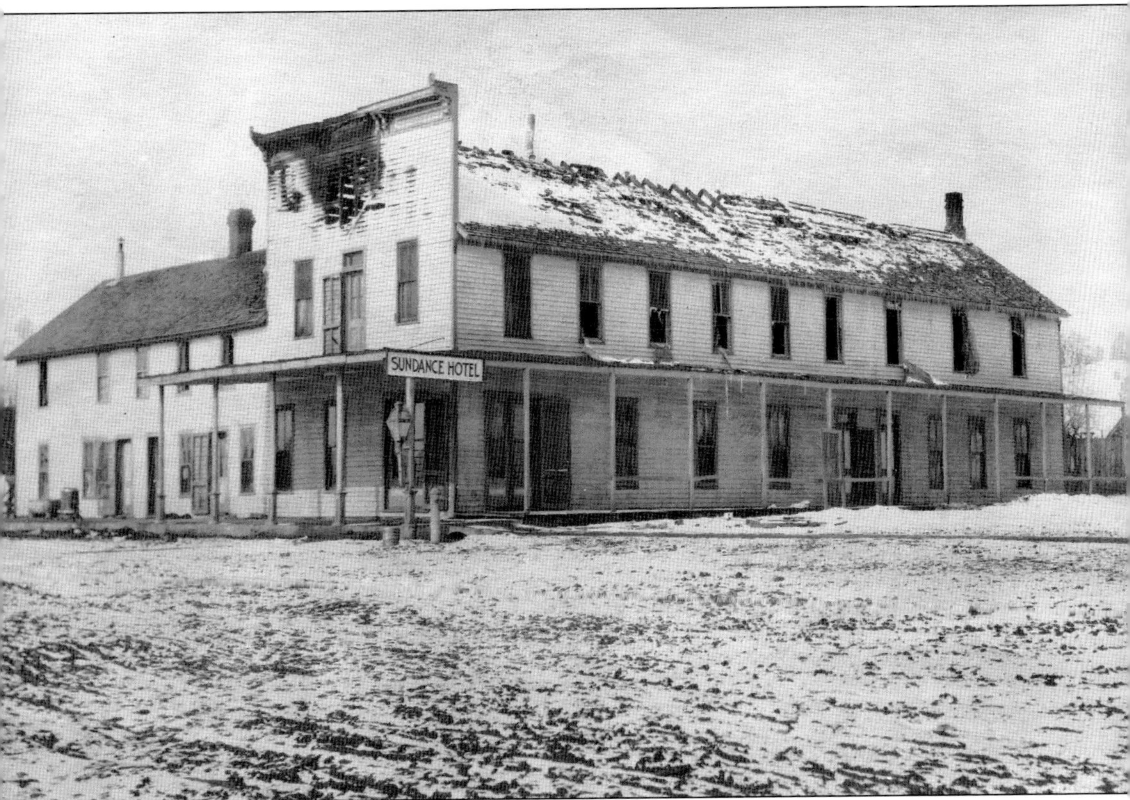

The Sundance Hotel would change its name and ownership many times during its history, but the hotel never lost its charm. Frank Hardy owned the hotel when it burned. At that time, it was an apartment hotel. The fire was reported at 2:30 a.m., and by that time it was too late to save the landmark. There were no fatalities, but all belongings were lost. It stood on the corner for many years and watched the town grow from a trading post to a thriving community before its demise.

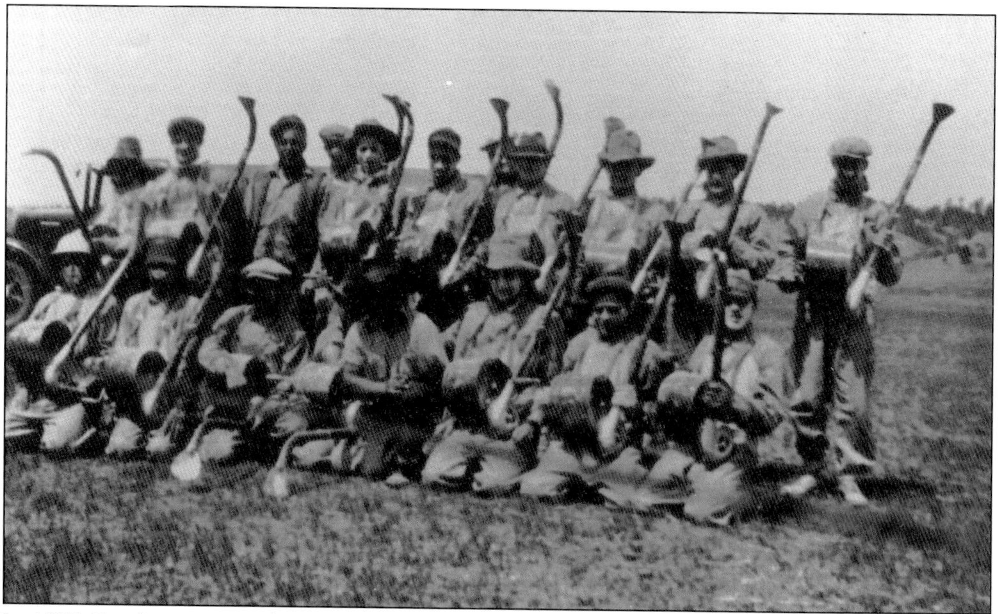

In 1937, Sundance erected a fence to keep out the hordes of Mormon crickets. Crickets moved across the land and covered everything in their path, even the strands of fence wire. Men built these fences using 10-inch strips of metal roofing that were tightly staked together in the ground in a continuous barrier. A shallow trench was then dug behind the fence. Every couple of feet, a container of water and oil was placed into the trench. The crickets would move along the fence and fall into the oil trap. This method was safer than poisoning the crickets, as this would not harm the workers or animals. Nothing would eat the oil-soaked crickets. Another means of combating the never-ending clouds of crickets was groups of men armed with club-like weapons, much like the team of unidentified men pictured above with their cricket stompers. Below, Art Knowles sits on his official United States Department of Agriculture Mormon cricket division car.

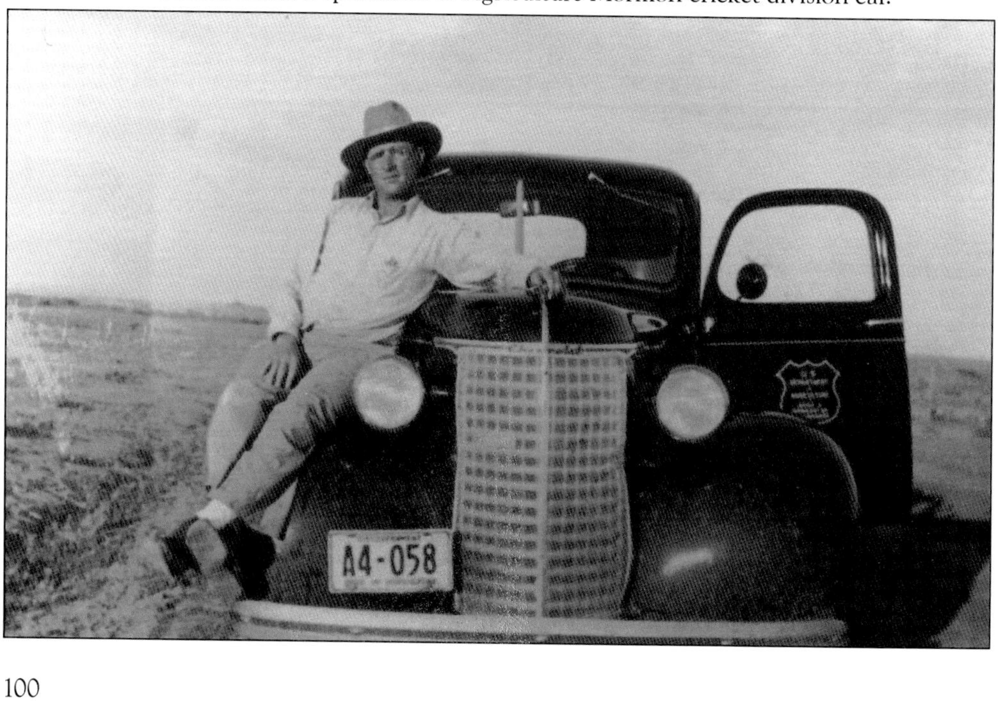

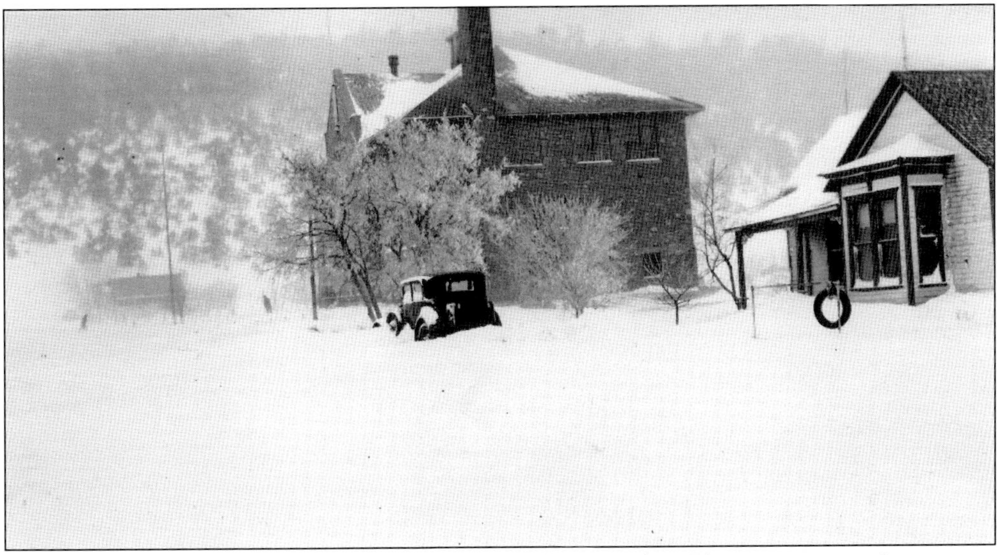

This is April 1938 in Sundance. There are no daffodils, nor tulips. The snow is up to the running boards of the car. It is almost as high as the bay window of the house. There are bare spots near the right back corner of the school, which means the wind is blowing. There are two poor souls out leaning into the wind as they try to walk home. Nothing else is moving. Oh, happy day—spring has arrived in Sundance.

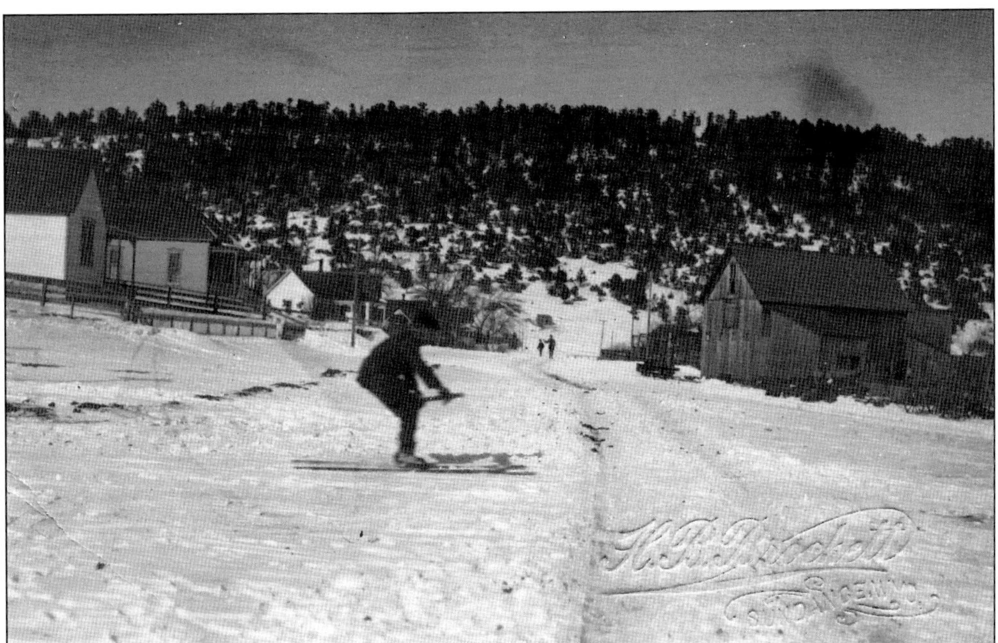

In Sundance after a heavy snowfall, people could get lost crossing from their homes to barns or outhouses. Lives were lost, and many suffered from frostbite. Not much is moving. Cross-country skis were one way to get about.

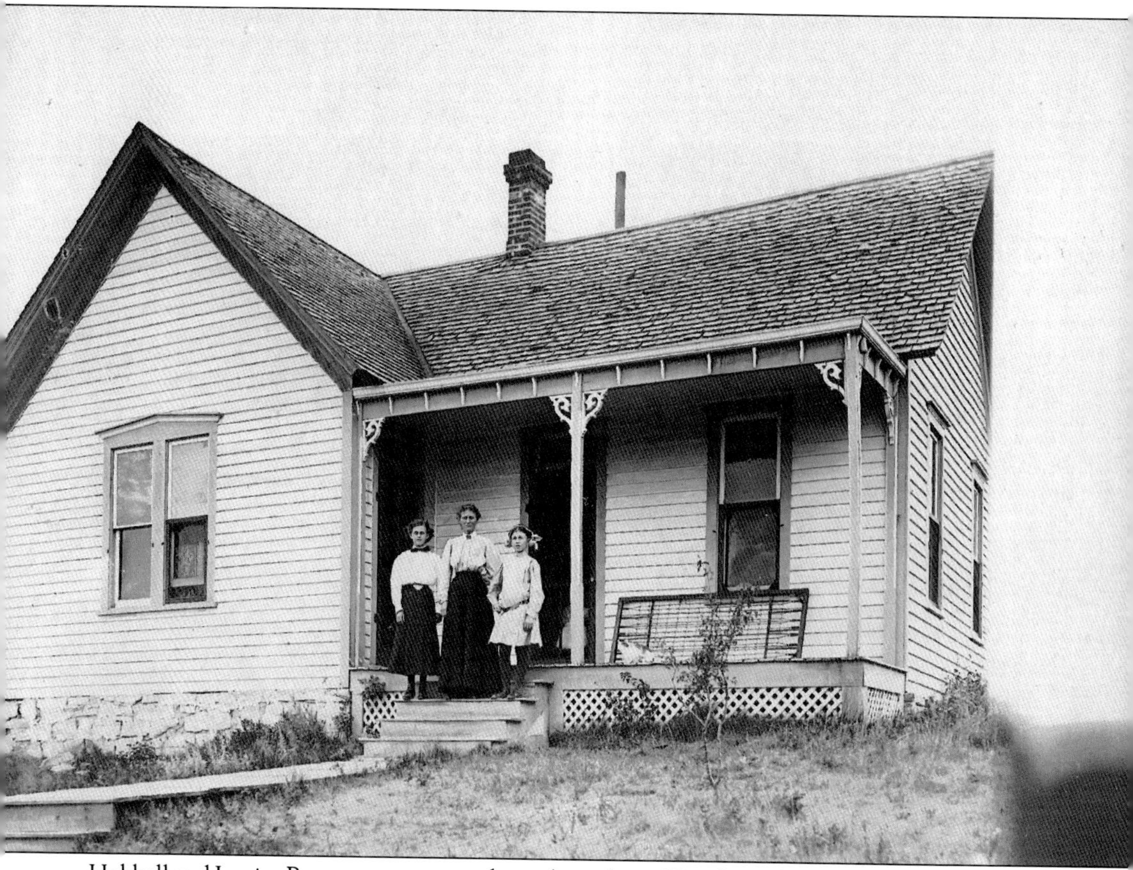

Hubbell and Louisa Brown were among the early settlers of Sundance located near Green Mountain in 1884. Before they moved here, they buried a four-year-old daughter who died of scarlet fever. In June 1890, four of the Brown's children died of diphtheria. Eight-year-old Orris and five-year-old Alvah were buried in the same casket. Eight other children of Sundance died of diphtheria between March and July 1890. In this picture, Clair McGuicken, Mabel Crewdson, and Imogene Thomas—friends of Hubbell and Louisa Brown's daughters—are standing on this porch.

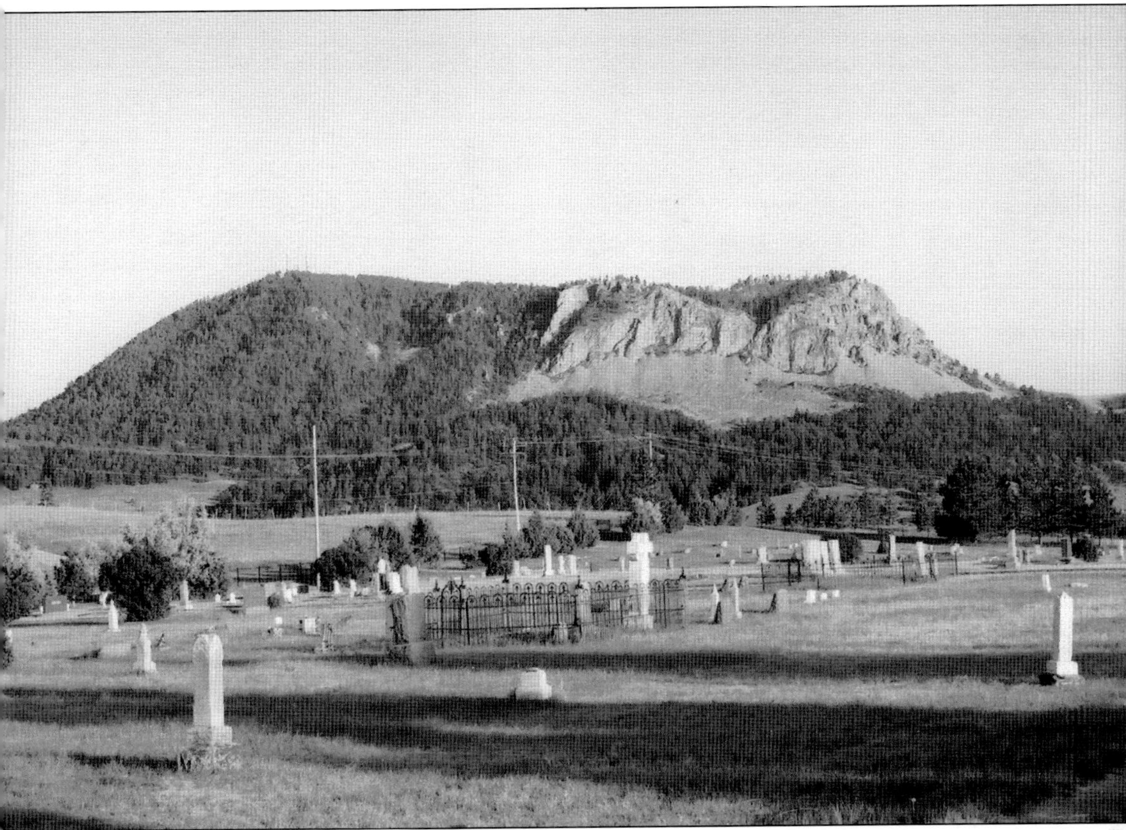

In 1890, the city was given 10 acres high on a hill west of town to be used as a cemetery. This plot of ground was named Mount Moriah Cemetery. W. E. Barlow, the nephew of William Draper, the land office agent, was the first one to be buried in the new cemetery. Young Barlow was killed in an accident with horses that happened near the site where the Church of the Good Shepherd sits on Main Street.

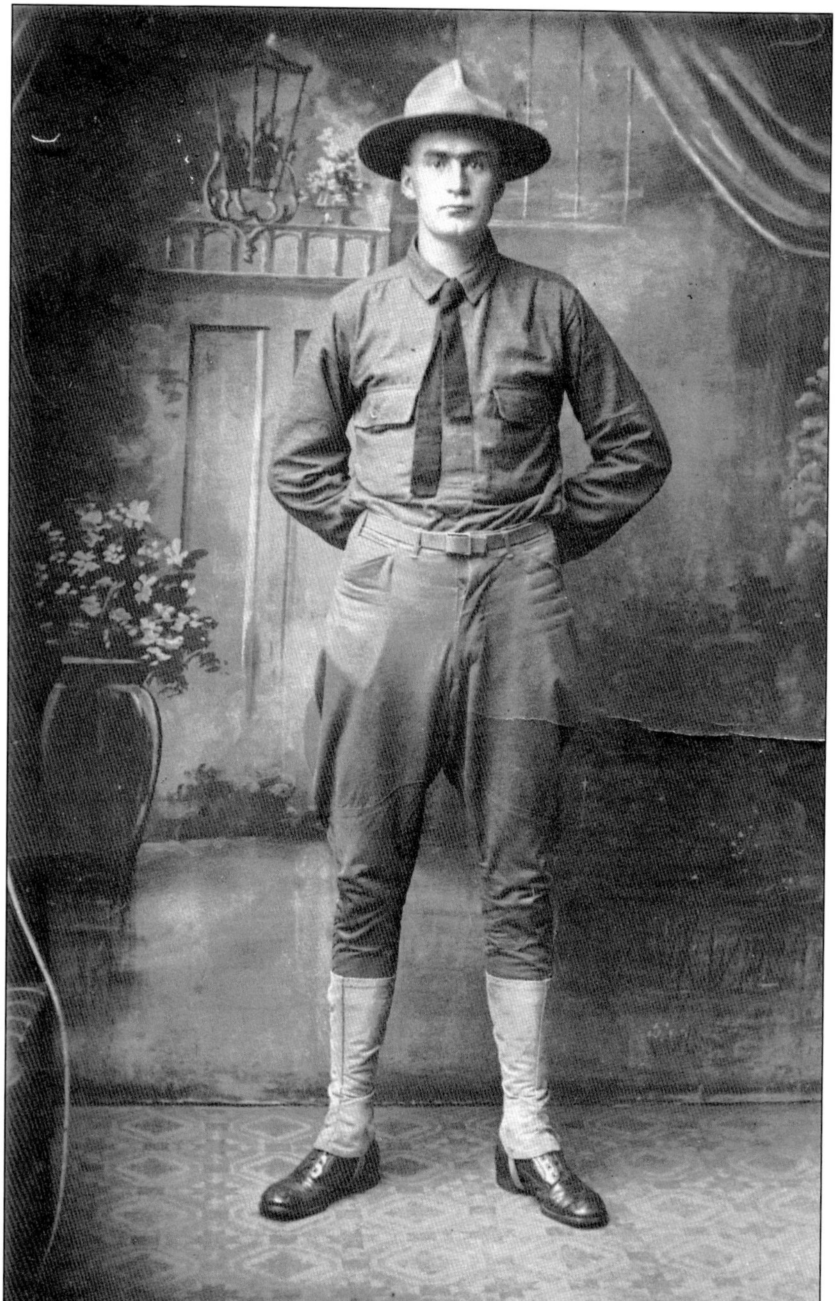

In 1917, front-page news became more concerned with the war in Europe. Articles in the papers called young men to sign up for the World War I draft. By 1918, the papers were listing draft calls. Among these local men that were called in May of that year were Glen William Cameron, Harold P. Fawkes, Fredrick R. Schloredt, William Atchison Thompson, Conda Chaffin, Melville Dudrey, Leomdas C. Hurtt, William Good, and Elmer Eaton. The man in this picture is Elmer Eaton. He represents all the men from Crook County that gave their time and often their lives to the service of their country. Sundance does not forget such an effort. In later years, a memorial would be placed on the courthouse square to remember all such valiant men.

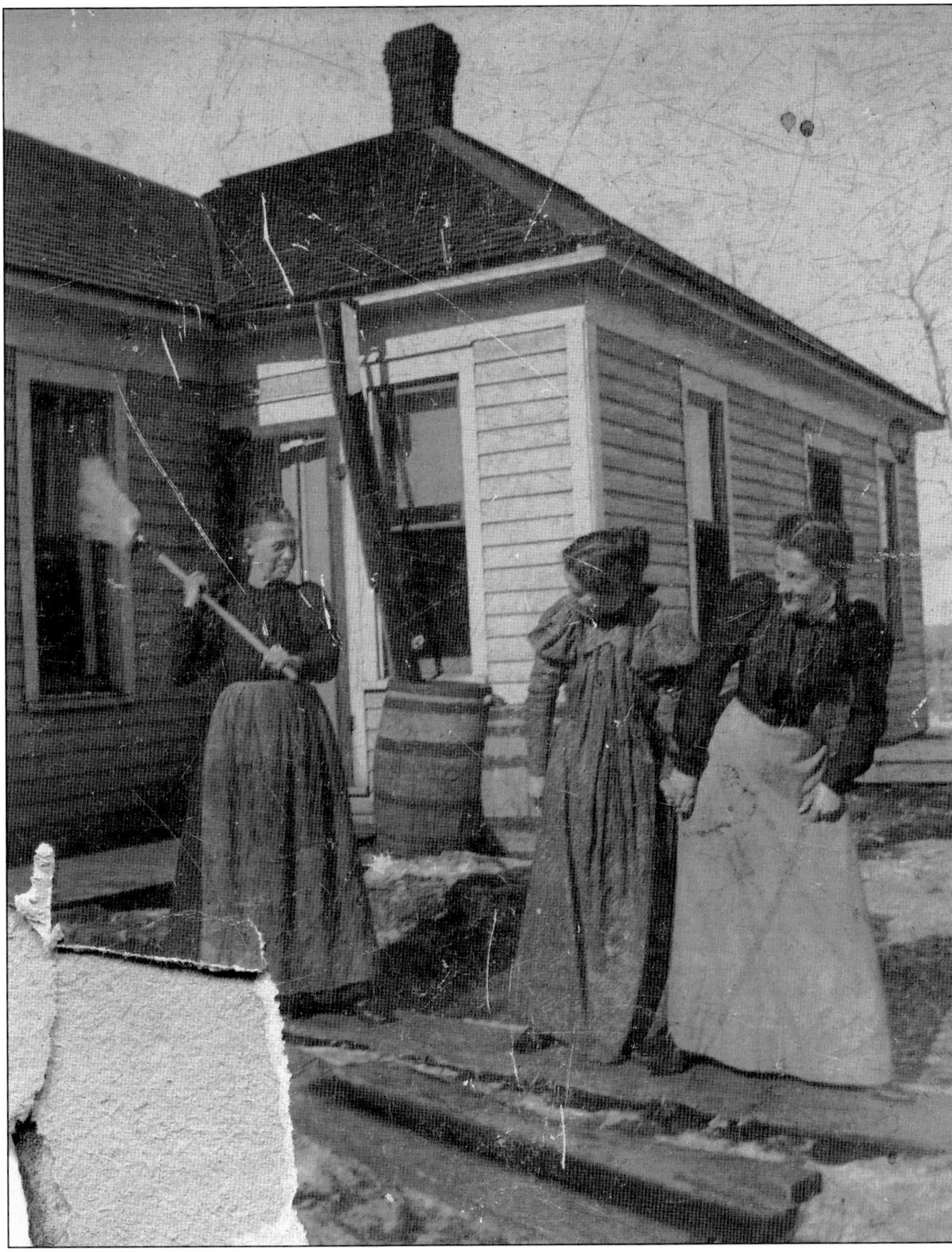

This unidentified lady of the house seems to be chasing two unwelcome pests from her home. Of all the pests that needed to be removed from family homes, these two seem relatively harmless. Bedbugs were a different type of unwanted pest. There were many ways to rid oneself of bedbugs. Placing the legs of the bed in cans of coal oil was one method. People got sick from the smell, but it did not bother the bugs very much. A can of raw formaldehyde set to boil on the back of the stove was a more effective method, but it was best to leave during the entire process. "Sleep tight, and don't let the bedbugs bite" was a serious goodnight prayer in those days.

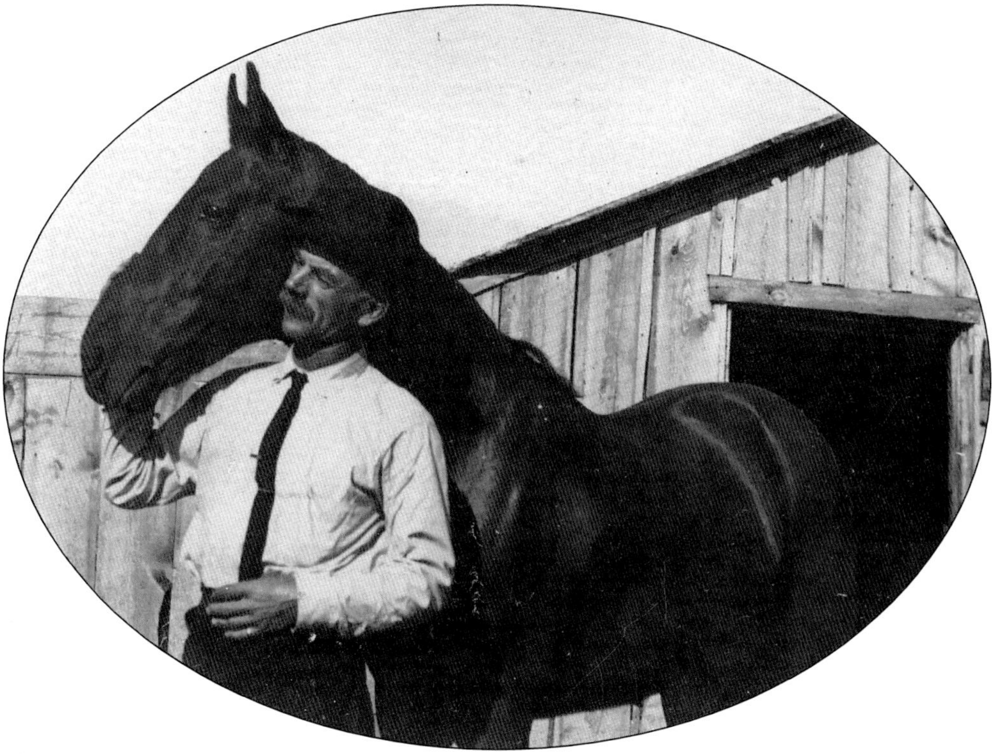

Shown is John L. Propst, former sheriff of Crook County. In addition to his daily duties of serving and protecting, he also went after horse thieves. Thomas Zimmerschied and Robyn Witcher were caught after having rounded up and driven horses belonging to the neighbors a considerable distance from their homes. The two men were quickly caught and brought into Sundance to appear before Justice of the Peace Roberts. They were found guilty and fined $35 each plus costs. These two were let off easy, as it was not uncommon to spend time in jail or even go to the gallows for such a crime.

Nine

The Games They Played

The work was hard and the hours were long, but there was still the need to relax and have some fun. The families that settled Sundance found a variety of ways to entertain themselves. There were large picnic gatherings like the Old Settlers Picnic, where everyone could get together for games and visiting. Sundance had a skating rink and a bowling alley as early as 1886. A brass band was formed, and as the band improved, they were asked to play for dances and concerts. There were dances in every little community. These would take place in dance halls or in private homes or barns. A band was a treat, but one or two instruments were all it took to get in the swing. People would travel for hours to attend dances. There were no such things as babysitters in those days. Everyone brought their children along. When the little ones got tired, they were laid down and covered with a coat to sleep. There was also racing. Horse racing was popular from the very beginning of the town. Races could be planned, or they could happen at the spur of the moment. All that was needed was fast horses and cocky riders. A racetrack was optional. Not many towns had a racetrack as the schoolyard. Baseball hit Sundance hard. Games were played in vacant lots, in the fairgrounds, on the schoolyard, or anywhere there was room to hit the ball. With seven saloons in town, some found their entertainment in liquid form. This would bring about many other forms of entertainment, and Sundance had them all.

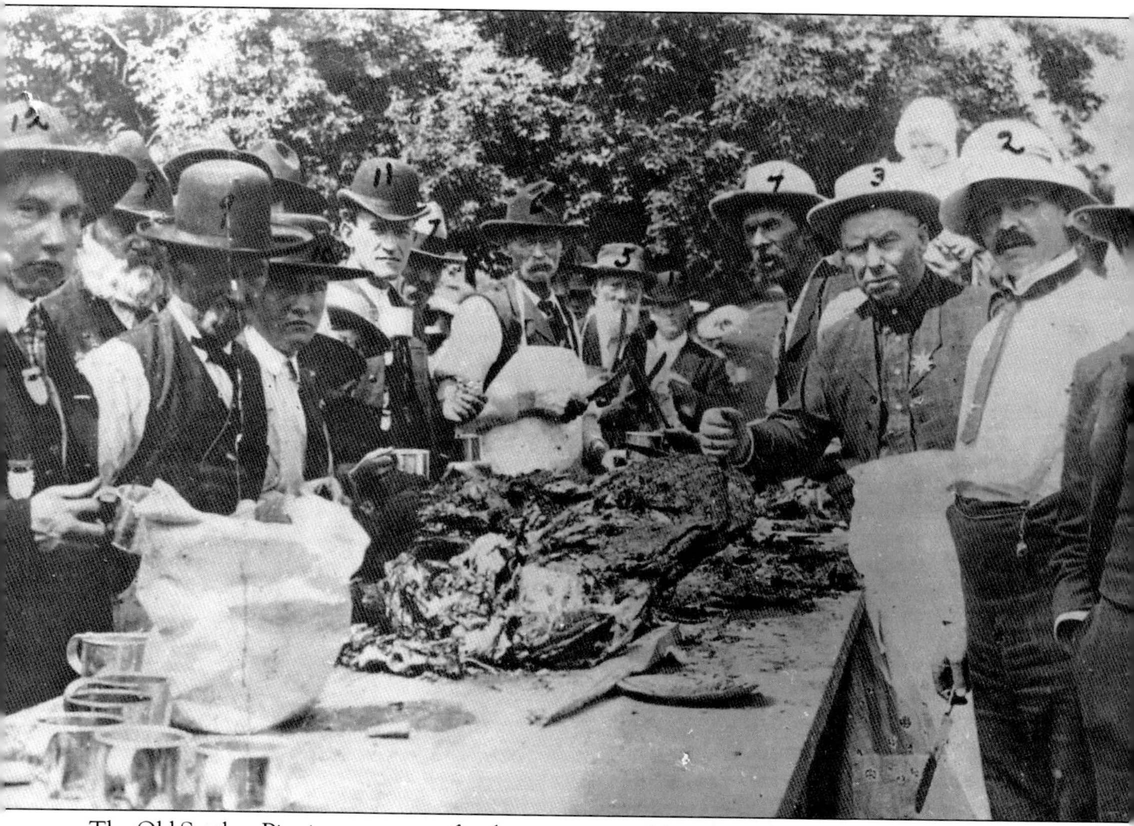

The Old Settlers Picnics were a way for the pioneers and founders of Sundance and Crook County to get together to visit, check up on one another, and to remember those that were not with them that year. There would be food and drink, games and contests, horse races, and baseball games. In the evening, there could be dances. Children would run and play and nap when they were tired. These gatherings were the way the community stayed connected to each other and their past. This picture shows the 1907 picnic. Charlie Sackett cooked the meat in the barbeque pit. Pictured here from left to right are Loyde Adams, A. E. Hoyt, George Ashdown, C. H. Dudrey, Richard Williams, John S. Vest, Fred Henerson, N. D. Townsend, James Schrivener, Shorty Severance, two unidentified, and Milo Adams.

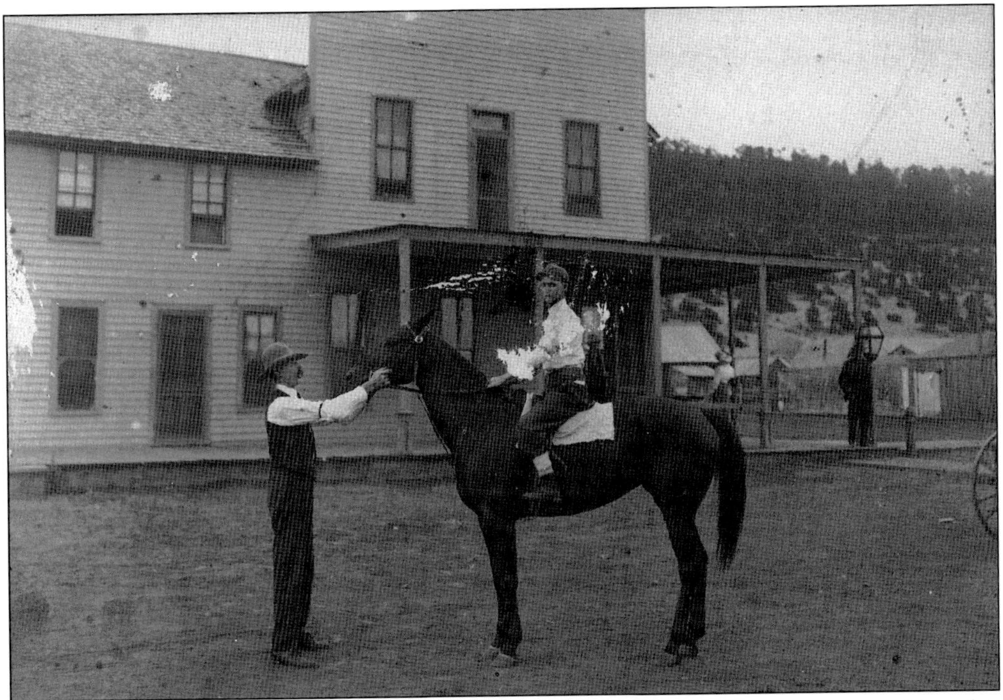

George Stotts is holding Whisper, with a jockey onboard. Whisper is just two years old in this picture but already making quite a name for himself in the county. In a few years, he would become *the* horse to beat, and people would travel great distances to see him race. They are standing in front of the Sundance Hotel. The July 6, 1900, *Sundance Monitor* said a horse race had been arranged during the Fourth of July celebration. The race was won by the famous mare from the 2 1 Ranch, and O'Hana's mare took second. Charlie Benn's bay saddler took first place in the pony race, and Whisper came in second.

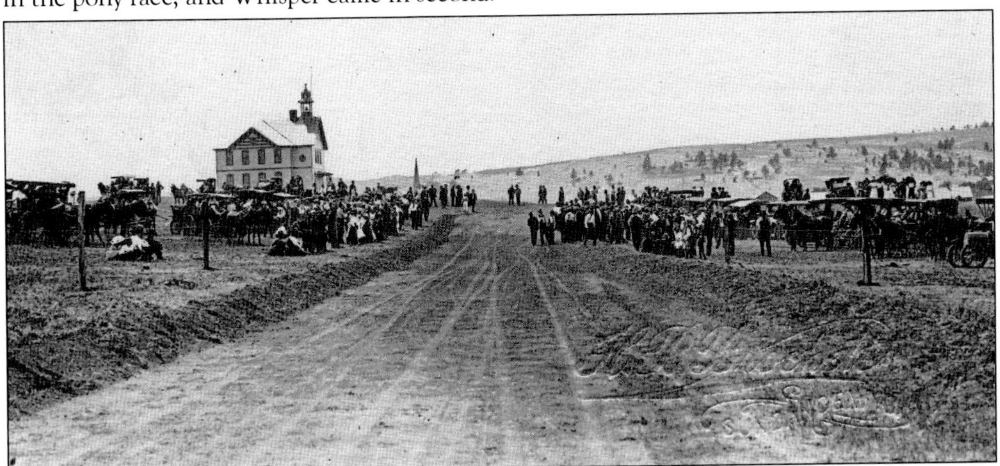

On the Fourth of July, 1911, the most important event was the race between Whisper and Gold Dollar, held at the Old Settlers Picnic. Al Storts owned Whisper, and Gold Dollar was owned by Tom Riley from South Dakota. A match between these two horses was inevitable, and there were heavy bets placed on both. It was run on a quarter-mile straight track in Sundance. This picture shows the track and the people gathered to watch the race. The large building to the left is the schoolhouse.

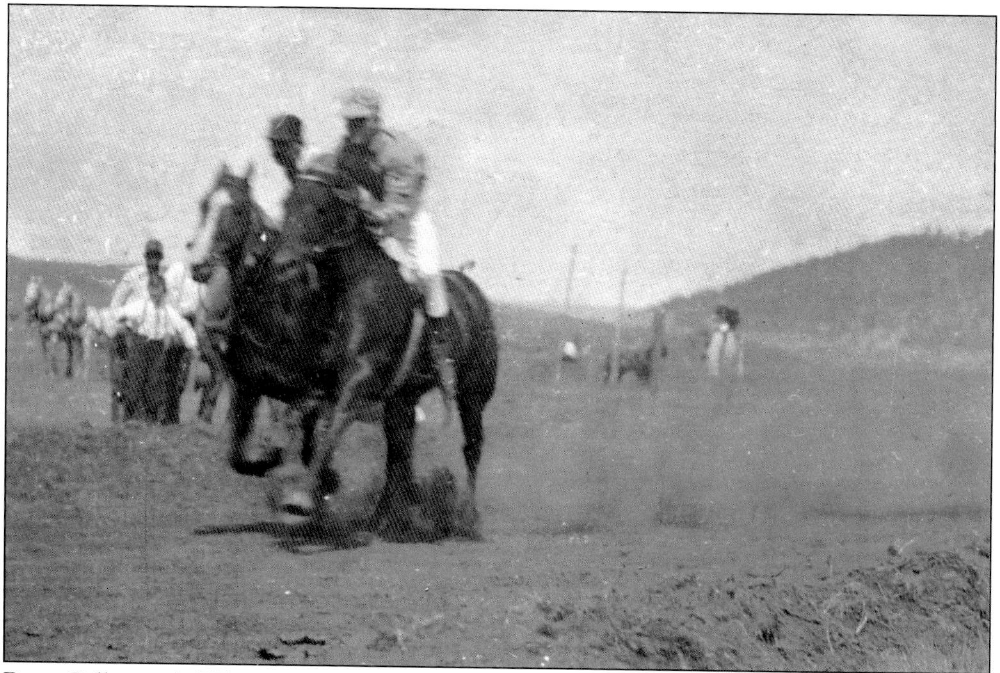

Dean Collins rode Whisper, and Romey Glover rode Gold Dollar. From start to finish, they ran neck and neck. The track was slightly uphill and was not groomed, but it did not bother the horses or the riders. As they neared the finish line, it looked like the race would end in a tie, but Whisper won the race by a nose. As a result, many South Dakota gold dollars came to Wyoming. A quote from one of the local newspapers stated, "Money talks, but on a day in 1911 on a race track in Sundance, a Gold Dollar could not be heard above a Whisper."

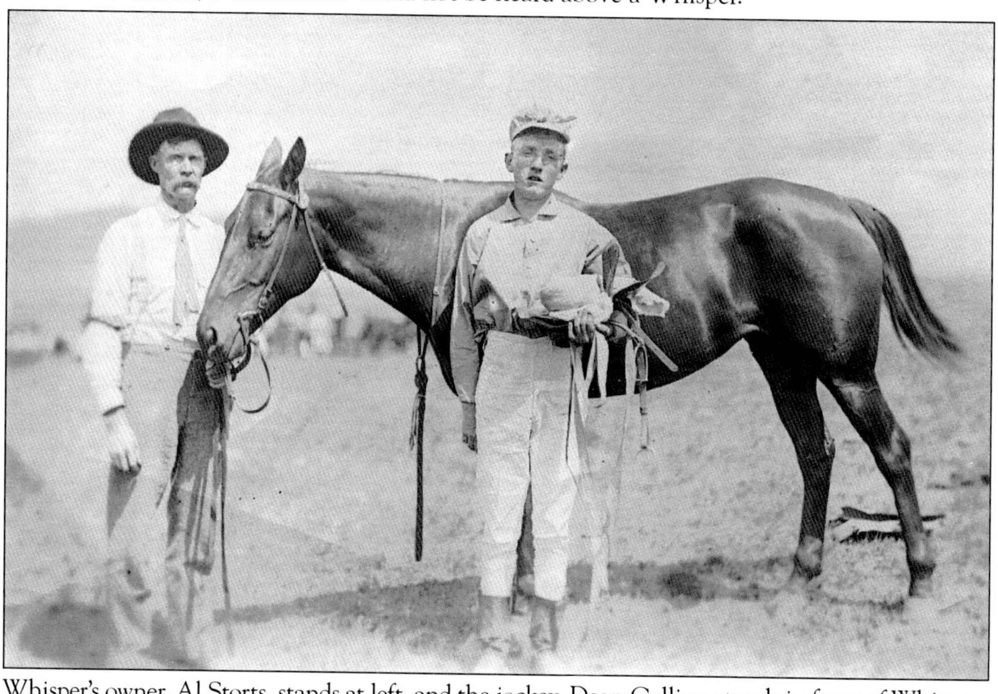

Whisper's owner, Al Storts, stands at left, and the jockey, Dean Collins, stands in front of Whisper.

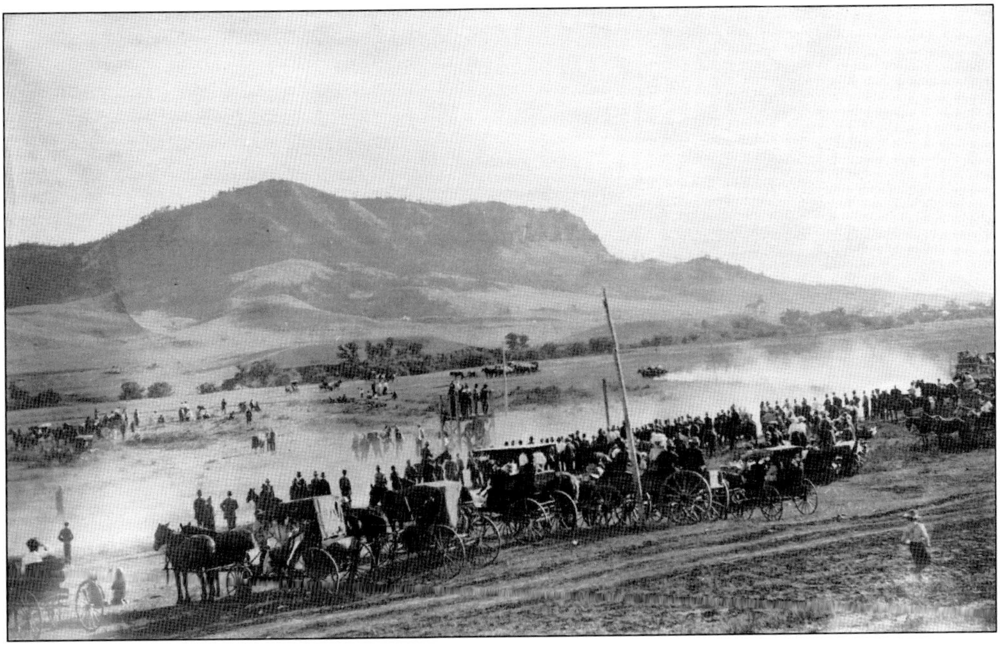

Pictured is the Old Settlers Picnic at the Kim Addition racetrack. There are three horses making the first turn, trailed by the whirl of dust. The next picture shows the dash for the finish line. Sundance had a few different sites for the racetrack. This one is situated on the east side of town. The racers would come from all over to prove that their horse was the fastest.

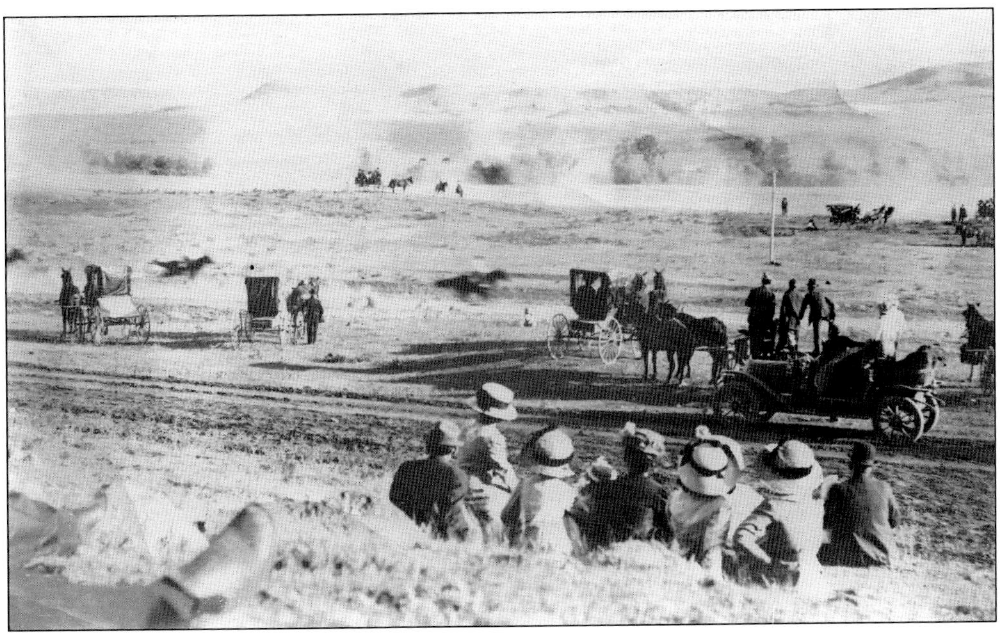

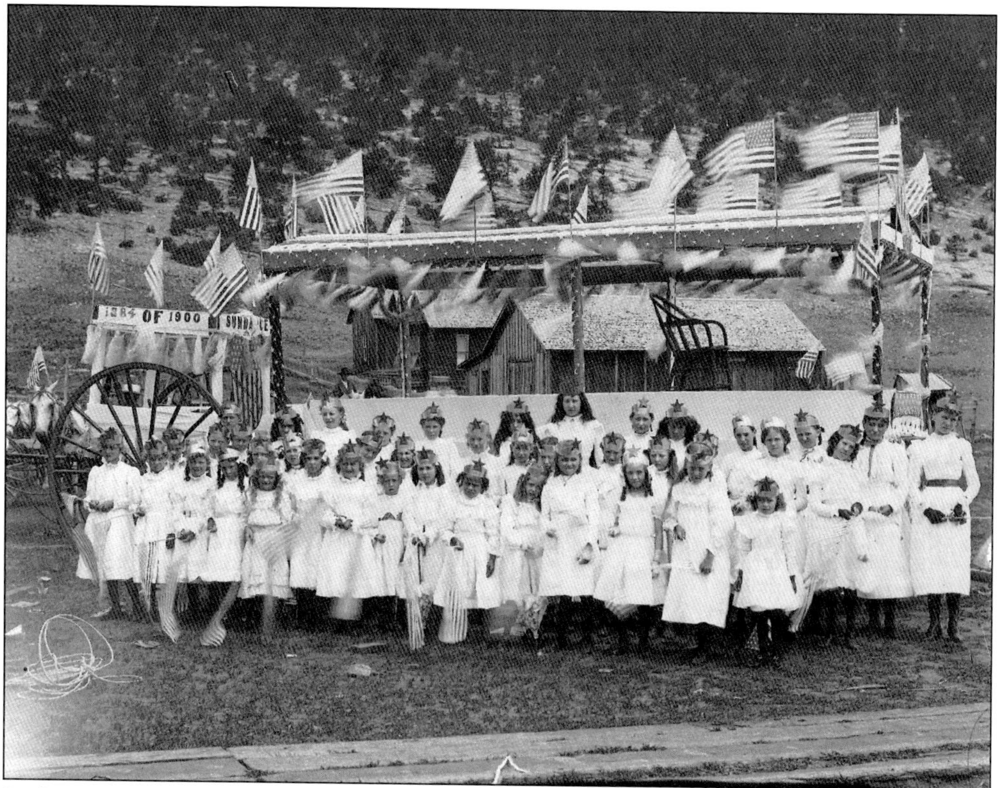

In the top picture, 46 schoolgirls dressed in white gather in front of the Odd Fellows float for the Fourth of July parade in Sundance in 1900. Each of the little girls has an American flag and a banner to wave. The bottom picture is a group of young lady cyclists lined up in front of the livery stable barn waiting their turn to ride in the Fourth of July parade. These pictures were taken by photographer Lock of Deadwood, South Dakota.

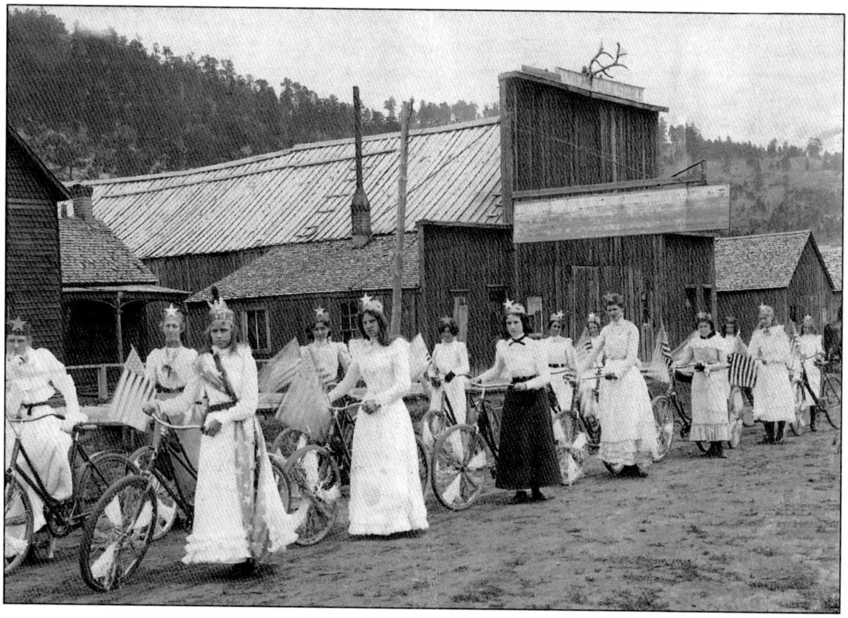

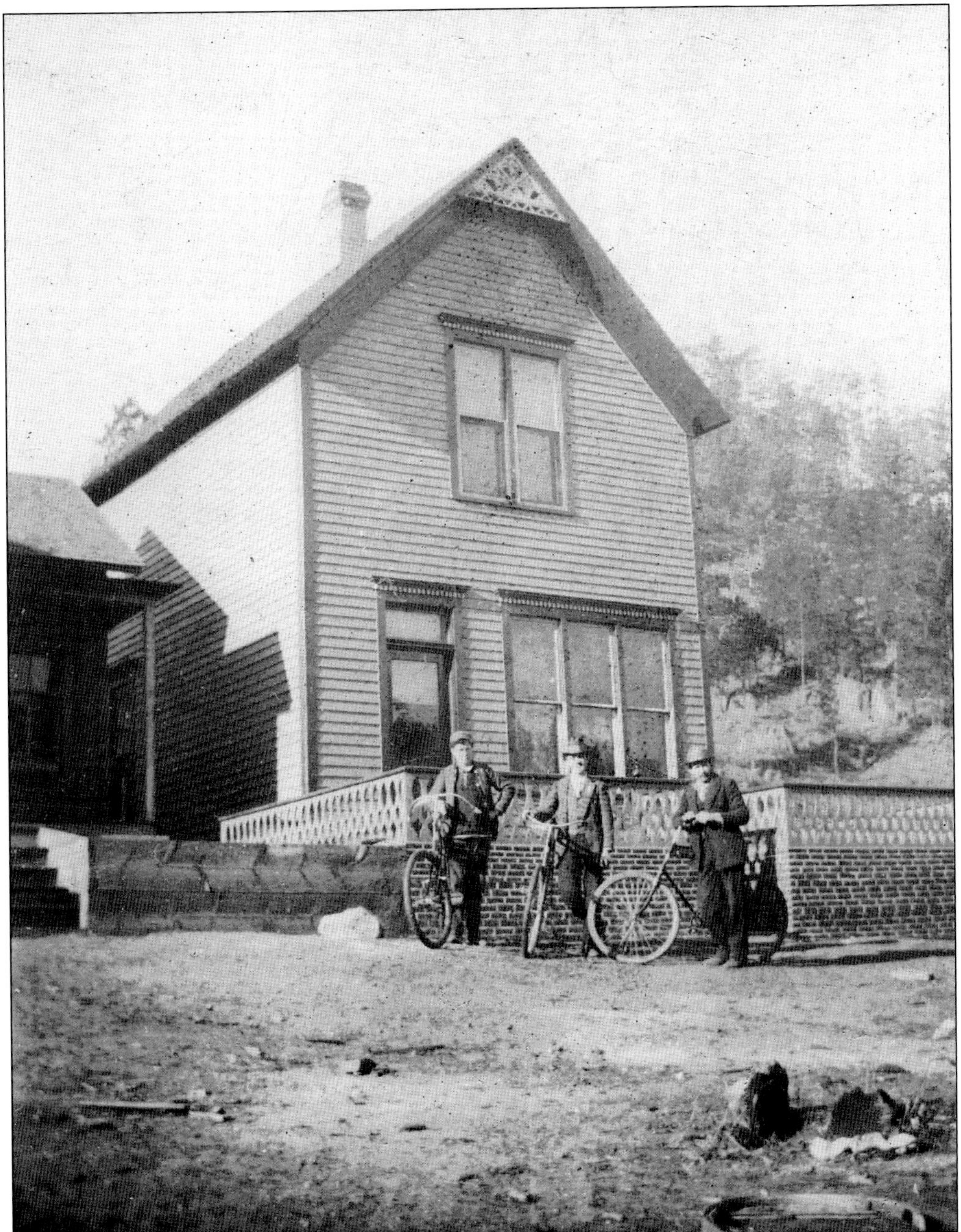

Pictured from left to right are Walter L. Nettlehorst, Frank Leget, and an unidentified man. The three gentlemen are about to enter a bicycle race on the Fourth of July, 1900. It was reported in the newspaper that Frank Legett won the race, and Walter L. Nettelhorst came in second. Nettelhorst, a Sundance attorney, had an opera house in a building just east of the Odd Fellows Hall. Frank had a shop where he made and sold bits and spurs, but bicycle repair was his specialty.

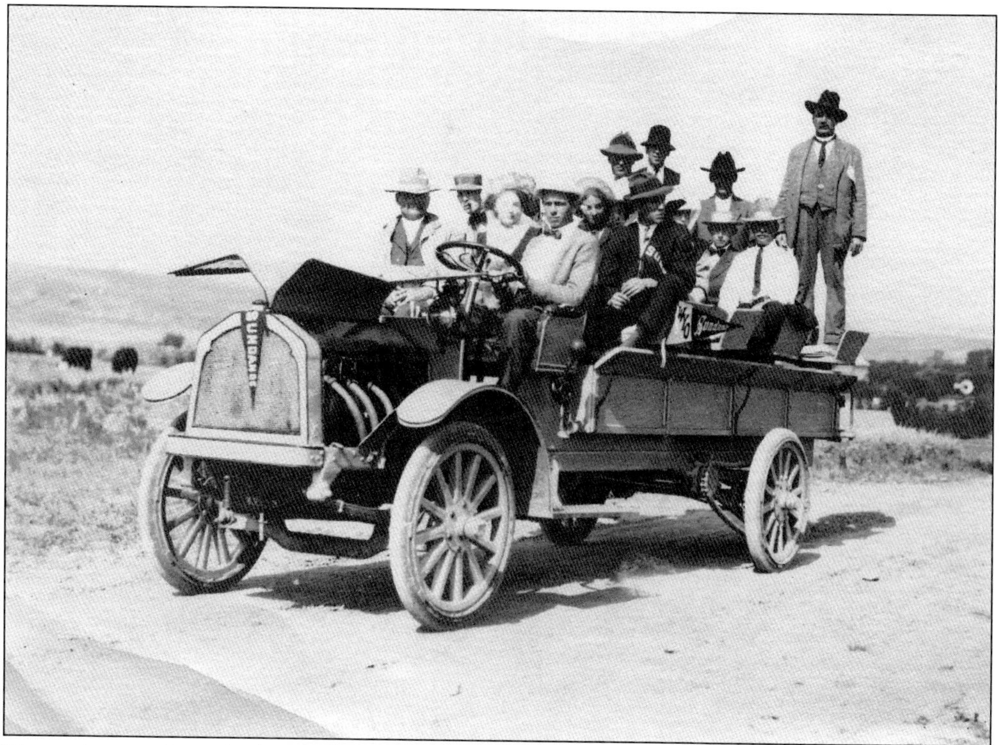

These pictures show the baseball team traveling to games in neighboring towns. To say baseball was popular in Crook County is an understatement. Teams were willing to travel any distance to "play ball." In the early 1900s, the tri-county league consisted of Sundance, Beulah, Moskee, Moorcroft, and Hulett teams. These teams played each other as well as teams from Lead, Deadwood, and Spearfish, South Dakota. One newspaper article reported, "The game with Moorcroft was not very interesting as they were simply outclassed by Sundance." The paper also stated that Moorcroft was generous with their bets and money.

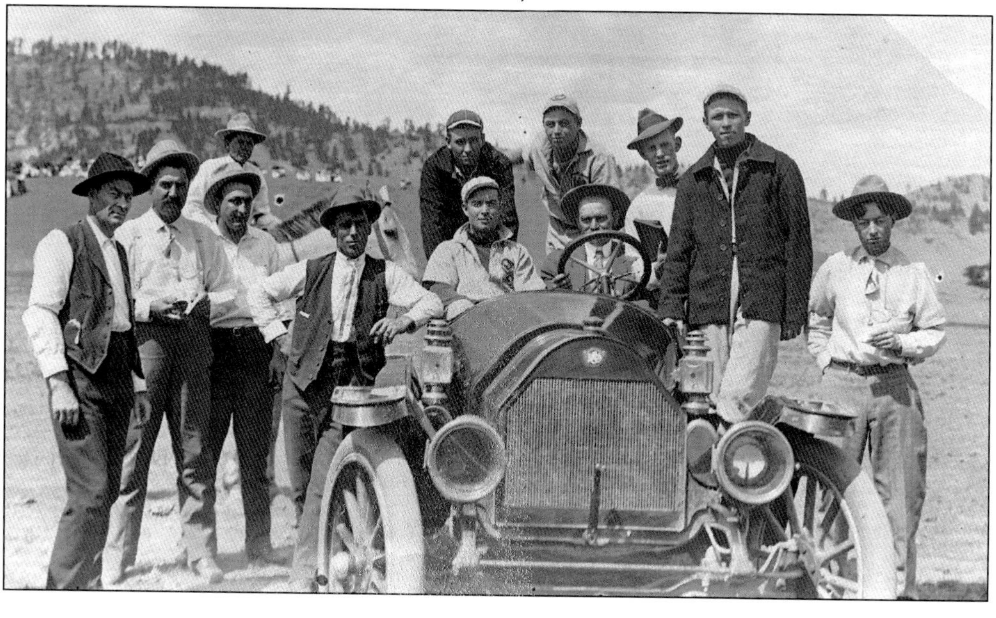

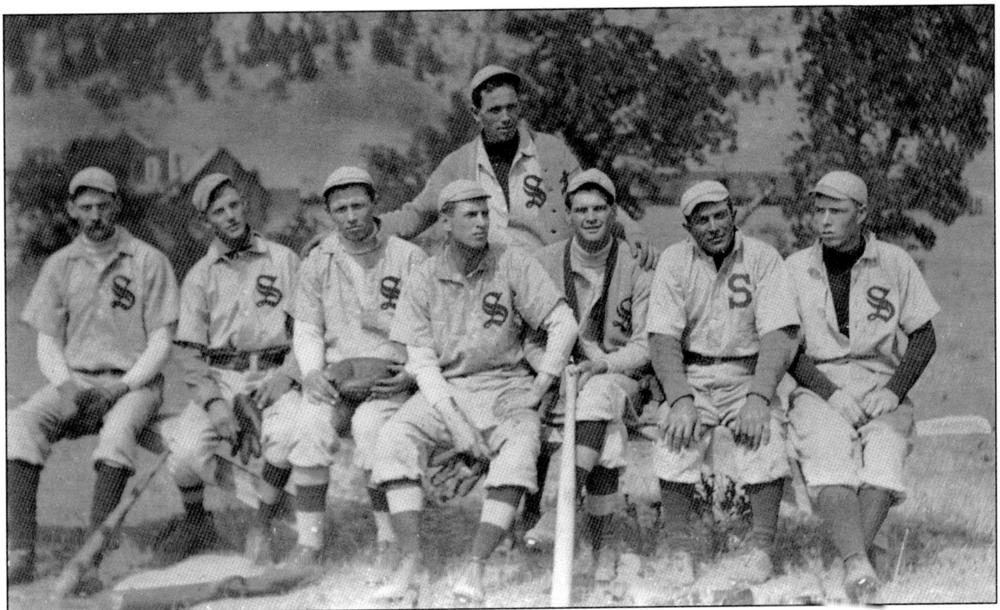

The base hits, the sliding runners, and the moments of glory for these players echo across the years. Pictured from left to right are J. W. Baker, outfielder; Edwin Rounds, manager and outfielder; Herb Brockett, catcher; Harry Ilsley, who played second and third base; a man named Hubbard, an outfielder; Harry Benson, back-up catcher; and Harry Atteberry, first baseman. Standing behind is Ted Brockett, the pitcher. In 1910, the Bearcats won tournaments with players like Francis "Red" Hejde, Irv Hejde, Jay Hejde, Ralph Neckleson, and Addison Dudry.

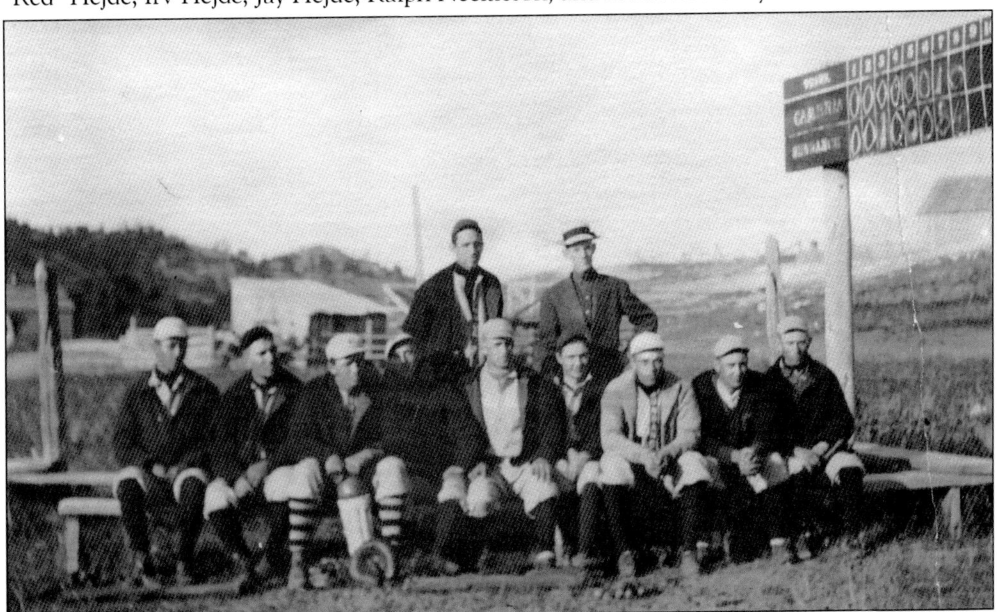

Moses Pettigrew mentioned in the May 29, 1886, *Gazette* that a baseball club of 23 men had been formed and that out of this, nine men would be chosen to form the first baseball team in Sundance. The team called themselves the Invincibles, but they soon changed that to the Bearcats. This team did win a lot of games, and this was due to the Brocket boys. Herb (seated, fourth from the left) was the catcher, and Ted (standing, left) pitched a curve that not many could hit.

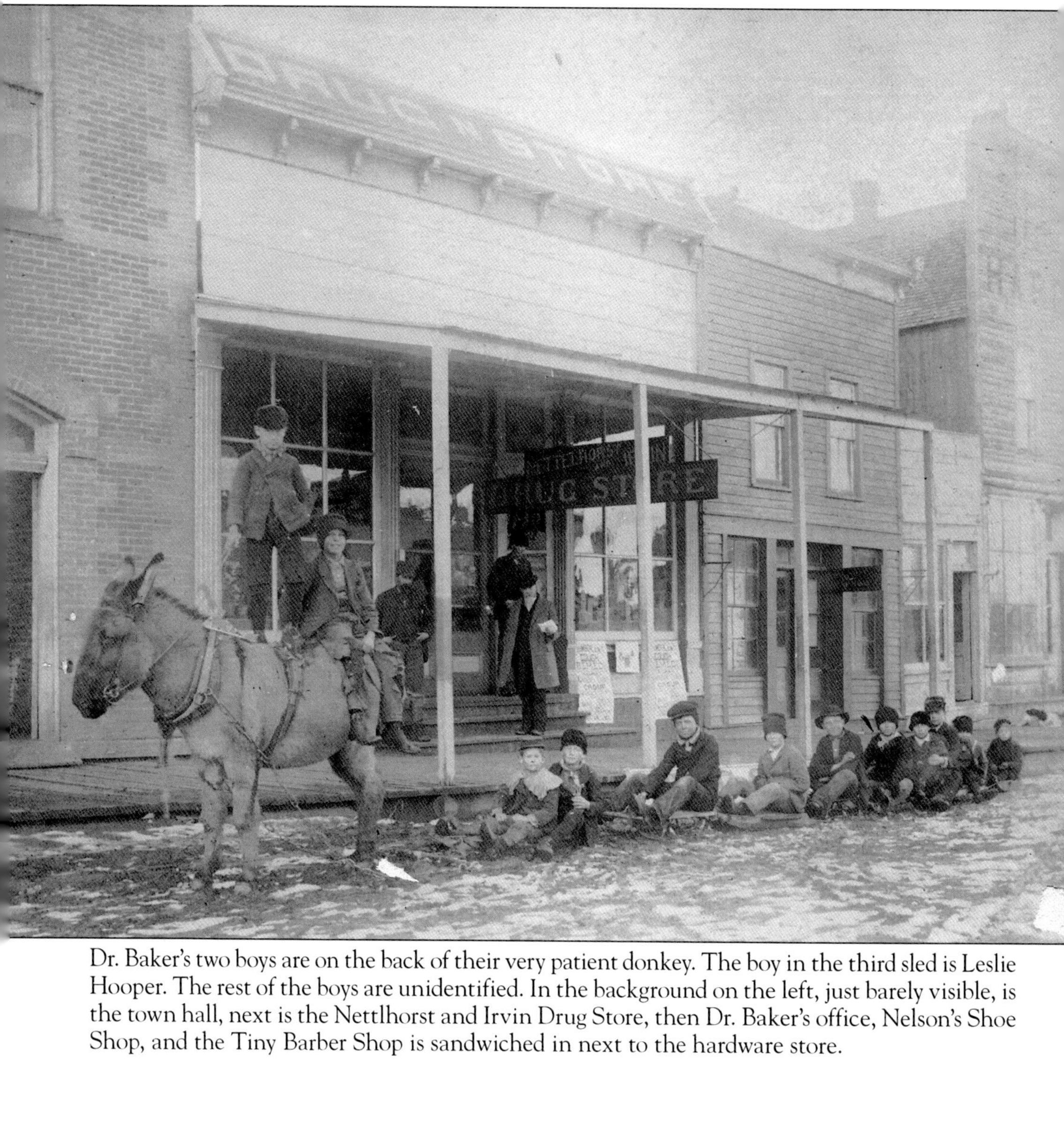

Dr. Baker's two boys are on the back of their very patient donkey. The boy in the third sled is Leslie Hooper. The rest of the boys are unidentified. In the background on the left, just barely visible, is the town hall, next is the Nettlhorst and Irvin Drug Store, then Dr. Baker's office, Nelson's Shoe Shop, and the Tiny Barber Shop is sandwiched in next to the hardware store.

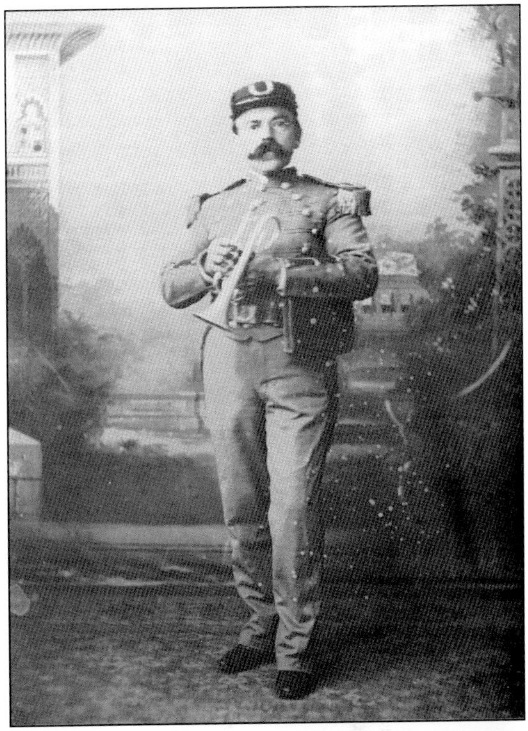

Fred Schloredt was a member of the Sundance City Band—he played the trumpet. This band consisted of any members of the community who liked to play an instrument. In November 1885, the newspaper reported that "our boys" were getting a brass band together. The editor warned that before anyone was ready, the tooting would begin. By January 30, the *Sundance Gazette* thought the band boys were looking pretty good and a band concert was scheduled for February.

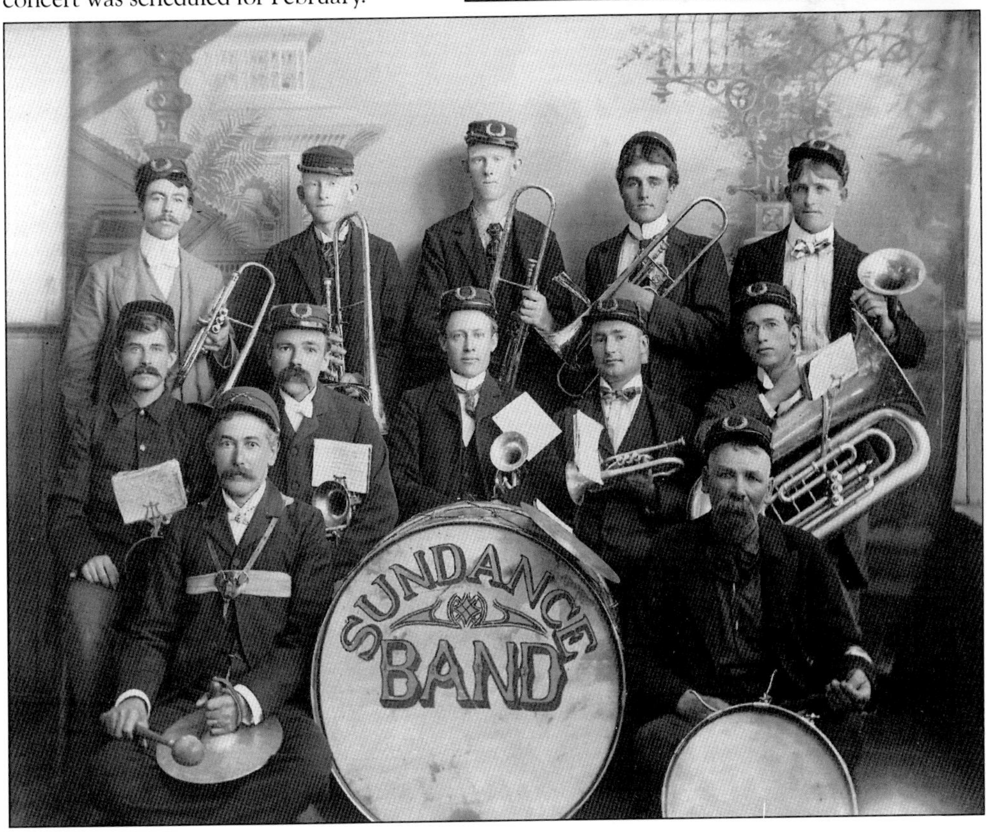

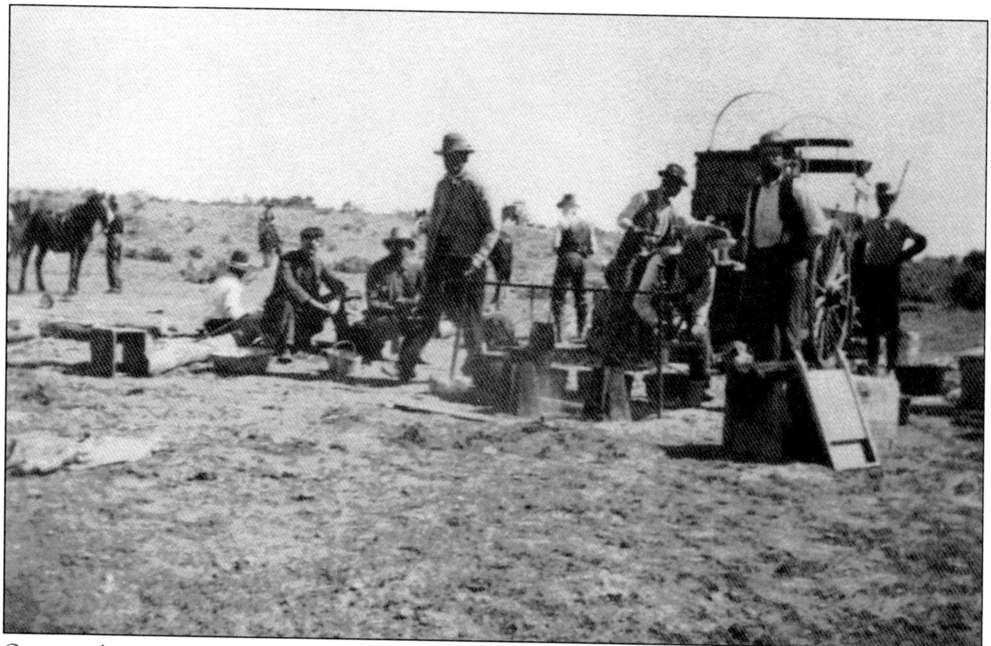

On a cattle camp's noonday break, much like the one pictured, the boys from the D and the L.A. ranches enjoyed a little mischief. Hugh Gainer and John Driskill decided to give a few wild horses some extra exercise. After the dust had cleared and everyone had a good laugh, the two picked themselves up from the ground only to realize that Hugh had several broken ribs and John had a broken collarbone. This was the end of the roundup for them, but they both healed quickly and went right back out.

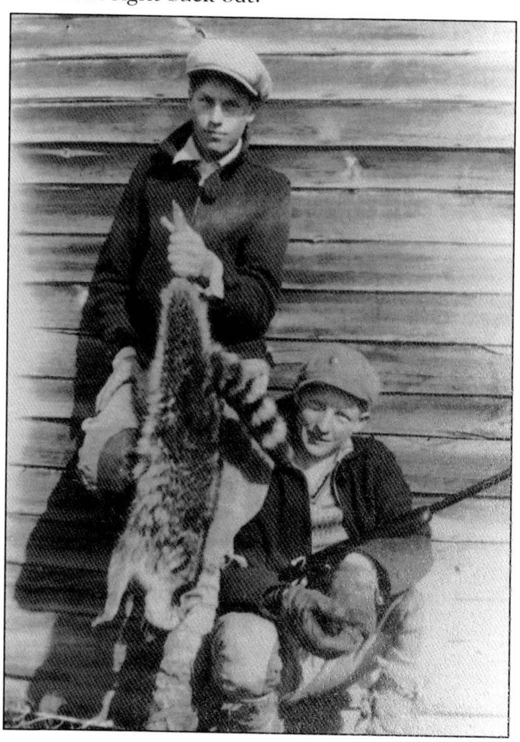

Living in Sundance in the 1900s was like living on the frontier. Being nestled between the Black Hills and the Bearlodge Mountains put Sundance in the middle of a natural trail system where town and nature often collided. Bear sightings and pesky woodchuck stories were common. Everyone, even children, was trained to use guns out of necessity. Pictured here are brothers Leon (left) and Rex Dillon in 1935 with a raccoon, a little worse for wear. Rex would grow up to be the owner of a hardware store on the corner of Main and Second Streets.

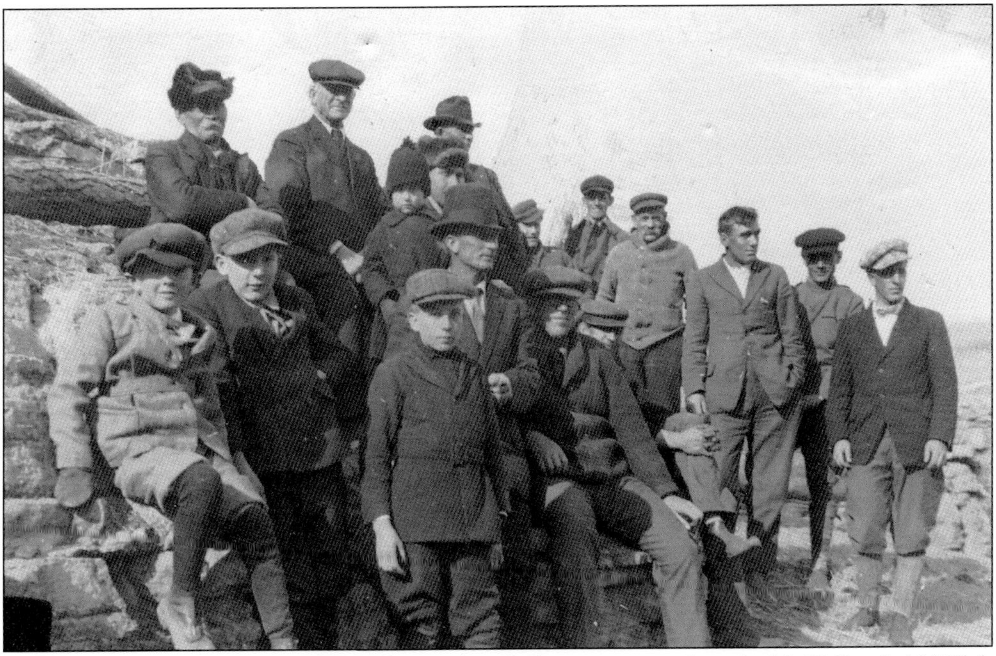

4-H Clubs began in the area in 1902. This unidentified group is attending the McClellends 4-H Club meeting in about 1920, where Augustus Gould was the leader. The idea from the beginning has been hands-on learning in conservation and nutrition. Their motto is "to make the best better."

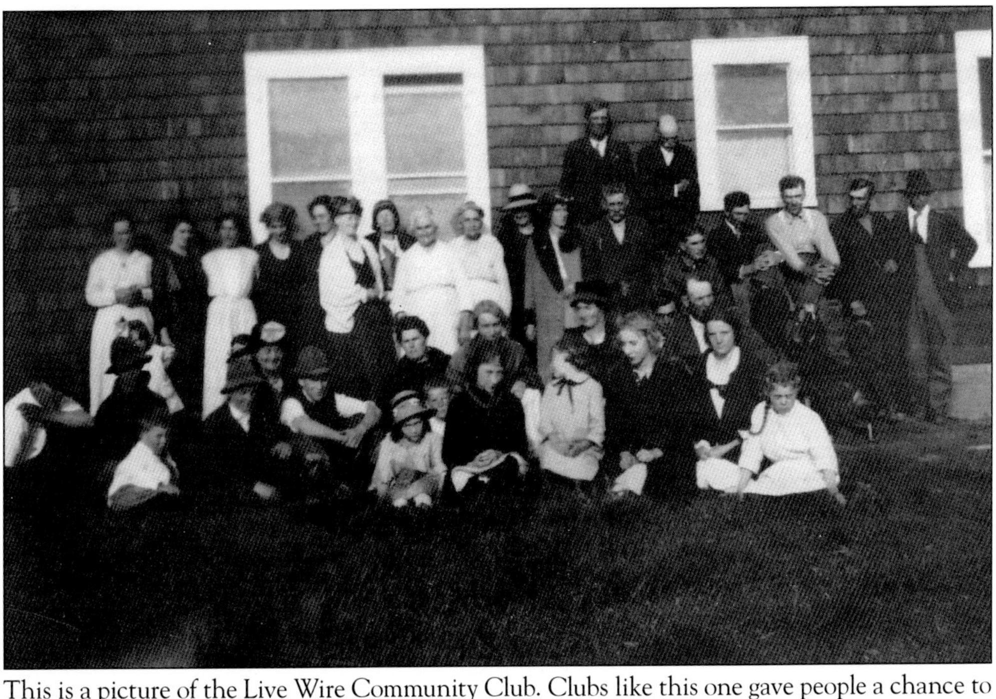

This is a picture of the Live Wire Community Club. Clubs like this one gave people a chance to visit, play cards, dance, and work together. The men would share the work that needed a helping hand or two. The women might have a quilt they worked on together. Many friendship quilts came from such a gathering.

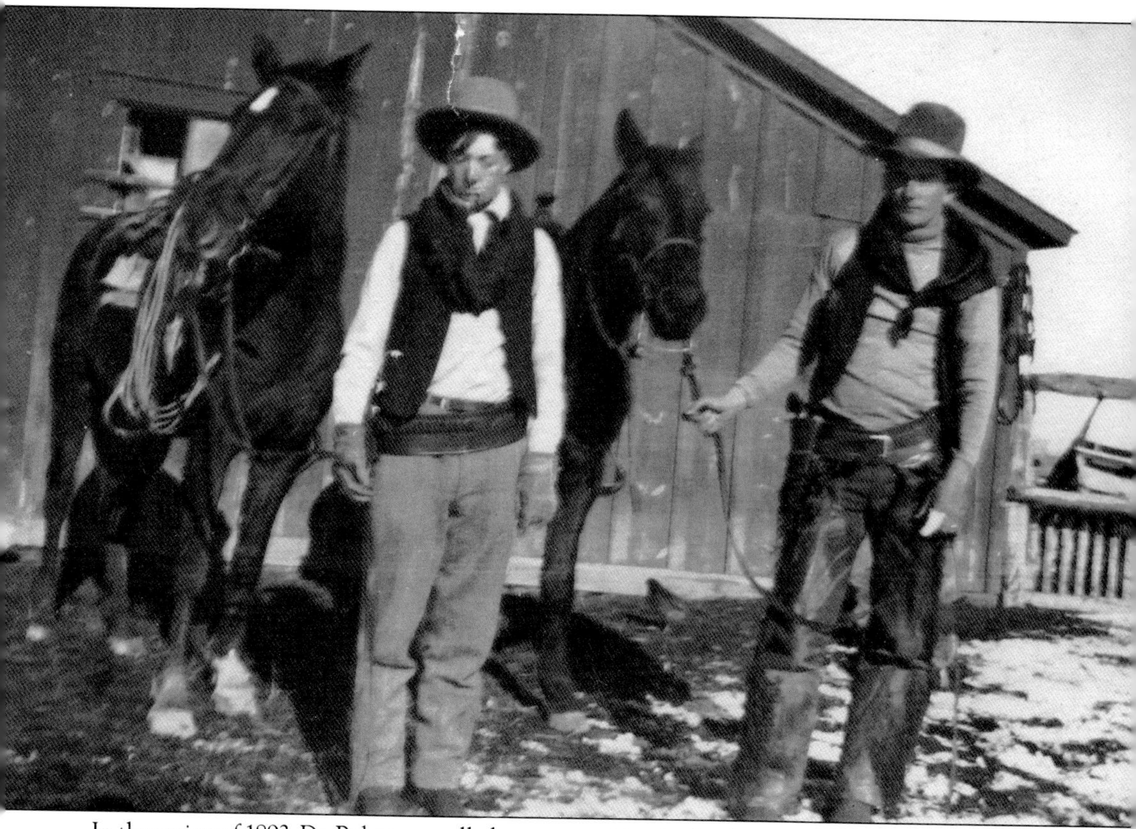

In the spring of 1893, Dr. Baker was called on to treat Gray Jack, who was suffering with inflammatory rheumatism. The doctor prescribed the mud baths in Thermopolis, west of Sundance. John Harper loaned Jack a wagon, and Lew Stone provided the team of horses. Mrs. Abe Settle found a feather bed and food from the Frank Grocery Store. All that was needed was someone to drive the team, and for a price, two customers from one of the saloons volunteered. These two unidentified cowboys are dressed much like the wagon drivers might have been. In Thermopolis, Jack was helped into the mud, and the drivers went to wash away the dust of the trip at the nearest watering hole. As the night set, Jack—all alone—became angry. He clawed himself out of the mud and went looking for his faithful wagon drivers. When he found them, they quickly agreed to start back to Sundance. Jack was cured!

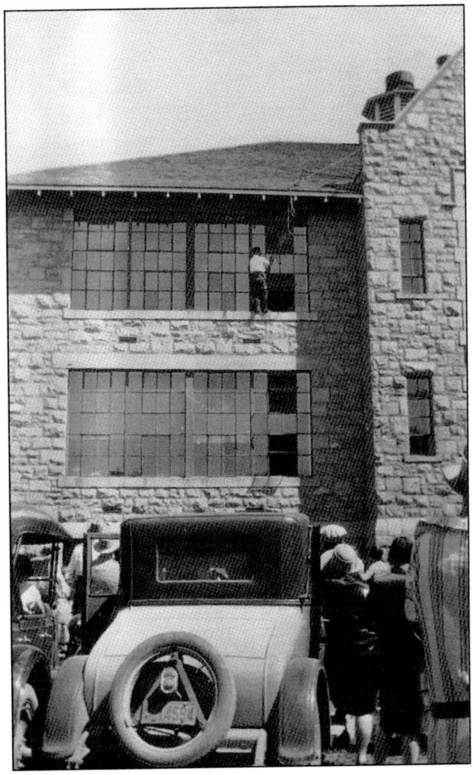

Babe White came to Sundance to show off his daring deeds. A crowd gathered in front of the Sundance School to watch with awe as he climbed the building. The first picture shows Babe just coming out of the third floor window onto the windowsill. The next picture, he has reached the roof and is pulling himself up over the eaves. We do not know how that rope got there before him.

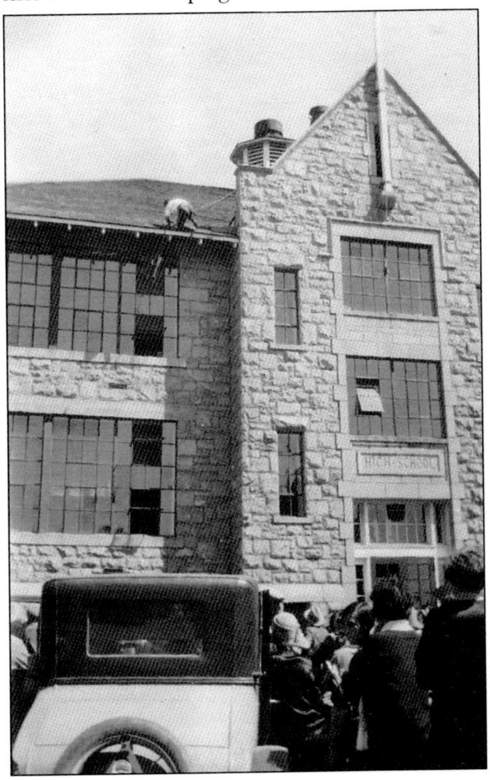

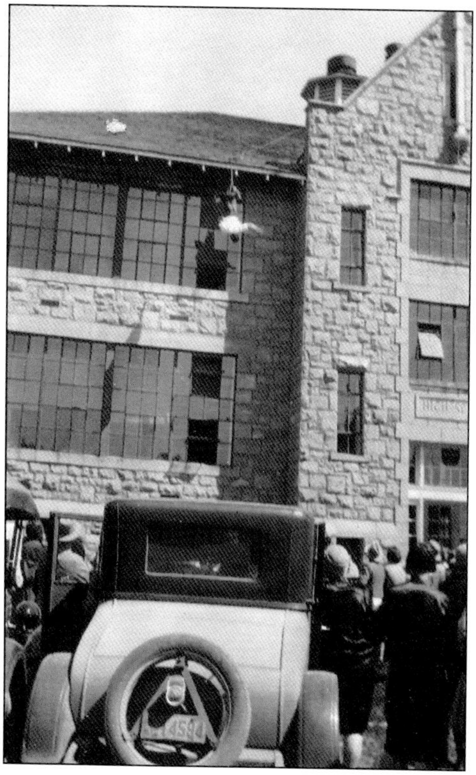

Babe White is still at it. The crowd has not moved, but Babe sure has. On the left, he is hanging by his legs. Afterwards he somehow got back on the roof, and in the next picture he has managed to shimmy up the flagpole. Who knows if there was a prize waiting for him at the top. Hopefully the city marshal or the sheriff was not waiting for him when he reached the firm, hard ground.

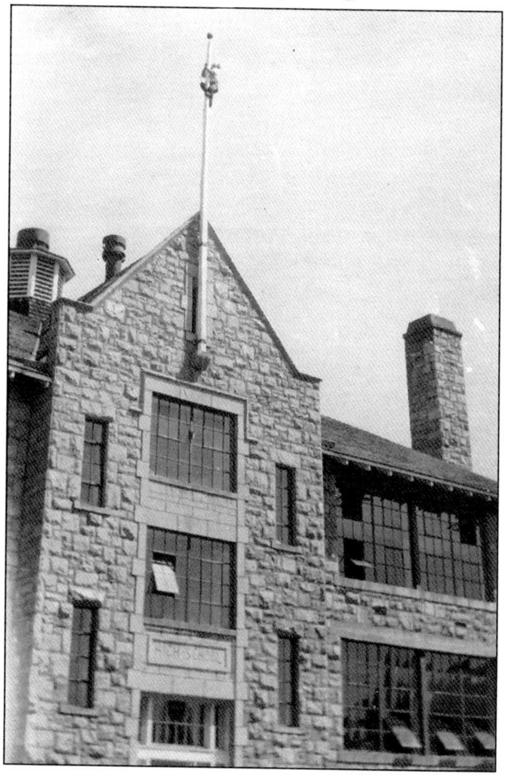

We cannot underestimate the value of a front porch. This was often the best place to feel a light breeze after a long, hot, summer day and spend time with friends and neighbors. Doing just that is Ella Schloredt on the steps, a Chaffin boy on the porch, Bill Irvin sitting on the rocking chair, and the older woman identified as "Uncle Frank's first wife."

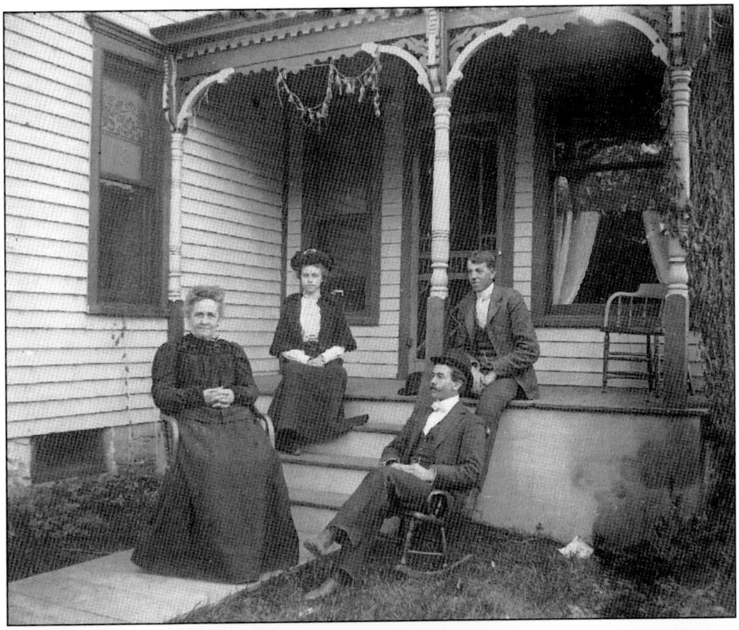

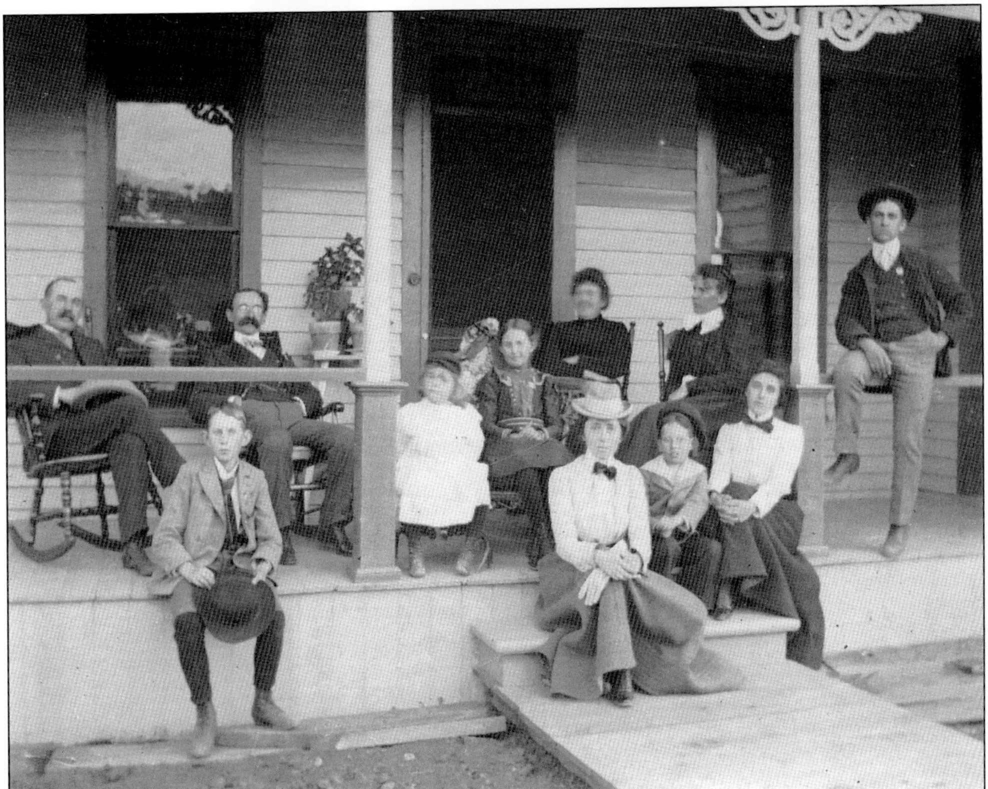

This photograph shows a larger group. Seated from left to right are (first row) Elmer Frank, Chasey Mchaffey in the middle front, unidentified, Pearl Foster, and an unidentified man sitting up on the ledge; (second row, up on the porch) Abe Frank, Meyer Frank, "chubby child not known," unidentified young girl, Florence Frank, and Marie Frank.

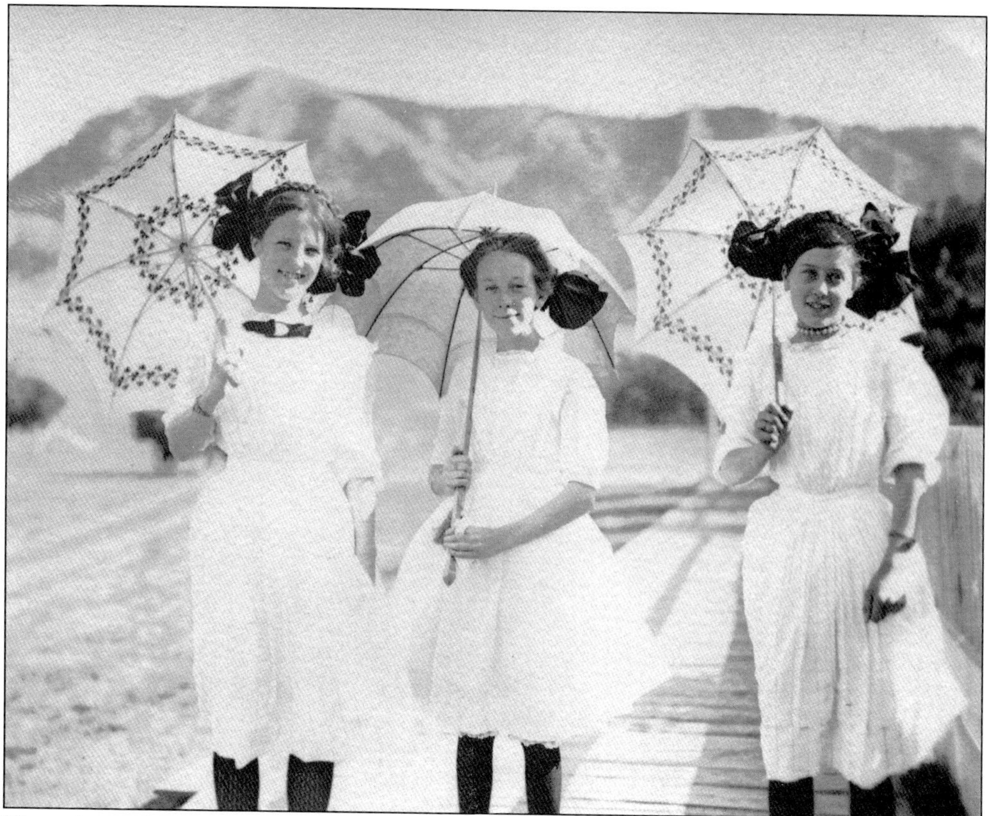

These three take a walk in the sunshine using their parasols to protect them from the Wyoming sun. Their braids are up to help keep them cool, and their hair ribbons are, without a doubt, something to behold.

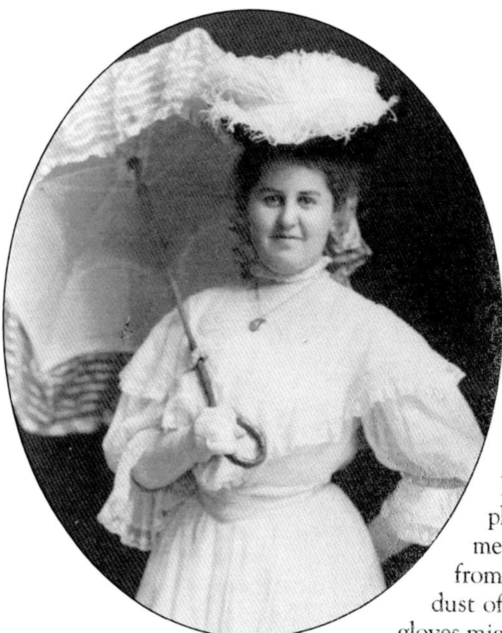

As the only surviving daughter of Abe and Marie Frank, Florence Frank, seen in this 1906 photograph, probably had first choice of the new merchandise that Uncle Meyer (Frank) would bring from New York City. However, with the winds and dust of Wyoming, a parasol, feather hat, and white gloves might not be exactly practical.

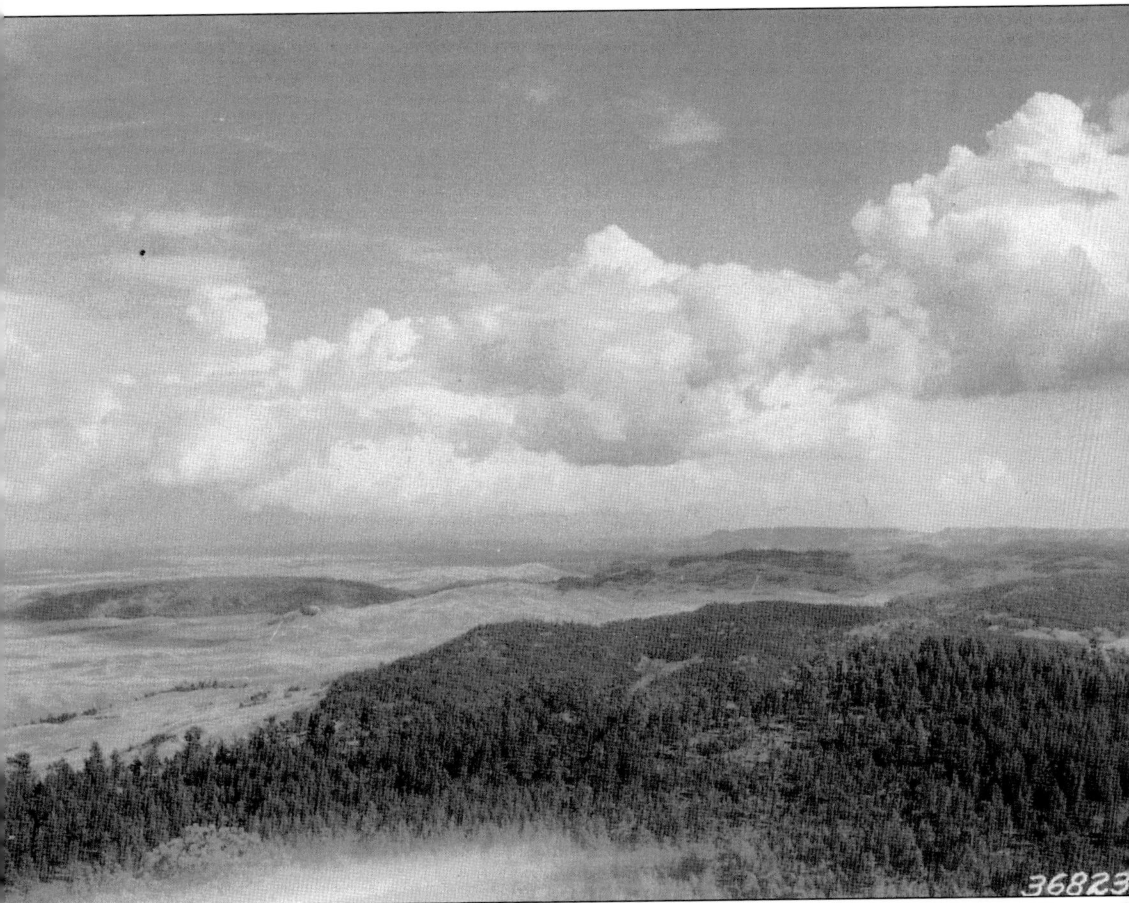

The Belshe coal mine is located in the Bearlodge Mountains. Several miners built a still in the mine and had it operating for some time, but word got out and a "revenuer" came to investigate the stories of whiskey coming out of a coal mine. He brought Jack Belshe along to help search the mine. Because of the time it took for them to find the still, the miners had time to spirit away a good share of the whiskey and store it elsewhere in the mine. Legend has it that whiskey is still buried in one of the mine shafts.

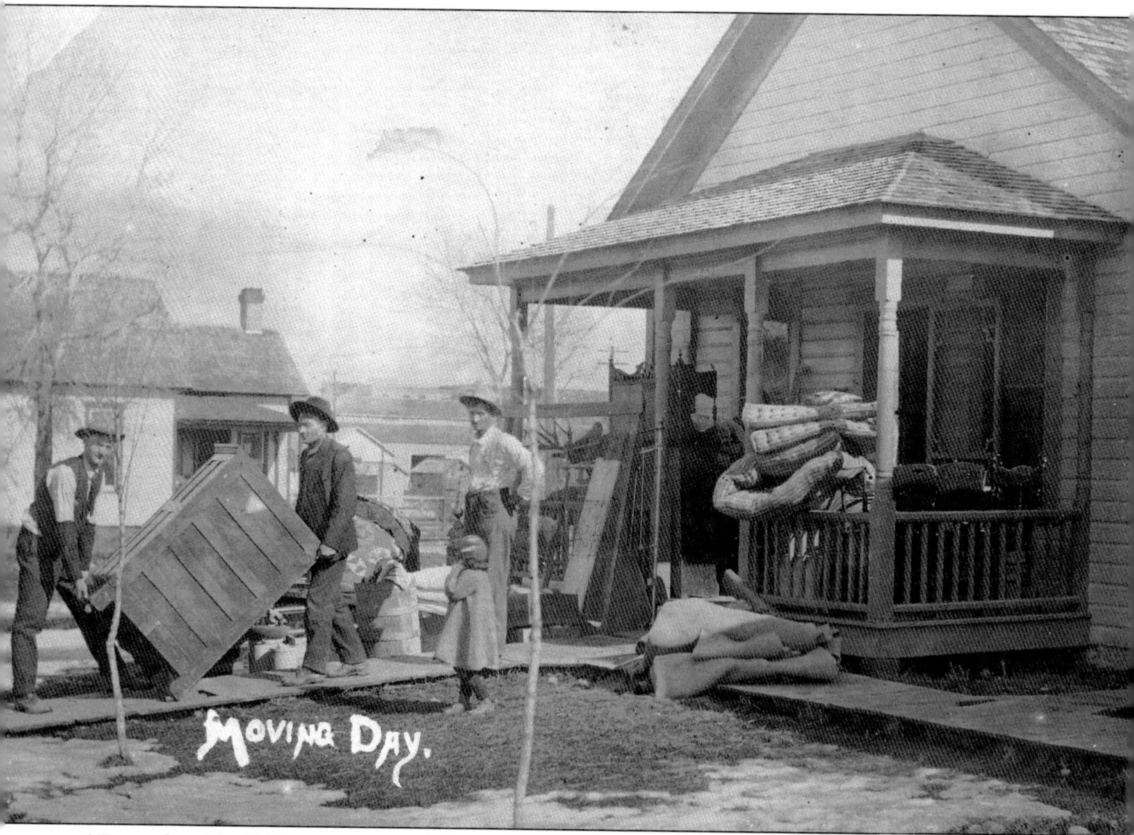

November 11, 1885, court records show that Maggie Madden and Rose Schaffer were brought before Judge Bishop's court on the charge of being prostitutes, because they were keeping a "bawdy house" in the northern part of Sundance. The two ladies were fined $50. Judge Adelber "Dell" Bishop's court gave them the privilege of leaving town. After much thought, the ladies took the judge's offer and made plans to leave Sundance. The fine was waived. This picture shows the type of help from friends and neighbors that the women could have used to load their wagon as they made their getaway from the fine city of Sundance.

Bibliography

Crook County Historical Society. *Pioneers of Crook County, 1876–1920*. Pierre, SD: State Publishing Company, 1981.

Fitzpatrick, George, and Edwin A. Tucker. *Men Who Matched the Mountains*. Washington, D.C.: U.S. Government Printing Office, 1972.

Garman, Mary. *Harry Longabough, The Sundance Kid: The Early Years, 1867–1889*. Sundance, WY: Crook County Museum Board, 1978.

Horsted, Paul. *Exploring with Custer*. Dakota Photographic, 2005.

Lageson, David R., and Darwin R. Spearing. *Roadside Geology of Wyoming*. 2nd ed. Missoula, MT: Mountain Press Publishing Company, 2004.

Lewis, Jon E. *The West*. New York: Garroll and Graf Publishers, 1996.

Massie, Evelyn Hepworth. *A Massie Family History*. Kennewick, WA: Evelyn Hepworth Massie, 1972.

Morris, Lesley R. "Plowing up the Past." *Range The Cowboy Spirit on America's Outback* (Spring 2010): 10–11.

Murphy, Robert J. *Devils Tower National Monument Historical File*. Sundance, WY: Crook County Library, 1965.

Raventon, Edward. *Island in the Plains*. Boulder, CO: Johnson Books, 1994.

Sodaro, Crag, and Randy Adams. *Frontier Spirit: The Story of Wyoming*. Boulder, CO: Johnson Books, 1986.

Consistent with our mission to preserve history on a local level, this book was printed in South Carolina on American-made paper and manufactured entirely in the United States. Products carrying the accredited Forest Stewardship Council (FSC) label are printed on 100 percent FSC-certified paper.